Palestinian Identity
in relation to Time and Space

Mitri Raheb

First Edition

**Palestinian Identity
in relation to Time and Space**

Mitri Raheb

Copy right © 2014 Diyar Publisher

*Art direction : Diyar Publisher
Designer : Engred Anwar Al-Khoury
Printing press: Latin Patriarchate, Beit Jala*

Supported by :
The Evangelical Lutheran Church in Amerika

All rights reserved. Except for brief quotations in critical articles or reviews, no part of this book may be reproduced in any manner without prior written permission from the publisher.

*1. Palestinian Arabs - Israel - Ethnic Identity
2. Palestinian - Diaspora - Exil*

w w w . d i y a r . p s

Contents

Foreword 7

1. **The Palestinian Identity: Historical Perspective"**
   Nazmi Al-Ju'beh 9

2. **Identity, Belonging, and Home (Land):**
   Diaspora People Engaging with Palestinians on the Question of Identity
   Eleazar S. Fernandez 29

3. **Palestinian Identity in Relation to Time and Space:**
   Palestinian Identity, Citizenship and the Role of Isa Al-Khuri Baseel Bandak in the British Era, (1919 - 1948)
   Adnan Musallam 45

4. **Palestinian Identity in the Diaspora**
   Qustandi Shomali 65

5. **The Impact of Place on Identity in the Works of Mahmoud Darwish**
   Liana Badr 81

6. **Biblical Narrative and Palestinian Identity in Mahmoud Darwish's Writings**
   Mitri Raheb 89

7. **Holy Places and the Formation of Identity:**
   The Case of Hebron / al-Khalīl
   Ulrike Bechmann 107

8. Land of Sprouting Twigs Vertical ecumenism in Palestinian art and culture
   Thomas Staubli 121

9. Reading Palestine Realities with American Indian eyes
   Robert O. Smith 135

10. "Exile as Identity:
    African Americans, Palestinians, and the Book of Ezekiel"
    Dexter Callender, Jr. 151

11. The text as a landscape and the landscape as a text:
    Reading Jeremiah 32 through Palestinian and Israeli eyes
    Dr. Janneke Stegeman 163

12. Religious Identity as Gift and Task: A Christian Perspective
    Ottmar Fuchs, Tübingen 175

13. Infiltrators or Next of Kin: Identity Negotiations around
    the Label 'Mistanenim' of African Migrants in Israel
    and its Connection to the Von Palestinians
    Mirjam van Reisen, Erik Borgman 197

14. Home, Land, and Homeland As Social Values
    George Rivera 223

    Biographies 233

    Endnotes 240

    Index 279

Foreword

This book contains the proceedings of the August 2013 conference, "Palestinian Identity in relations to Time and Space", which was held at Dar Annadwa (the International Centre of Bethlehem) and organized by Diyar Consortium. The conference brought together more than 60 professors and researchers from over 15 countries including Europe, USA, Latin America, and Asia, and had a good number of local Palestinian participants.

This conference was the seventh in a row that Diyar Consortium has organized. The idea of a conference that is deliberating Palestinian identity in relation to time and space is indeed pertinent. The development of the Palestinian identity has been the focus of many studies and conferences. However, all of the studies so far concentrate on the emergence of this identity in the last hundred years. Although several papers in this book continued to deal with the development of the Palestinian identity in late Ottoman and early British Mandate Palestine, another focus was placed on analyzing the understanding of the Palestinian identity in relation to the biblical story, history and archeology and how this understanding has been reflected in poetry and art. The self-understanding of the Palestinians in relation to time and space and their relationship to other marginalized groups is a question of high political and social relevance.

The participation of scholars from different parts of the world in this undertaking did not only bring an international scope, persuasions and perspectives, but helped fostering an ecumenical, interdisciplinary, multi-ethnic and multi-cultural environ, dialogues and philosophy.

I would like to thank all the authors for participating in the conference and for their valuable time, energy, and thought-provoking papers that they presented at the conference and here for publication. My thanks also go to the Diyar staff that helped in organizing the conference and collecting the papers, especially Ms. Rania Salsa, Ms. Fida' Ghareeb, Ms. Angie Saba, Ms. Hiba Nasser Atrash, Christina Sawatzki, and Tobias Abromeit. Special thanks go to Ms. Sarah Makari for doing a great job in editing this book. This conference would not have been possible without the generous sponsorship of the Division of Global Mission of the Evangelical Lutheran Church in America, and the Evangelical Church of Westfalia, The Church of Scotland, and the United Church of Christ/Disciples of Christ.

Rev. Dr. Mitri Raheb
Diyar President
August 2014

1

The Palestinian Identity:

Historical Perspective

Nazmi Al-Ju'beh

Introduction

It is very difficult, perhaps impossible, to tackle the identity of a people, as if exploring one homogeneous entity, for a clear-cut definition, accepted comfortably by the community/communities that formulate the society/the state/the nation.

History is considered to be the main and most important container of identity. Nations rewrite their history/histories in order to explain and adapt contemporary developments, events, and phenomena, to employ them in the challenges facing society, and also to reflect the ideology of the ruling class. It is, indubitably, a difficult task, to trace the identity of a people through history; hence, identity, like any other component of society, is highly flexible, variable, mobile and, of course, reflects historical conditions.

The formation of identity/identities commonly takes place in an intensive manner during conflicts and challenges; since it is important, at time of challenge, to clarify and to underline the common elements among a certain group of people which can be mobilized to face the specific challenge.

Naturally, it is not accurate. As well understanding will not be precise if the formation process of a nation is limited to conflicts and challenges only; such an "identity" is a temporary one. It has to include much more than that; in most cases, other elements, mainly historical background, and historically shared experience, in addition to other components. Shared interests are usually an essential element in the process of formation. "Normally," the effect of such developments spread over a long period of time, and in some cases, form a myth. In this case, identity becomes far more important and is an essential political abstract, uniting people. Building on that, the intellectual elite in a society begins to formulate the different elements of that society, and the creation of new elements is in history, fairly common.

It's not rare to find that identity/identities are intensified through symbols, mainly national symbols, as they are easily utilized, marketed, and converted into a popular character. National symbols are also subject to continuous change, due to socio-economic and political developments of society, and its need for self-expression. Symbols can be created, shaped, and carved; but they can also be a reflection of the realties and needs of a society. The intellectual elite or/and the ruling class can impose created symbols; in this case, symbols can last for a long time, or disappear when the need for them diminishes.

Finally, symbols can be formulated within societies, but they later become impossible to change or to reshape and sometimes can become a real burden on society.

1. The Terminology

It is very difficult to present a single identity of any society. Each society has different identities of various levels, regardless of sub identities. Identity can have geographic, cultural, ethnic, religious...etc dimensions (not simply a single dimension). We have to look at these components in a complementary manner rather than in a contradictory one. Various identities are supported with a multi-colored multi-shaped historical arsenal.[1] Again, certain basic elements need to be clarified before we can present Palestinian identity and in its cultural heritage context: Palestine, Palestinians, borders, historical context, and different components of identity.

The meaning of the word "Palestine" is unclear; as there are different interpretations of what Palestine means.[2] As administrative terminology, it has been used since the Greco-Roman period in the first and second centuries BC. It is worth mentioning that Herodotus (ca. 490-430 BC), the Greek historian, had already written about Palestine long before, it meant, the land of Palestine. The name was taken from a group of people called "the Philista," who settled in the Iron Age (around the twelfth century BC) along the shores of Palestine. Their origin, Aegean or Semitic, is disputed among scholars.[3] Therefore, the southern coastal strip (today's Gaza Strip) in Assyrian texts (eighth century BC) was called "Pilaschtu". With Herodotus, the Greek historian there emerged the term "Palestinian Syria" for the entire coastal strip between Phoenicia (today's Lebanon) and Egypt. The Greek term "Palestine" was then transferred to Latin: "Palestine". This Latin term, first used in 135 A.D, for the Romans, meant the entire province of "Judaea" was introduced in order to erase the use of the term "Judea" and the entire realm from the memory of the Jews after putting down the Jewish rebellion against the Romans. Jerusalem was then given the name "Aelia Capitolina." [4]

It is true that the Palestinians, those who were living in Palestine, were mostly part of a greater regional or international political entity, which usually housed several nations, ethnic groups and cultures. Belonging to great powers did not convert people culturally. This does not exclude the influence of the dominating culture. Roman Palestine left many influences not just in the cultural heritage of the land, but also deeply influenced its population.[5] These influences did not convert the people of the country (Palestine, in this case) into Romans, in spite of the fact that some members of the elite of Palestine were influenced heavily by and even adapted imperial Roman culture, including personal names.[6] Yet this way far from what happened among the masses in general and among the peasants (the majority of the population), in the countryside in particular.

We have evidence in the major cities of Roman Palestine of imperial Roman architecture (Caesarea, Bisan/Scythopolis, Jerusalem...etc.) which while it reflects the soul of Rome, of course, with some local influence, is still Roman. Leaving this aside and focusing on the rest of the country, mainly on the countryside, we discover that the continuity of the cultural materials existed before the Romans and continued afterwards.[7]

The invasion of the Crusaders in 1099 AD meant that a good number of Palestinians left their homeland, some for Damascus, the major metropolitan city of the region. These immigrants, mainly scholars (the elite) settled in a newly established quarter on the slopes of Mount Qasioun. The quarter was called (*Salhiyya*), and its inhabitants were called *al-maqadisa*, (the Jerusalemites), in spite of the fact that we know no Jerusalemite lived among them. They were mostly from the area of Nablus and mainly from the village of *Jamma'in* or *Jamma'il*, and thus were also called *al-Jamma'iny* or *al-Jamma'ily* (a prominent family of them were Banu Qudama). "*Al-Maqadisa*" (Jerusalemites) played a major rule in the intellectual life of Damascus for centuries; some of them are still called *al-Qudsi*. This can be explained as a form of blessing, but also as belonging. Most of the countryside of Palestine, as well as its major cities, except Jerusalem, remained Arab, both Muslim and Christian. Even in the later period of the Crusades Arab Christians lived in the walled city of Jerusalem. The Crusaders left the country in large waves, but some of them remained and integrated with the local population.

Much earlier, even directly after the Islamic conquest of Palestine, some scholars from Palestine were called *"al-Filastini"*. The most interesting discussion about this Palestinian belonging (identity!!) is to be found by the Palestinian geographer (al-Maqdisi /al-Muqaddasi) of the tenth century AD, who uses the terminology "Palestine" and "Palestinian" not to express spirit, but as a clear-cut form of geographic belonging and identity.[8]

2. Geographic Definition

The geographic definition of "Palestine" went through tremendous changes and developments. What is called "Palestine" today is but the British Mandate geographic definition of borders, which resulted from agreements with France after WWI.

The highlands of Palestine during the Bronze and Iron Ages were called the "Land of Canaan"; hence, the coastal plains were Philista. In the Roman period, the land was divided into three administrative areas: Palestine I, II, and III, which included most of east Jordan, southern Syria (*Hauran*), south Lebanon and the Golan Heights. In the Early Muslim period (late seventh century), it was divided into two major administrative sections: the northern parts including southern Lebanon and the Golan Heights expanding to *Hauran* and northern Jordan; this was called Jordan (*Jund al-Urdun*) with Tiberius as the administrative capital. The second part expanded from the south, Mount of Carmel, to the south of the Negev including southern

Jordan, and was called Palestine (*Jund Filistin*) with Ramla as a capital. This division did not influence the importance and centrality of Jerusalem to the Umayyad dynasty (r. 660-750 AD). Jerusalem was, during this period, a de facto capital, the major political events during this period occurred there, and Jerusalem exceeded Damascus[9], the officially declared capital.

Later, the terminology became very complicated according to which ruling power controlled this strip of land, which was mostly administrated from either Damascus or Cairo. For example, in the twelfth century, during the Crusader period, most of Mandate Palestine (but not just this part) became the Kingdom of Jerusalem. The British Mandate fixed, as mentioned above, the borders between the years 1916-1923. The borders created by the British have not followed any geographic, historical, cultural or demographic concepts. As well, the Mandate borders were also not sensitive to the needs of the population of the area. These areas (Jordan, Palestine, Syria, and Lebanon) had not experienced state or national borders, as mentioned above, so the socio-economic consequences of such an artificial division were of no interest to the local population of *"Bilad al-Sham"* (Great Syria). The British and the French defined borders according to their needs as well as for the needs of creating a Jewish state as promised in the Balfour Declaration.

At the turn of the twentieth century, the land area of Palestine underwent several changes. It began with the Sykes-Picot Agreement, which created the states of Syria, Jordan, Lebanon, and Palestine paving the way for the British Mandate over Palestine as well as implementation of the Balfour Declaration on November 2nd, 1917. Both have influenced Palestine and the entire region until the present.

3. The Formation

The Palestinian people are no different from the rest of the peoples of Great Syria. They are the result of accumulated ethnic, racial, and religious groups, who once lived, conquered, occupied, and passed through this strip of land. Wars and invasions have never totally replaced the local population in any period of history; rather, they added to, mixed with, and reformulated the local identity. The Palestinian people are the Canaanites, the Fillister, the Jews, the Jabousites, the Assyrians, the Babylonians, the Egyptians, the Aramairs, the Greeks, the Romans, the Byzantinians, the Arabs, the Turks, the Crusaders, and the Kurds, who once settled, conquered, occupied or just passed through Palestine. All of the above, regardless of the extent to which they affected the land and its population, left their mark in forming the Palestinian people and their identities. From the fourth century AD, the peoples in Palestine went through an *Arabization* process, which was strengthened in the Arab-Islamic invasion of the country in the first half of the seventh century.[10] Since then this process has given Palestine its "Arab identity," whatever this terminology means. This *Arab identity* encompassed several religions; Islam being the religion of the majority at least from the tenth century, as well as Christianity, and Judaism with all of their sub-religious groups. These three religions were, until the rise of Zionism, the main religious components of the Palestinian people.

As mentioned above, the term "Palestine" went through several stages of development. There is enough historical evidence of the formation of Palestine, tackling parts of it, or even going beyond Mandated borders; sometimes even including parts of "others" lands. Palestine, throughout history was parts of a greater empire, and we shall never discover a clear trend, in history, that defines Palestine as a geographic entity in its, Mandate borders. This historical context does not differentiate between Palestine and the rest of the countries/lands surrounding it (Jordan, Syria and Lebanon); all of them were connected to each other, in one way or another, and they were collectively parts of great empires. Some of these countries/lands, including Palestine, have enjoyed a certain level of independence or autonomy inside the empires (the Assyrian, Babylonian, Persian, Greco-Roman, Byzantine, Arab-Islamic...Ottoman). During the eighteenth-nineteenth centuries (the Ottoman period), however, a semi-independent state, under the leadership of Dhahir al-'Umar az-Zaidani, was established in the northern parts of Palestine, and sometimes included the center of the country, with Acer as a capital.[11] This phenomenon continued in different ways until the Egyptian invasion of 1831-1840. Some historians consider Dhahir al-'Umar to be the founder of the concept of a modern Palestinian independent state. Others reflect on the revolution of the Palestinian notables (1884 A.D.) against the Egyptians as the beginning of the formation of a Palestinian entity and identity. The discussion continued until the end of the nineteenth century, when more and more Palestinians, including those representing Palestine in the Ottoman Parliament, joined the critique of the polices of the Ottoman Empire in converting its subjects (including the Arabs) into Turks (at least from cultural point of view). These policies continued until the beginning of the twentieth century, thus producing more and more "localism" (local character as opposed to Ottomanization) including a Palestinian one.[12]

4. Identity and Conflict

A large number of historians have raised the question about the relation of the "Palestinians" to the land of Palestine. This question, far from being innocent, should be understood in the context of the denial of political rights, rather than a serious discussion of identity. This school believes that Palestinian identity is nothing but a reaction to the Zionist movement and its claim over Palestine.[13] Here we must differentiate between *identity* in its historical, social, and cultural dimensions and *identity* that grew up resulting from the mobilization of reaction, struggle and crucial abnormal realities. There is no society that has not reformulated, reshaped, and restructured its identity during long-lasting challenges. In the last century Palestinian identity went through tremendous changes and developments; all of which took place, of course, under the influence of Zionist claims. This identity can be described as very lively, with great adaptation and integrative power, just like any other identity facing denial and depression. The Palestinian struggle against Zionism and later against the State of Israel has left a tremendous influence on the Palestinian people in general and on their identity in particular. There is no way to understand this identity apart from the conflict.

Regardless of geography and history, Palestine has become well-known, at least from the 1960s on, all over the world in general, and in Latin America, Africa and the Middle East in particular, as a symbol for liberation and a symbol for anti-colonial struggle. The picture of the late Yassir Arafat with his *kufiyya* was portrayed internationally, symbolizing Palestine, which made him a familiar global personality. In this context, an internationally recognized Palestinian identity was reflected clearly; regardless of whether the Palestinians themselves liked it or felt comfortable with the image. This "identity," which reflects part of Palestinian identity, was not the only Palestinian identity, but rather was a symbol of the struggle for independence; it was a symbol of revolution, exceeding the importance of Palestine itself.

With the aaftermath of the 1967 occupation, there has been a rekindling of national interest among Palestinians in preserving material culture as a way to affirm "national identity" and attachment to the land. This *"Palestinian Awakening"* arose in the 1970's in the form of safeguarding what remained of local heritage, historical buildings, monuments, archaeological sites and ethnographic remains, personal belongings, art objects, etc.

Initially begun by individuals, this interest in salvaging, promoting and collecting different sorts of "heritage" objects, mainly embroidered clothing, later developed into a more structured practice. In the absence of a governmental body, it was the NGO's, mainly women's charitable societies and other national establishments - who initiated this drive. In the visual arts, symbols of Palestinian cultural heritage, pottery, embroidery, architecture, designs and landscape became intrinsic to the themes chosen by the artists. These symbols were supposed to emphasize issues of national identity, pride, belonging, and deep-rootedness to one's history and traditions.

5. National vs. Regional

The question is whether Palestinians can reflect their identity in different ways than they do now? I think the answer is yes. The artificial division of Great Syria was imposed on people. If there had been no Sykes-Picot Agreement, I am not sure that the Palestinian people would choose an independent state for their identity. However, statehood does not have much to do with identity; a state can include several peoples and a variety of identities. The idea of an independent Palestinian state was raised quite recently. In fact, the Palestinian national movement continued to market the conflict as an "Arab-Israeli" one and not as a "Palestinian-Israeli" one. The idea of a Palestinian independent state was raised in 1973 in the aftermath of the October War and after certain international, regional, and national political developments; while in 1974 the idea became the vehicle of the political program of the PLO.[14] Since then and up to the present, (but for how long I don't know) Palestinian has been completely organized accordingly.[15]

With the establishment of the PLO and different resistance organizations, mainly in the 1960s, the Palestinian identity went through an intensive politicization process. The PLO has exceeded its national and regional importance reaching wider circles all over the world. With the PLO, the Palestinian identity became, or was at least known as "revolutionary." The Palestinian became a young man/woman wearing a *kufiyya* and carrying a machinegun. The PLO has faced a complicated challenge, namely how to unify a nation and how to develop a shared identity for people(s) living under different political regimes and in different socio-economic contexts. Palestinians living in the West Bank were under the Jordanian regime, Palestinians in the Gaza Strip were under the Egyptian regime, and Palestinians in the north (1948 territories) remained under Israeli control, in addition to Palestinians in the Diaspora living all over the world. The PLO has actually implemented different political, cultural, and social programs and worked very hard to strengthen, shape, reshape and develop a national identity, vis-à-vis an Arab identity, with the aim of creating a nation fighting for freedom. This, in the mid-1960s, was a dreamy approach, but it led to tangible results. Shared political aspirations, which are not easy to maintain and to gather people around, were efficiently used. These aspirations became the major vehicle in forming the current "*Palestinian Identity*".

The PLO, in addition to the above mentioned facts, has managed to create communication systems connecting, under very difficult circumstances, different Palestinian groups/communities all over the world living under different terms. The hard work, regardless of the means and tools, which were implemented also led to the recognition of the Palestinian people, first by the Arabs and then, slowly, by the rest of the international community. This recognition was not really meant to acknowledge identity, but rather recognize the aspirations and political rights. In order to understand the meaning of that, it is worth mentioning the famous statement made by Golda Meier, the late prime-minister of Israel who denied completely the existence of the Palestinian people. Now Israel recognizes, even officially, the Palestinian people as such, regardless of their right to self-determination, which is internationally recognized. It will surely not be too long before Israel officially recognizes that also in spite of the fact that some argue that this recognition had already been made in the Oslo Peace Accords of 1993.

6. Identity and Cultural Heritage

The Palestinian people have had, like any other nation, a long experience in the process of integration in the surrounding environment; thus producing a rich cultural heritage, which became an essential part of their identity. The components of this heritage vary from archaeological and historical sites, through an incredibly rich vernacular architecture, holy shrines and sanctuaries, songs, dancing, ethnographic instruments and tools, embroidery...etc. These components have been utilized, reproduced, restructured and sharpened in the last five decades, mainly as a reaction to the denial of the existence of a Palestinian identity and as a reaction to the destruction of more than four hundred Palestinian villages and towns in the aftermath of the War of 1948.

The losses in cultural heritage in that wave of destruction are tremendous and mostly irreversible. The only remains of this destruction are the maps built-up areas, which were prepared by the British Mandate, the memories of people and, luckily, a few pictures. The rest: buildings, mosques, churches, plazas, *maqams* (holy saints and sanctuaries), the cultural landscape, land use, memories related to place and space, cemeteries, holy trees and caves...etc.[16] Different components of cultural heritage and identity (identities) are lost forever.

We need to note that most of these components are of a rural origin. Palestinian urban centers are actually very difficult to differentiate from those of Great Syria and were not represented in this *identity*. Therefore, on one hand, people tend to use cultural symbols of the village because they were mostly targeted by destruction; while on the other hand, village symbols are ideal to reflect the relationship between the Palestinian people and their land, a theme that stands at the center of the Palestinian – Israeli conflict.[17] Praise of the land was also used as a vehicle for cultural identity, reflected in literature, dance, fine art, and of course in political education.

We must bear in mind too that the expulsion of Palestinians in 1948 from their homeland was detrimental, as is evident in the expropriation of hundreds of towns and villages by the State of Israel. The Zionist nature of Israel led to crude attempts to acquire political, historical and cultural legitimacy in Palestine. This hegemony resulted in the exploitation, destruction and manipulation of existing Palestinian cultural heritage. Thus, in a deliberate attempt to minimize all memory of the history and existence of Palestinians on their land, more than four hundred towns and villages with their typical Palestinian architectural character were demolished or eradicated. Most of the physical aspects of Palestinian life and tradition, houses, furniture, personal belongings, photographs, documents etc. were lost. In the rush of leaving, people sadly chose to take just the necessary possessions, leaving behind households and public places full of belongings and memories, which represented centuries and centuries of the history, taste, beliefs and social life of Palestinian society.

Above all, most Palestinians were forced to leave behind the historical, archaeological and natural heritage of their ancestors. Whoever remained in the land occupied by Israel had to struggle to retain their identity as "Arab" and/or "Palestinians."

7. Identify and Cultural Heritage Symbols

Most of the well-known Palestinian symbols of identity are drawn from the fact that the majority of Palestinians are refugees. The identity of the refugee was a movable identity: *kufiyyah*, embroidery, traditional songs, *dabka*, a house key, a picture, a land registration document, a Palestinian passport (British Mandate), a map of Palestine, a picture of the Dome of the Rock and many stories about space, which are colored by nostalgia. The immovable cultural heritage played a minor part in the formation of identity. These components of identity could be carried by the refugee and Diaspora Palestinians wherever they went and could be easily shown and demonstrated.

Prior to 1991, the Occupied Palestinian Territories had witnessed a growth of interest in material culture, mainly ethnographic collections in the form of museums. These museums were mostly established by women's charitable organizations such as *In'ash al-Usra* in al-Bireh, *Dar at-Tifl al-'Arabi* in Jerusalem, and *Baituna al-Talhami* in Bethlehem...etc. These were strengthened through the challenges of the 1967 Israeli Occupation of the rest of Palestine. In parallel, a series of publications appeared to highlight Palestinian cultural heritage and identity. Most prominent was *Majallat at-Turath wal-Mujtama'* (Heritage and Society), published by *Jam'iyyat*

In'ash al-Usra. This phenomenon was dominant in Palestine (both 1948 and 1967 Palestine) as well as among Palestinians in the Diaspora. Still, until 1991, the most important elements of Palestinian cultural heritage were movable objects and relevant research. This is of course an influence of the PLO, as a Diaspora Liberation Organization, Heritage was merely a tool to fortify the united identity of different Palestinian groups spread across the Middle East in addition to Palestine and elsewhere in the world. This tool was used efficiently in the conflict and mainly for the right of return and the right of self-determination; hence, it is understood that the owners of such a heritage are the owners of such rights.

The PLO, as mentioned above, was mainly a diaspora representative, so immovable cultural heritage was not the focal point of its activities, hence it cannot be reproduced, or exhibited and is difficult to research unless it is conducted by Palestinians living under Israeli occupation. This was not really achieved in the first two decades of the Israeli Occupation; hence, inside Palestine, the ideologies as well as the practices of the PLO prevailed.

One component of the immovable cultural heritage of Palestine, namely archaeology, was a subject of intensive research from the second half of the nineteenth century; even so, it too was a victim of ideological possession. In spite of that, extensive research has produced a tremendous amount of information on major sites all over Palestine. It reconstructed the main historical periods, produced thousands of publications (books, articles, maps, illustrations, reports… etc), uncovered a countless number of archaeological artifacts (exhibited or stored in museums, academic institutions, and private collections all over the world)…etc.

Archaeologists came from the West, and dug up archaeological sites, using local Palestinian workers, but did not communicate with the communities around the sites. They were hunters of objects as well as publishers of the results of their research in their mother languages.[18] The local population was a very important element of anthropological reference in understanding the discoveries. Therefore, the level of attachment between the local population and their historical sites was marginal. The local tendency, in spite of the establishment of the Palestinian Department of Antiquities, has not changed much even today.

The other component of immovable cultural heritage in Palestine, namely architecture, failed to attract the same level of interest as archaeology. Three different kinds of architectural heritage in Palestine can be examined in order to clarify the issue.

Historical monument buildings: These monuments, which fall under the judicial definition of archaeology, mean buildings which were built before 1700, which are protected by the current antiquities laws. These buildings in general have attracted the interest of both authorities and researchers: Greco-Roman, Byzantine, Early Muslim, Crusader, Ayyubid, and Mamluk. Recently, Ottoman buildings have also become a subject of research.[19]

Religious buildings: Muslim, Jewish and Christian holy sites, regardless of their judicial level of protection, were also a subject of interest by the relevant authorities (mainly religious authorities) as well as researchers.[20]

Vernacular architecture: Very little attention was given to vernacular architecture, which can be considered a major component of the cultural heritage of Palestine. Early studies and documentation were conducted by C. T. Wilson[21] and G. Dalman[22] with the aim of reconstructing biblical traditions rather than examining the relationship between the people in Palestine and the environment. These studies, which are of key importance and vital for reconstructing traditional life in Palestine, are loaded with biblical and Talmudic citations. The Palestinian physician, Tawfiq Canaan noted the connection between man and his environment for better than previous researches.[23] In the aftermath of 1967 with the gradual growth of a Palestinian local intellectual elite, the need for further ties between man and his environment began to grow slowly. The need, under the pressure of Israeli settlement policies to rediscover Palestinian heritage, made more and more people interested in the cultural landscape.[24]

When Western researchers arrived in Palestine in the nineteenth century, the concept of a cultural landscape did not exist. Since those researchers worked in the framework of historical geography, places were only linked to historical or religious events. Discoveries in the cultural landscape of Palestine started with the Palestinian Excavation Fund, and the Survey of Western Palestine. Palestine was divided into twenty-seven sections on maps with a 1:100000 scale; cultural and geographical landmarks were referred to by their local and biblical names. Other surveys were implemented parallel to this one. It should be mentioned that the most important survey was carried out during the French invasion of Palestine in 1799. The problem with these surveys however, is that they failed to produce realistic maps. Instead, they indicate geographical and cultural landmarks without linking them to geography, sea level, or scale maps. In addition to the surveys, many of the foreign missions wrote of their travels in accounts that interwove documentation of Palestine from geographical, ethnic or historical concepts.[25] The value of these texts relies on their depiction of the cultural landscape of Palestine prior to twentieth century technology.

The focal point for research gradually changed from that of the cultural landscape to historical and cultural sites. This came about for the following reasons: 1. The main interest was on historical sites connected with Old Testament events; 2. The influence of urban archaeology, which studies cultures and civilizations existing in the same area from antiquity to the present by studying indications of change in pottery. Thus, a site's connection to its environment, its cultural landscape, was neglected. The field of cultural landscape remained relatively intact, and was influenced to a certain extent only by the Bible. This makes it a key for future development in archaeology and other sciences of history, in view of the development in modern scientific technology, and theories connected to sciences of cultural landscape especially geology, which enabled the expansion and increase in its areas of study.

Archaeology in Palestine was, and still is, a very sensitive, ideologically and politically tainted issue. This is because archaeological research in Palestine has been intricately tied to the region's historical development since the 1850s. Thus, it is essential to review this context in order to properly assess the current status and its perspectives for the future. The aim of this assessment is not just to reflect shortcomings, failures, and successes of past efforts, but also to trace the history of those tendencies which led to today's more scientific, objective and modern archaeology, which still struggles to free itself from the ideological pressure and influence of political conflicts.

8. Final Remarks

To target the relationship between cultural heritage and identity it was necessary to revise the history of research in relevant fields. It is clear that the Palestinian people were very marginal in effecting the development of these sciences and applying them in Palestine during the last fifteen decades. The relatively long history of research in Palestine managed to establish strong foundations of historical writing. This development led to the marginalization of certain ethnic groups, certain historical periods, certain materials of culture and above all certain legitimacies.

It is also obvious that the tremendous number of publications on Palestine/the Holy Land/the Land of the Bible/Israel/Canaan etc. deal mainly with the land as if there are no people living on it, or at least those who are living on it have no historical relationship with the land.

Treating the history of Palestine starts with abstaining from deliberately marginalizing or even erasing the history of others. I believe that a particular Palestinian strength resides in the traditional cultural and religious pluralism that shaped its history in the past. With accepting the concept of pluralism, balance in historical research becomes possible. This understanding, of course, includes a critical assessment of the written sources on which research relies, and which present the country's history as a mere history of generations of sovereigns governing Palestine. Modern history, in contrast, considers the history of large social groups with varying cultures. For the sake of greater precision, the history of cities and countries cannot be reduced to kings and dynasties; it is also the history of collective social groups and their varied identities. Palestine from a cultural perspective is an essential part of the region and not isolated form it, regardless of its religious merits. Palestinians are the result of all the nations, religious, or ethnic groups who ever settled in Palestine or passed through it. Therefore the history of these peoples is the history of Palestine.

2

Identity, Belonging, and Home (Land):

Diaspora People Engaging with Palestinians on the Question of Identity

Eleazar S. Fernandez

"If the Olive Trees knew the hands that
planted them,
Their oil would become Tears."

Mahmūd Darwīsh

My contribution to the conversation on the topic of Palestinian identity is through the lens of diasporized communities. I seek to bring global diaspora literature into conversation with Palestinian diaspora literature on the issue of identity and homeland for the purpose of helping to sharpen intra-Palestinian conversation on the issue and of forging an alliance between Palestinians and other members of the global community, particularly the diaspora. Diaspora literature will be explored, especially as it touches on the issues of identity and homeland, and attempts will be made to relate them to the Palestinian articulation of identity. What are the experiences of other diaspora people that may help sharpen Palestinians' naming and articulation of identity? What are some of the perspectives from diaspora studies that bring something to bear on the Palestinian issue of identity and homeland?

1. Identity, Belonging, and Home

Diaspora triggers an intense articulation of identity, belonging, and home. These three dimensions are intertwined and inseparable. In diaspora the once considered stable identity experiences tremors as individuals or communities undergo the travail of uprootment, dispossession, displacement, and marginalization. Diaspora pushes one to the edge or to the border of life in which the once considered stable and constant center no longer holds. As diasporized persons encounter others who make a claim on shared and fluid space, the issue of identity comes to the fore and becomes a contested issue. Diaspora brings instability and fluidity to the notion of self and leads to such questions as: "Who am I?" or "Who are we?" (And conversely, who are they?)

The matter of identity cannot be separated from the matter of belonging. If diaspora leads to the question of "Who am I?" or "Who are we?" it also leads to the question, "Where do I belong?" or "Where do we belong?" The question of belonging intensifies as a group, particularly when the dominant group, feels threatened and the issues of security and loyalty are raised. One is forced to take account of one's primary allegiance, and equivocation is not acceptable: "Are you with us?"

Moreover, the issue of identity and belonging leads to the question of home. What is home? Where is home? What constitutes home? How shall we relate the experience of diaspora and home? How does the experience of diaspora contribute to the notion of home as well as homeland?

The issue of home (and homeland) becomes intense as those in the diaspora are forced to take account of home by those who also stake a claim on the same shared space, especially by those considered long-time inhabitants of the place. But it can also be the reverse: long-time inhabitants may be forced to take account of home as newcomers themselves, particularly when recently arrived newcomers assume the form of occupiers/colonizers, displacing, uprooting, and disempowering long-time inhabitants. Long-time inhabitants may then experience diaspora/exile in their homeland; they may even experience being prisoners in their homeland.

This is how many Palestinians see their situation. As Saddik Gohar has noted, by the end of the catastrophic year (1948) the concept of land took two forms in the eyes of the Palestinian people: exile and prison. Exile includes all countries where Palestinian refugees live, whether inside Palestine or outside it; while prison involves Palestinian land that is under the Israeli flag.[1]

2. Diaspora Identity:
Constructed, Fluid, Shifting, and Multiple

Michael Lapsley, a priest from New Zealand who went to South Africa during the apartheid era, shares some thoughts that help us understand the fluid, shifting, and multiple characters of identity, belonging, and home. He said: "Before I went to South Africa, I thought of myself as a human being. On arrival in South Africa, my humanness was removed and I became a white man."[2] Lapsley experienced a fluid and shifting identity as he moved from one socio-geographical location to another, an experience that is revelatory of the character of our lives.

My awareness of the politics of identity was heightened during an Israel-Palestine immersion trip in 2012, which I co-led with Peter Makari, area executive for the Middle East and Europe of the Global Ministries of the United Church of Christ USA as well as for the Christian Church—Disciples of Christ. One day our immersion group went to the Golan Heights (a territory which belongs to Syria, and has been occupied by Israel since 1967). Its terrain and resources (e.g., water, vegetation, etc.) make it strategic in a comprehensive sense, not just militarily. Our group stopped by a cherry farm and I had the chance to ask a few questions of a farmer by the name of Jamil. I asked Jamil if he had been in the area during the war with Israel and if he was Syrian. He confirmed that he was Syrian by birth and nationality and that he also carries an Israeli ID. Afterwards he spoke about his love for his land, and why he did not leave the place even during the war that led to its occupation. As a person living on land (his own) under Israeli occupation, he said that he is loyal to whomever is the ruling power (currently the State of Israel). He abides by the rules of the occupier in order to survive. But, at the end of the conversation, he expressed his longing for the return of the territory to Syria.

Israel-Palestine is one of the best places in the world to study the politics of identity. Identity is a construct and it shifts. One does not have to move physically in order to experience shifting identities and location. In some instances, it is the boundary of the nation-state that moves. One's identity is subject to political vicissitudes, and it can be terribly oppressive. This has been the plight of Palestinians and Syrians in the Golan Heights.

This discourse of shifting identity is not always welcome, particularly by those who are invested in "nativistic" politics. As much as possible, they want to hold to any semblance of solid, pure, and stable identity. Nativistic claims are played out by various groups to varying degrees for different purposes. Indigenous communities are not exempt from this tendency; perhaps a reaction to the threats they have experienced from the settler-colonialists. The irony, however, is that the more a solid and stable identity is asserted, the more it reveals its constructed and fluid nature. At the core of its claim, if we may speak of a core, is the construct of a power-knowledge nexus.[3] Power-knowledge constructs identity for various reasons. Counter-hegemonic hermeneutics does not escape becoming a new hegemony by claiming that it is devoid of a power-knowledge nexus. What counter-hegemonic hermeneutics must do is to expose the power-knowledge nexus of all forms of discourse.

Identity is not only fluid and shifting, it is also multiple. We assume multiple identities across time as our geographical and social locations change. One expression of our multiple identities may gain prominence depending on our geographical and social context. If we have multiple identities and they shift across time and place, then we assume multiple and shifting positions in power relations. Our position in power relations is not constant. This is important as we think of the plight of Israeli Jews in relation to the Palestinians. Furthermore, to pursue the point of shifting and multiple identities, we also must recognize multiple and shifting narratives or stories.

Diaspora places people at the borders (geographical, political, and cultural) which enables the diaspora to hear multiple and, sometimes, conflicting and overlapping stories of various communities. Being at the borders, the diaspora is exposed to the narratives that various groups share about their understanding of who they are and their perception of others. This has important implications as we explore ways of dwelling together in a shared place. We will pursue and articulate the implications of this in the last section of this essay.

3. Identity and Relations: The Evolving and Shifting Palestinian Identity

Identity is a relational concept. Identity exists and develops in relationship with others. It is a constant dance with others. Identity always develops in relation to its surroundings, particularly in relationship to people and social events. There is no space outside of this relationship in which we become who we are. Social relations constitute the main ingredients for identity formation. Our relationship defines who we are. Identity evolves through the process of differentiation. Several factors contribute to the process of differentiation. The development of national consciousness, for example, may be triggered and hastened by outside political forces, such as conquest and colonization by foreign powers. The loosely defined and scattered multi-ethnic groups may feel the need to bond together in response to invaders. As time evolves, a national consciousness or a nation-state may be born.

Human communities see and construct difference in the process of identity formation. The constructions of "we" and "they" and "us" and "them" are all part of identity formation. There may be difference/es, but difference is not the problem. The main problem is our attitude toward difference and how we deal with difference. As Audre Lorde puts it succinctly, the main problem "is rather our refusal to recognize those differences, and to examine the distortions which result from our misnaming them and their effects upon human behavior and expectation."[4] To be different from another is not the same as be against. The good news is that we can be different but not necessarily against each other.

Sadly, the dominant identity formation in our society is that of being "over against the other." It seems easy to fall into this destructive pattern which basically is finding an identity set in opposition to the other. Even more, it elevates one's primary identity marker over another. In the context of unequal power relations, it can be individually and corporately imposed on others. When one's identity is equated with the cultural norm, the worst of systemic violence results. Various forms of fundamentalism, whether religious or secular, can be interpreted as an expression of an identity posed "over against the other."

Unfortunately, the evolution of contemporary Palestinian and Jewish identities has been such that, in many ways, they are yoked and defined against each other. The "Day of Independence" for Israel is *al-Nakba* (the great Catastrophe) for Palestinians. "Settlement" for the Jews is "occupation" and "displacement" of Palestinians. "Security" for Israel is "imprisonment" for Palestine. The partitioning of the land called Palestine into two states to accommodate two peoples is also the beginning of contemporary articulation of antagonistic and polarizing identities. This polarization of two identities, however, is more disadvantageous to Palestinians. Rashid Khalidi contends that "it often means that permission cannot be granted for a Palestinian voice to be heard—even on matters having absolutely nothing to do with Israel—without the reassuring presence of its Israeli echo. The opposite, of course, is not exactly true: a Palestinian voice is not necessarily required when exclusively Israeli or Jewish concerns are aired."[5]

Beyond the antagonistic definition of each other's identities, larger forces are at work shaping the articulation of identities. The interaction between the Arab world and the wider global context has influenced the way Palestinians articulate their identity. I hear an echo of Mahmūd Darwīsh, the poet: "Israeli repression transformed me into an Arab, and that disappointment with the Arabs transformed me into a Palestinian."[6]

It is indeed true that Zionist repression turned Palestinians into Arabs. Palestinians identified with the Arabs and had high hopes that the Arab world would stand steadfast by their side. They were disappointed, to say the least. Even in the Arab countries where Palestinians live in exile "a knight stabs his brother in the chest" and there "my dream leaves me only to make me laugh/or make people laugh at someone leading a dream like a camel in a market of whores," says Darwīsh. In their exiles in the neighboring Arab countries, Palestinian refugees were slaughtered by Arabs (such as the Lebanese, the Syrians, and the Jordanians), just as they were massacred by Zionists in Palestine. Palestinians living in refugee camps in Lebanon were brutally attacked by the Israeli army and its Lebanese allies, right-wing Christian militias with the support of Israel.[7]

Disappointment with the Arabs, following Darwīsh, turned them into Palestinians. Even as they have continued to identify themselves with the Arab world, the Palestinian experience is distinctively theirs. Palestinians must articulate their own unique identity, for no other people, much as they seek to be in solidarity with them, can live their lives, mourn their losses, and die their deaths. It is only as Palestinians are able to articulate their own experience and identity that they will survive and thrive as a people. The power to articulate this Palestinian identity is critical, especially as the more dominant forces surrounding them have the means and power to impose their definition of Palestinian identity. The Zionist propaganda machine, with the help of the U.S. and other Western countries, has been aggressive in defining Palestinian identity.

In many ways, Jewish Zionists and their Western allies have been effective in shifting the world's opinion of Palestinians from refugees to desperate and primitive insurgents to terrorists. When Palestinians are cast as terrorists, the massacre of civilians is less likely to generate much sympathy and support, because people find it difficult to understand the notion of the "massacre of terrorists." There is no such thing as terrorists being massacred. When one is portrayed as a terrorist, the humanity of the person is taken away. Michelle Saracino makes the point that "[a]s long as Palestinians, or any other for that matter, are unilaterally typed as terrorists they cannot be acknowledged as flesh-and-blood human beings with particular stories, memories, and feelings that must be heeded."[8] We can find something similar in the plight of the prisoners in Guantanamo or Abu Ghraib. If the humanity of prisoners is removed, it is difficult for people to hear their cries or hear them as victims of torture.

Hence, there is a need to intensify efforts to articulate a different portrayal of Palestinians; there is a need for concerted action to articulate and project a different identity. There seems to be a shift in the way Palestinians have been perceived by the global community in recent years. Today, many have moved to recast the Palestinians not as perpetrators of terror but as the underdogs and the victims of Israeli politics. These shifts in the public image of Palestinians demonstrate how the portrayals of Palestinians are dependent upon their interaction with Israel and other communities throughout the world. We need to articulate and lift up the cries and stories of Palestinians. We need to let the public know of the pain and suffering of the Palestinian people, especially in a world in which they are prevented even from expressing their laments in public.

4. Al-Nakba:

Reclaiming the Right to Mourn

The creation of the State of Israel is *al-Nakba* (the great Catastrophe) for the Palestinians. Palestinians were forced to leave their country twice, once in 1948 and again in 1967, after the occupation of all Palestinian territories. In their third exodus in 1982, Palestinian refugees in Lebanon were subjected to more suffering. Darwīsh cries: "The sea cannot take immigration/oh, the sea has no room for us." Some Palestinian refugees who survived the genocide of the camps, whom Darwīsh calls "the generation of the massacre," are doomed to move from one exile to another exile only to be killed: "Every land I long for as a bed/dangles as a gallows."[9]

The *al-Nakba* and its consequences must be mourned. The prophet Jeremiah reminds us that there is no hope without mourning. We cannot jump into hope without the freedom to weep. Jeremiah tells his people that only as they lament their pain will they be able to imagine new beginnings or new possibilities. He summons his people to grieve or mourn. This permission to weep and mourn freely may startle the people, but Jeremiah longs for an even fuller expression of grief to be possible, that his head would be a spring of water and his eyes a fountain of tears so that he could weep day and night for his suffering and fallen people (Jeremiah 9:1)

Adding cruelty to suffering, the Palestinians have been prevented from lamenting in public, because the Jews have made a monopoly of suffering (the Holocaust). "Is there anything more cruel than this absence: that you should *not be the one to…lament your [own] defeat?*" [10] The State of Israel has censored the rights of Palestinian refugees to express their feelings about their plight. Their poetry of lamentations and elegies have been considered forms of political protest.[11] The attempts of the colonizers (the Zionists) to erase the history and culture of colonized peoples (Palestinians) by dismissing their poetry of exile as propaganda is, in the words of Edward Said, part of "the moral epistemology of imperialism." [12]

The lamenting or mourning that I am speaking about needs to be distinguished from melancholy. Melancholy causes one to get stuck in a state of narcissism; thus, one may speak of narcissistic mourning. Narcissistic mourning festers like an "open wound." Narcissistic mourning is the inability to mourn with and for others because the only suffering that counts is one's own suffering. On the other hand, the mourning of lament pushes people to move on; it is a prelude to hope or it is an integral part of hope. Without the courage to mourn, Palestinians would not be able to articulate their soaring hopes.

5. Land, Memory, and Nostalgia: Living in the "Future Imperfect"

Land remains central for the identity of the diasporized. Perhaps the intensity of attachment to the land or the desire to return to the land becomes stronger because of one's separation, especially when forced out by invasion and occupation. Forced separation from one's homeland is a traumatic experience. Palestinian poets speak of the loss of homeland as tormenting the soul and splitting the body "*into two halves,*" which may be described as "existing between a loved but dead past and a living but agonized present. At the same time, these words point out that the past and the present cannot be simply separated from one another."[13] In the lines of Safiq Kabha, "We became an intoxicated people who go to sleep and wake up in the love of their homeland. Oh […] you, my body that is torn into two halves, a living one and another that lived, and the living half is left for pain and suffering."[14] This resonates with Said's account of exile: "Exile is strangely compelling to think about but terrible to experience. It is the *unhealable rift* [emphasis supplied] forced between human being and a native place, between a self and its true home."[15] "Unhealable," indeed, because "nothing," says Darwīsh, "will bring [him] back from my free distance to [his] palm tree: not peace, nor war... Nothing takes [him] away from the butterfly of [his] dreams back into [his] present: not earth, nor fire." [16]

Darwīsh speaks of exile as an experience of a profound "insubstantial existence." Its effects are far-reaching, so much so that Darwīsh articulates this transient experience as a form of weightlessness: [The exiles] "have become weightless,/as light as our dwellings in distant winds." He describes it: "We have both been freed from the gravity of the land of identity." Western postmodern sensibility must not be too quick to pick up the positive connotation here because, for Darwīsh, to be "freed" from the land is like unmooring a ship, or perhaps, more appropriately, cutting off a tree at the roots. In Darwīsh's lines: "Nothing is left of me except you./ Nothing is left of you except me." [17]

In "The Desert Exile," Jabra Ibrahim expresses a sense of nostalgia for his homeland in Palestine: "Our land is an emerald/but in the desert of exile/spring after spring/only the dust hisses in our face." Ibrahim refers to the suffering of the Palestinian refugees who live in exile appealing to a homeland they feel they have lost forever: "remember us/with our eyes full of dust/that never clears in our careless wandering." [18] Palestinians are attached to their homeland because Palestine, to Ibrahim, "is a reality that exists; it is a land that has been usurped by a ruthless enemy, a mother, a sister, a wife raped by the colonizer..." [19]

Palestinian exiles and the diaspora seek and dream of returning to the land. However, as circumstances make it more and more difficult to speak of immediate return, their discourse assumes the tone of a remote and distant future. Fawaz Turki speaks of 'living in the future imperfect.' Living in the future imperfect—when next year, next time, next speech, the wrong will have been righted, when grievances removed, and our cause justified... Godot for whom we waited never arrived."[20] What is it like to live waiting for something that you believe may never come, or you have already believed will not arrive?

6. Diaspora / Exile as a Permanent Habitat: Living on the Threshold as a Permanent Home

As the possibility of physical return to the once upon a time Palestine becomes more and more remote, the literal return shifts to a more symbolic articulation of land, identity, and home. This is not to discount place (geography), but the sense of place expands to embrace something beyond geography, and the meaning of being a Palestinian also expands. Maybe, as Helena Lindholm Schulz puts it in her account of diaspora identities, "we don't live in places after all," but "maybe learn to live in lives." [21] Palestine is a practice or a way of living wherever one is located, which is not a negation of the importance of place, but an adaptation in the context of forced displacement.

"After twenty-five years of living in the ghourba, of growing up permanently reminded of my status as an exile, the diaspora for me, for a whole generation of Palestinians, becomes the homeland. Palestine is no longer a mere geographical entity but a *state of the mind*," [22] says Fawaz Turki. In exile Turki has learned to live on the "threshold" as a "permanent habitat." Obsession with return means the reconstitution of a Palestinian integrity and the regaining of his place in history.[23]

Exile/diaspora has become a state of mind for many diaspora Palestinians. Even in the event of the possibility of peace and return, something cannot be undone because exile has become, for Darwīsh, a state of mind that he carries wherever he happens to be. In fact, it has become who he is; diaspora/exile has become his identity. "What will I do? What will I do without exile, and a long night that stares at the water?" [24]

Palestine, for those in the diaspora, is much larger than the land of Palestine even as it is always connected to the land. It stretches far beyond the geographic confines of the land of Palestine. Palestine reaches to every corner of the world where the Palestinian diaspora are present and have found a home, that is, where they are thriving and finding their voices, singing their own songs, and dancing their own dances. This home is where they re-enact the life of Palestine away from the homeland and engage in political and religious practices that support the aspirations of the Palestinian people. It is in the diaspora that the possibility of a *transnational identity* is emerging. Members of the diaspora form new lives in new settings and the idea of homeland becomes important, but it is not the only source of identity.

Extending Palestine beyond geography to a category of practices wherever one is located (whether in the Occupied Territories or in the diaspora) cannot be underestimated if the diaspora are to speak of their survival as a people in the context of a vanishing homeland. As the struggle for homeland continues, so must the struggle to articulate a narrative of the Palestinian people continue if they are to survive and thrive in the face of *al-Nakba* and its continuing consequences.

7. Moving Beyond Trauma: A New Identity

"A pain that is not transformed is transferred," Richard Rohr so aptly says.[25] The wounded may develop what Marc Gopin calls "negative identity," which is an identity that has developed out of a negative or traumatic experience. As he puts it, "If the rule of deep identity of the stranger is 'Love your neighbor as you love yourself' (Leviticus 19:18), then the rule of superficial identity or negative identity is 'Do unto others what they have done unto you, or before they do it unto you again.'"[26] Sadly, the formation of the dominant Jewish identity has taken this direction. Palestinians need to avoid falling into a similar trap.

We have witnessed ugly expressions of this negative identity formation in the monopolization and elevation of suffering (the Holocaust) by the Jews at the expense of others, particularly the Palestinians. As Rosemary and Herman Ruether articulated so well, "The effort to elevate Jewish suffering to unique status, incomparable with any other suffering, is self-defeating. It signals to other people a lack of generosity and solidarity with their suffering. It evokes a response of like ungenerosity."[27]

The wounded/pained must experience healing before she or he becomes a "wounded-healer." More appropriately, we must move beyond "wounded-healer" to "mending-healer." Only those who are "mending" can be "healers." One cannot lead out of a damaged self. Indeed, as Gillian Rose reminds us, "[p]olitics does not happen when you act on behalf of your own damaged goods but when you act, without guarantees, for the good of all—that is to take the risk of the universal interest."[28]

The formation of negative identity is a common outcome of a negative or traumatic experience. When we should expect the opposite, what we often encounter is ungenerosity and inhospitality. However, although the formation of negative identity seems a common outcome, it is not the necessary outcome of a painful and traumatic experience. When woundedness undergoes healing, one develops a greater ability to understand the wounds of others and become mending healers. When pain undergoes healing, one develops the ability to listen to the pains and voices of others. Similarly, out of one's experience of displacement and being pushed to the borders one may develop a greater ability to listen and understand the stories of others.

Being within the borders gives us the privilege of hearing the stories of others and, perhaps to our surprise, we may discover the overlapping of our stories. Within the borders we may come to the awareness that there is no pure single story, but a cacophony of stories vying to be heard. Within the borders we may come to see the binaristic stories of good and evil we have created of each other, which have prevented us from seeing the complexity of our identity. Within the borders we may discover that a part of our story is implicated in the other. The best antidote to stories becoming pathological is to put ourselves within hearing range of the stories of others. Perhaps, Within the borders, we may learn to let go of a single story identity and begin to embrace the complexities of our identity and the overlapping of our stories. I hope that within the borders we will hear our calling, which is to be open to the call of another's story.[29] I hope that in the hearing of another's story our hearts begin to embrace the life and stories of others. When this happens to us, we may discover that we are already living in the present, no matter how fragile and limited, and the future that we are longing for.

3

Palestinian Identity in Relation to Time and Space:

Palestinian Identity, Citizenship and the Role of Isa Al-Khuri Baseel Bandak in the British Era, (1919 - 1948)

Adnan Musallam

Introduction
Important Dimensions of Palestinian Arab Identity

Eternal attachment to the soil of Palestine, Islamic and Christian collective identities, Arab consciousness, dispersion throughout the world, anger and alienation, a vision of return, steadfastness on national soil, resistance and uprising the quest for self-determination and for a just and lasting peace... all these are important dimensions of Palestinian Arab national identity. This identity gives Palestinians everywhere, in the areas controlled by the Palestine National Authority (PNA), in the occupied territories or in the Palestinian Diaspora, a clear sense of a unified self hood.

Palestinian identity is neither a child of yesteryear, i.e., a child of World War I or World War II, or the 1948 Palestine War, or of the 1967 June War or of the Intifada. This identity is a result of the amalgamation of peoples and cultures and is an accumulation of cultural and human experiences which span human history from the dawn of civilization, and especially since the beginning of the third millennium B. C. when the Canaanites settled in the country and built highly fortified and developed city states. Palestine, as an integral part of Greater Syria/Bilad Ash-Sham, was always a crossroads of peoples and cultures connecting Europe, Asia and Africa.

Following the appearance of the Canaanite city-states, Palestine saw wave after wave of peoples who conquered and or settled in the country. With the establishment of Arab and Muslim rule in Palestine under the leadership of the second caliph 'Omar ibn Al-Khattab (634-644 A.D.), in 638 C.E.., an Arabization and Islamization processes began, leaving a permanent cultural legacy as seen in the present Arabic speaking peoples of Palestine including the modern inhabitants of Bethlehem who are Christian and Muslim Arabs. Arabization was manifested in the Arabic language and culture and gave Palestinians their predominantly Arab identity. Arabic became the native tongue and Arab culture supplanted the existing accumulated cultures of the peoples and conquerors who had inhabited the land since the dawn of history. Islamization, on the other hand, transformed the spiritual and social life of the majority of Palestinians.[1]

1. Modern National Awakening and Zionist Colonial Settlements

Before the emergence of national awakening, several identities already existed. The common Arab ethnic tribal background of both

Muslims and Christians in Palestine often transcended religious affiliations. This was seen clearly in the division of Arab society into southern Arabs (Yeman) and northern Arabs (Qays). In the ensuing alliances and conflicts during the decline of the Ottoman Empire from the latter seventeenth to the early nineteenth centuries one could see, for example, a Muslim town like Hebron and a Christian town like Beit Jala, both Qaysis, stand together to face their rivals among the Christians of Bethlehem and the Muslims of Jerusalem, both Yamanis.

Otherwise, Palestinians lived in harmony in the Sunni Muslim Ottoman state as loyal Ottoman subjects. However, the People of the Book (Christians Jews and others), had their religious identities as well within the Millet System and as Dhimmis/Protected People. The common Arab roots of Christians and Muslims, based in language, history, etc., would, become re-enlivened with the advent of Arab nationalism in the nineteenth century as nationalists wanted to liberate themselves from the Millet and Dhimmis systems. They wanted to be first class citizens like their fellow Muslims.

The Arab cultural renaissance of the nineteenth century and the deteriorating Arab Turkish relations on the eve of World War I played a key role in furthering Arab national consciousness among the Arabs of Palestine. Nakhle Zuraiq (18611921), a native of Beirut and a student of the leaders of Arab national renaissance, Butrus al Bustani, Nasif al Yaziji and Yusuf al'Asir, came to Jerusalem in 1889. He is credited with reviving Arabic language and literature in the schools of Jerusalem and Palestine. His students would become future Palestinian Arab national cultural leaders, including Khalil asSakakini, Ibrahim Touqan, Musa Aqel, and Saleem alHusayni, to mention a few.

Najeeb Nassar, another colorful Arab personality from Lebanon, who settled in Haifa and founded "al Carmel" newspaper in 1908, drew the attention of his fellow Arabs to Zionist settlements and the dangers of selling land to them. He translated the article "Zionism" (found in the *Encyclopedia Judaica*) into Arabic and published it in sixteen articles. In 1911 all of those articles were included in a booklet titled *Al-Sihyounia* (Zionism). It should be noted that the Palestinian dimension of Arab nationalism and identity began to crystalize gradually at this juncture, having gained momentum from the increased tempo of Zionist colonization in Palestine and the resulting deadly Arab- Zionist struggle over the land, which can be traced to 1882, and the establishment of "The First in Zion" colonial settlement in Ottoman Palestine.[2]

2. World War I (1914 - 1918) and its Long lasting Impact

The story of World War I and its impact on the Arab East has been treated in depth. Suffice it to say that despite Western promises to help Arabs attain independence, and despite the key role Arabs played in tipping the military balance in favor of the Allies in the region, geographical Syria (Bilad al-Sham) was divided by the same Western powers into small entities: Palestine, Lebanon, Syria and Transjordan (1916-1921), while the Balfour Declaration came into being in Palestine on 2 November 1917 and Palestine came under total British rule in September 1918.

Resentment of the West was felt mostly by Palestinian Arabs whose country was entrusted to Britain at the San Remo Conference of April 1920 with a proviso putting the Balfour Declaration (the establishment of a Jewish national home) into effect. From that time on anti-Western sentiments have been kept alive in Palestinian Arab national consciousness. These feelings were to become an integral part of Palestinian identity and the Palestinian national movement from the early 1920's on.

The solidarity of the people of the Bethlehem area with their fellow Palestinians was deeply entrenched, and was apparent in the activities of the various sectors of society. Thus, when the American King-Crane Commission of Inquiry arrived in Bethlehem on 17 June 1919 to ascertain the wishes of the local inhabitants regarding their future, they found that "in that old Biblical city all the delegations showed a very careful organization. They were in general agreement concerning the unity of Syria and Palestine, wanted complete independence if possible, and were opposed to Zionism and Jewish immigration." Even the phenomenon of Bethlehem area emigration to the Americas, which was given further impetus by the continued uncertainties of the Palestine problem throughout the twentieth century, became a political issue closely related to the emergence of Palestinian identity and the Arab Jewish conflict.

3. Palestinian Citizenship and the Question of the Return of Palestinian Arab Immigrants from Latin America

It is worth mentioning that a considerable number of immigrants living in Latin America desired to return to their country because they did not emigrate for the love of emigration but to improve their economic conditions or in an attempt to flee the horrors of continual conflicts. After the end of the First World War, many decided to practice their natural right of return to their birthplace. The

British authorities, however, closed the doors in their faces at a time when the doors of Palestine were wide open to Jewish immigrants. The Palestinian Citizenship Law was ratified in 1925 with the main aim of facilitating the granting of Palestinian citizenship to Jews coming to Palestine, according to Item 7 of the Mandate Charter.

Lauren E. Banko states that "The process of 'inventing' Palestinian citizenship was unlike anything else Great Britain had done in their colonial empire, especially because they had to take into account international treaties and regulations, Ottoman laws and the Balfour Declaration as it was included in the Mandate's charter."

Banko adds that the British saw Arab inhabitants as Ottoman citizens during the military and civil administrations during the period the Allies were at war with Turkey. The international recognition of Palestinian nationality became operative in light of the peace treaty (Treaty of Lausanne) between Turkey and the Allies on 24 July 1923. Concerning Palestinians residing abroad, Article 34 of the Treaty clearly mentions that these persons had two years to apply for the Palestinian nationality.[3]

Excerpts of immigrants' quests for Palestinian citizenship and the many problems encountered in their host countries as a result of not having citizenship were reported, discussed, and documented in leading Palestinian newspapers, mainly Jaffa's *Filastin* (Palestine) and Jerusalem's *al-Jami'ah al-'Arabiyyah* (The Arab Union) between 1926 and 1933.[4]

4. The Committee for the Defense of Immigrants Rights to Palestinian Citizenship

Notables of the Bethlehem region took up the case, under the leadership of Khalil 'Issa Morcos from Bethlehem, 'Atallah Hanna al-Najjar from Beit Jala, and 'Issa al-Khury Basil Bandak from Bethlehem (owner of the newspaper "Sawt al-Sha'b" and later Mayor of Bethlehem and one of the founder of "The Committee for the Defense of Immigrants Rights to Palestinian Citizenship" in 1927). The Committee led the campaign against the oppressive British policy that allowed incoming alien Jewish immigrants to obtain citizenship under the easiest conditions, while placing numerous obstacles in the face of native-born Palestinians who wanted to return to their country. The Committee launched an appeal to the British people in the form of a booklet on the question of the emigrants and the obstacles created by the British authorities preventing Palestinians abroad from obtaining Palestinian citizenship.[5]

'Issa al-Bandak, Mayor of Bethlehem (1934-1938), raised the question before "Lord Peel's Royal Commission" that came to Palestine in 1936 to investigate disturbances and rebellion in the country, and to recommend the partitioning of Palestine in 1937. The Royal Commission recommended in its report the facilitation of measures of return for those emigrants with genuine intentions who kept continual personal contact with Palestine.[6]

The Defense Committee demanded in its campaign that all Palestinian immigrants residing abroad should be considered, at their request, Palestinian citizens, and that all Palestinian emigrants who returned to Palestine or had temporarily stayed away should obtain their right to Palestinian citizenship as soon as they submitted official applications to the relevant departments. The Defense Committee demanded that orders be circulated to all British government representatives throughout the Palestinian Diaspora to defend and protect the interest of all Palestinian Arabs until the government acknowledged their right to Palestinian citizenship. "The government should consider these applications indicative of the feelings of Palestinian Arab public opinion in the country and abroad…"[7]

5. Isa Al-Khuri Baseel Bandak (1898 – 1984)

The Beginning

'Isa Basil Bandak's Palestinian activism began to emerge in 1919 with the founding of Al-Nadi Al-Adabi (Ethical or Literary Club), and **Bayta Lahm** a monthly review. Al-Nadi Al-Adabi, was the first non-sectarian organizations whose members shared indignation at the outmoded social customs and unchecked power of alien Church hierarchies and espoused as well the nation-state of United Arab Syria. **Bayta Lahm**, the first printed mass publication in Bethlehem's history, which lasted for two years, appeared on September 11, 1919 as a general monthly review. It was published from September through June; for July and August subscribers were offered a short novel written by Yuhana Khalil Dakkarat, one of the founders and editors of the journal and president of Bethlehem's Literary Club. These short novels dealt with social issues facing Arab society and included **Zulm al-Walidayn** (*Injustice of Parents*), 1920, and **Asl al-Shaqa'** (*Source of Misery*), 1921.

Bayta Lahm was not so much a moneymaking scheme as it was an outlet for the secular views of its founders, Yuhanna Khalil Dakkarat and 'Isa Basil Bandak, and the Literary Club, which both men helped to found and lead. It was also a tool of expression for the literary, political, educational, and social views of fellow Arabs in the Bethlehem area, in Palestine and Syria, and in the Diaspora in the Americas.

Yuhanna Dakkarat's colleague in both the Literary Club and **Bayta Lahm**, 'Isa al-Khuri Basil Bandak, was born in 1898 to Father Basil Bandak, an Eastern Orthodox Arab clergyman, and to Mariam Bandak. 'Isa attended the local Orthodox elementary school as well as the Christian Brothers (Freres) school and continued his preparatory and secondary education in the Christian Brothers School in Jerusalem. Unable to acquire higher education due to the outbreak of World War I, young Bandak joined the Ottoman telegraphic service where he served in various Syrian (including Palestinian) cities such as Hums, al-Salt and Jerusalem. Upon British entry into Palestine in 1917 'Isa returned to Bethlehem where for the next few years he taught in the local Orthodox and Christian Brothers' schools. He took an active part with others in the community in the rising tide of the Palestinian Arab nationalist movement which found expression in secular clubs and societies, peaceful agitation and journalism. In 1920 'Isa married Zahiyya Ibrahim Zayid. They had eight children: Yusuf, Olga, Su'ad, Riyad, Ghazi, May, Mazin and Jihad.[8]

6. Bayta Lahm:
From Idealism to Reality

With limited financial resources Dakkarat and Bandak were unable to purchase a printing press. Instead, the proximity of Jerusalem's press facilities and low printing costs offered the two Bethlehemites unprecedented opportunity to put their idealism into practice.

Bayta Lahm's founders and editors organized the journal's monthly content, scrutinized and proofread the articles with the aid of their mentor and guide, Father Yusuf Kalis, made the ten-mile round trip to Jerusalem's Greek Convent Press and printed, addressed and readied the journal for delivery to the post office and various ad hoc distribution outlets in Bethlehem and Jerusalem. The monthly focused as well on the Diaspora in Latin America.

It would be erroneous to judge **Bayta Lahm** harshly because of its amateur financial arrangements. If mediocrity characterized the financial dealings of the journal, the same cannot be said of its diversified content. Although the journal followed the same format in its two-year history, from cover to cover the content was rich with literary, social, political and educational topics, designed, according to the editors, for the betterment and enlightenment of society. The contents included editorials, news and features culled from Arabic publications, news and features from and about Palestinian emigrants in the Americas, literary contributions by the editors and other local and national writers, and local news from the Bethlehem sub-district as well as including highly critical commentaries on problems facing local society in the educational, social and health fields.

The policies and major goals of **Bayta Lahm** remained unchanged throughout its two-year existence. Whether advocating a secular democratic state, calling for improved sanitation in the community, attacking outmoded social customs, promoting secular schools, or providing an outlet for literary talents, the journal maintained its crusading zeal. It is ironic that such zeal and idealism, shared by Bandak and Dakkarat, which gave birth to this pioneering journalistic experiment in the Bethlehem community was also a contributing factor in its premature death.

For as soon as the content of the second summer novel of Yuhanna Dakkarat, **Asl al-Shaqa'**, became known to the religious authorities in Jerusalem, **Bayta Lahm's** editor came under attack for the anti-clerical views presented in the novel, such as the attribution of society's miseries to the existence of religious hierarchies. The Latin Patriarchate demanded an immediate stop to its publication, and took Yuhanna to the Court of First Instance. There he was found guilty of libel and was fined. The case, however, was appealed in higher courts by two leading Arab lawyers in the Jerusalem area, D'ebis al-Murr and Moghannam Moghannam. The lower court ruling was overturned and Dakkarat was declared innocent. Dakkarat was not in Palestine, however, to celebrate his victory and the victory of freedom of expression for local authors and journalists as he had left Palestine impatiently, shortly before the appeal was heard and joined his brother, in the Palestinian community of Santiago, Chile. Dakkarat departed without fulfilling his major goal in life which was the transformation of Arab society into a strong and viable society as championed by the Literary Club and **Bayta Lahm.**

The hasty departure of Yuhanna Dakkarat to the already familiar world of the diaspora – he had spent the early years of his life in Argentina – was indeed a tremendous loss to Bethlehem and Arab Palestine. Both Bayta Lahm and the Literary Club succumbed upon his departure to South America.

As for 'Isa Bandak, his two-year experience with Bayta Lahm and the Literary Club and his active participation in national politics through the Muslim-Christian societies, marked a stepping stone in his emergence as a national political figure, journalist, and unchallenged and highly respected leader in the Bethlehem community during the Mandate.

7. Sawt ash-Sha'b (Voice of the People) (1922 - 1948)

On May 11, 1922, Bethlehem's first and longest lasting weekly newspaper began publication with considerable national publicity and high expectations. It was founded by 'Isa Bandak, one of the founders of the Literary Club and the now defunct monthly *Bayta Lahm*, in collaboration with fellow members of the former Literary Club, Dr. Yusuf Abu A1-'Arraj and Yusuf Ya'qub Dabdub. *Sawt ash-Sha'b*, like its predecessor *Bayta Lahm*, was established in order to serve as an outlet for the secular and nationalist views of its founders as well as a tool of expression for the literary, political, and social views of fellow Arabs in Palestine and the diaspora. Abu al-'Arraj and Dabdub's roles were restricted to the administrative and financial aspects of the paper. 'Isa Bandak, on the other hand, was in charge of the editorial decisions and the overall content of the paper. Abu al-Arraj's association with the weekly lasted for a few months only, ending with the August 31,1922 issue, while Dabdub remained until 1925.

A glance through the pages of the bi-weekly clearly indicates that the front-page editorial played a major role in promoting Bandak's ideas on current issues facing Palestinian Arab society. Thus, in the May 16 and 19, 1928 issue, Bandak hammered at the theme of the need for national unity, and the necessity for holding a national unity rally that would save the national cause from the prevailing state of divisiveness and deadlock.

Bandak's ideas were also evident in the front-page section entitled "Public Forum." For example, in the May 16 and 19, 1928 issue, readers were reminded that the nation was in danger as a result of the prevailing reactionary currents spearheaded by sectarianism in Arab society. **Sawt ash-Sha'b,** according to Bandak, did not hesitate to raise the banner of nationalism in order to rally true nationalists under it... and repel the danger, i.e. religious fanaticism that threatened its existence. The nation would have to choose one of two things: either religious fanaticism, which would result in divisiveness, deadlock, death, and extinction... or religious toleration, which would result in unity, life, and rejuvenation.

Bandak was also an active member of the Palestine Arab leadership, represented by the Palestine Arab Executive, the acknowledged spokesmen of the Palestine Arab Congresses, and lobbyists of the Arabs of Palestine between 1920 and 1934 led by Musa Kazim Al-Husayni, father of martyr 'Abd Al-Qader, grandfather of the late Faisal Al-Husayni. Bandak's position in the Arab Executive could thus only be enhanced by this repeated demand for national unity on the front pages of his paper.

Sawt ash-Sha'b, in addition, devoted much space to coverage of local events in Bethlehem. For example, the activities of the Bethlehemite Young Men's Club were reported continuously, as seen in the issues of the 5th, 23rd, and 30th of January, 1929. Such coverage included the Club's public reception given to the Chicago industrialist, Charles Crane (of the 1919 King-Crane Commission), which was attended by Palestinian Arab leaders including Amin al-Husayni, and other items related to the Club's internal elections, the Club's intentions to form a Boy Scout group, and the Club's planned evening adult school. The issues of January 30 and February 2, 1929 also devoted much space to the proceedings and conclusions of a local trial, which was attended by a large segment of the community, and held in the Young Men's Club's meeting hall. Founded in 1927, as a secular educational medium for young men of the community, such as 'Isa Bandak, Oscar Dawid, Mishil Talhami, Yusef Habib Qattan, Iskandar Shahin, Yusef Miladeh, and Khalil 'Isa Murqus like its ancestor, the Literary Club, the Young Men's Club's chief purpose was the advancement of Arab society and the replacement of sectarianism in the community with the common bond of Arab nationalism. In its first two years under the leadership of Khalil 'Isa Murqus, al-Nadi (the Club), as it commonly became known, opened an evening school to fight illiteracy, held public lectures and discussions, sent its theatrical troupe on a tour of Palestinian cities and towns and held several welcoming parties for prominent national and international figures. Following Murqus's departure for Latin America in August 1929 the presidency was assumed by 'Isa Bandak. Political instability and fragmentation of Arab society in Bethlehem and Palestine finally led to the downfall of the Club in the early 1930's.

The publication continued on a bi-weekly basis until August 1929 when disturbances broke out in Palestine in the aftermath of the Western/Buraq Wall riots. The Palestinian press came under attack by the members of the Shaw Commission, which investigated the disturbances. According to the Commission, "too great a liberty of expression has been allowed to the Press in Palestine and ... at some stage an example should have been made of one of the papers in which exciting articles appeared." In the list of exhibits entitled "Arabic Press Extracts—incitement," the Shaw Commission report cited, among others, the **Sawt ash-Sha'b** of August 24, 1929, for allegedly taking part in public incitements which led to the disturbances.[9]

The content of the paper continued to reflect Arab nationalist views and to devote a great deal of space to related issues. For example, much coverage was given to the October 16, 1929 general strike in Bethlehem. The strike had been highlighted by the dispatch of telegrams to the British authorities protesting British policies in

Palestine and declaring their unity with fellow Arabs in Palestine in their stand against a Jewish national home.

8. 'Isa Bandak Mayor of Bethlehem and a National Figure, (1934 - 1948)

Extensive coverage was also given to 'Isa Bandak's increased responsibilities on the Palestine Arab Executive. For example, the issues of August and September, 1930 covered Bandak's trip to the Americas to solicit support for the Palestinian Arab cause on behalf of the Arab Executive extensively.[10]

By 1934, when Bandak was elected Mayor of Bethlehem, *Sawt ash-Sha'b* had reverted to an irregular weekly schedule, because Bandak's local and national political career left him less time for the paper, as more time was needed for the pressing problems facing Bethlehem's administration and Palestinian Arab leadership. However, Bandak continued to write and to decide the overall content of the paper.

Upon the death in 1934 of Musa Kazim al-Husayni, the Chairman of the Palestine Arab Executive, the representative body of the Palestinian Arab People, Palestinian Arab leadership proliferated, with several political parties appearing in 1934 and 1935. On June 22, 1935, 'Isa Bandak joined with the mayors of Gaza, Ramallah, Bayt Jala and other personalities to form the Reform (Islah) party, in collaboration with the Mayor of Jerusalem, Dr. Husayn Fakhri al-Khalidi. The Executive Secretariat of the party consisted of Dr.

Khalidi, 'Isa Bandak, Shibli al- Jamal and Mahmud Abu Khadra. The Reform Party's program was to a large extent similar to those of the leading Arab nationalist parties. The party attracted the support of Arab mayors, government officials and teachers and others who did not want to fall under the influence of the traditional leading political camps of al-Husayni and al-Nashashibi. **Sawt ash Sha'b** became, for practical purposes, the forum through which the program and ideology of the new party were publicized, especially in 1935.[11] **Sawt ash-Sha'b** also reported local political activities such as the formation of the National Struggle Party (al-Jihad al-Watani) under Antun Ya'qub Lama, Muhammad 'Id Hamidah, Nasri Jasir, and Ayyub Musallam in May 1935.[12]

In the wake of the Arab revolt of 1936 **Sawt ash-Sha'b** began to appear irregularly. In June 1936, during the Arab strikes, the paper was ordered closed for six weeks. On July 25, 1936 the paper reappeared and continued to be published on a weekly basis until March, 1937 when it was closed temporarily for reorganization.

9. Paper's Reorganization and 'Isa Bandak's Arrest and Deportation, (1937 - 1938)

On April 4, 1937, issue 980 of **Sawt ash-Sha'b** reappeared in a much improved magazine format with the aid of a modern press owner in Bethlehem and a relative of Bandak, by the name of 'Abd Allah Hanna Bandak. Saba Bandak, brother of 'Isa, continued to manage the financial and administrative aspects of the paper, a duty he took over from Khalil 'Isa Murqus in the late 1920's. On November 28, 1937 young Yusuf, son of 'Isa Bandak, a recent graduate of al-Rashidiyah school in Jerusalem and a student activist during the 1936 Arab disturbances, assumed the editorial slot vacated earlier by 'Abd Allah Bandak. Yusuf Bandak was not new to the paper. As early as the spring of 1936 young Bandak had been contributing to the weekly literary features.[13]

Aside from the attractive appearance of the reorganized weekly and the improved paper quality and print, the tone of **Sawt ash-Sha'b** was as before politically oriented with editorials and running commentaries occupying the largest space.

In addition, there was a noticeable emphasis on the humanities. Advertising was also present, solicited in the magazine by the short caption: "Advertise in **Sawt ash Sha'b**, the nationalist paper with wide circulation and you will secure the circulation for your commerce."

'Isa Bandak continued to utilize the front page of the weekly to express his point of view and to reiterate the Arabs' views concerning the Arab-Jewish impasse. For example, in the issue of April 18, 1937, Bandak's front-page editorial ridiculed the rumors of British Lord Peel's partition plan to divide Palestine into Arab, Jewish and mandatory sectors. He called the plan short-sighted because it did not take into consideration the Arab character of Palestine or the Palestinian Arabs' ability to determine their own way of life. The thought of partitioning Palestine, according to Bandak, was the acknowledgement of the policy of imposing the Jewish National Home on the Arabs, and thus only affirmed the Arabs' fears of a conspiracy to uproot them from their nation in order to replace them with intruders. Every solution that did not guarantee Arab sovereignty over their country would remain only ink on paper.[14]

In the midst of the continuing anti-British Arab rebellion and the accompanying chaos prevalent in Palestine's cities and countryside in 1937 and 1938, *Sawt ash-Sha'b* managed to appear for sixty-five weeks in its new format before events in Palestine and Bethlehem overtook it. In August 1937, the paper's editors received official warning from the Deputy Governor of the Jerusalem District for publishing matter that would likely endanger public peace. The British official was referring specifically to an editorial which included the passage: "Every Arab, Muslim and Christian should recite mornings and nights the dangers of the Jewish Nation..." Finally, the wrath of British officials caught up with Bandak's editorials and commentaries. In June 1938 'Isa Bandak was arrested for his journalistic and nationalist agitation and was sent to al-Mazra'ah (Farm) detention camp near Acre where he spent two months. He was then deported and went to Greece, remaining in exile in Europe until 1940. In July, *Sawt ash-Sha'b* was closed by the authorities for one year, allegedly for "publication of matter likely to endanger public peace." Of the several Arab daily and weekly papers that were suspended in 1938, Bethlehem's weekly received the longest suspension.[15]

10. The Reemergence of the Paper, (1939 – 1940), (1947 – 1948) and 'Isa Bandak as Mayor of Bethlehem, (1946 - 1948)

In 1939 'Isa Bandak's eldest son, Yusuf, continued to edit and publish the paper. However, the return of 'Isa Bandak to Palestine and the restriction on his activities, in addition to the paralysis of life during the war years, except for a few pro-British publications, made the reactivation of *Sawt ash-Sha'b* very difficult. The paper thus laid dormant from 1940 to 1946. Further delays in its resumption resulted when 'Isa Bandak and his slate of supporters won the municipality elections in 1946. Bandak replaced Hanna Qawwas as Mayor of Bethlehem; Qawwas had been appointed mayor upon Bandak's arrest in 1938.[16]

An exceptional event took place in Bethlehem in 1946 under the leadership of Mayor Bandak who was also President of the National Orthodox Society in Bethlehem. Bandak rallied the people's support and action in repossessing the Eastern Orthodox graveyard for the National Orthodox Society, now the building complex of the Palace Hotel and the orthodox Society. The Greek Synod and bishops thought that the land belonged to the Greek Orthodox Church. The people of Bethlehem answered the call of their mayor and were able to construct a small building, with lights on the spot, etc.. during the night. Having seen what the people did, the Greek Synod and Patriarch went to the Court of Justice but did not possess any documentation to prove their ownership. The land, therefore, reverted back to Bethlehem and the National Orthodox Society.[17]

In the closing months of the British Mandate, which ended on May 15, 1948, Bethlehem's weekly resumed publication under the editorship of Yusuf Bandak amid the war that accompanied Britain's decision to withdraw from Palestine and the ensuing United Nations' partition scheme of November 1947. *Sawt ash-Sha'b* was highly critical of the American role in the passage of the United Nations General Assembly partition resolution 181 of 29 November 1947. It described the threat and pressure America exerted on small countries as Nazi like and accused America's mind of being under the total control of Zionist illusions. It concluded "that America's politicians will be awakened by the spilling of blood which they are primarily responsible for; and in their awakening they will realize that Palestine cannot but remain Arab even though America itself had become Jewish".[18]

The state of bloody Arab-Jewish confrontation, which followed, made it impossible for 'Isa and Yusuf Bandak to continue publication. On the eve of the Nakbeh, *Sawt ash-Sha'b* again came to a halt.[19]

Mayor 'Isa Bandak of Bethlehem wrote a highly negative report concerning the impact of the 1948 Nakbeh (Disaster) on Bethlehem, its refugees, its residents and the economy.[20]

4

Palestinian Identity in the Diaspora

Qustandi Shomali

The question of identity has become a major theme in social history, literature, and cultural studies. This study focuses on Palestinian identity as it emerged and evolved in the literature produced by Palestinians in the Diaspora[1] and their treatment of the homeland. In fact, these authors' representation of the voice of their people is an important key to understanding the shape Palestinian identity takes in their works, which may be regarded as documents of Palestinian political, cultural and social life. In fact Palestinian identity has passed through several stages. It emerged initially as a literary movement with the main aim of reviving Arabic language, literature and culture. This movement at the beginning of the twentieth-century may be commonly referred to as part of the "Islah' Movement."

In the early twentieth century many Palestinians migrated to Europe and the Americas; among them a number of intellectuals and writers. While living in those remote places they expressed their feelings of attachment and longing for their homeland in different written forms. It is important to point out from the beginning that this subject is both expansive and multilayered. This study is limited to a specific historical time, and to specific places and sources. The aim of this presentation is to identify the characteristics of Palestinian identity which emerged in Diaspora literature in the first half of the twentieth century through the writings of four prominent Palestinian intellectuals. The use of "Diaspora" here conceptualizes the Palestinians as a temporary community settled in a number of host countries and longing for their homeland.

Although Palestinian migration to the Americas began in the last quarter of the nineteenth century, the mass exodus did not begin until the twentieth century. This migration took the form of four major waves: migration during the Ottoman period before the outbreak of the First World War; migration during the British Mandate in the wake of the bitter conflict resulting from the Balfour Declaration, and the influx of Jewish Zionist immigration primarily from Europe; migration after the Nakba (catastrophe) in 1948, with the displacement of roughly 750,000 and inhabitants; and migration after the Naksah contributed to the defeat of the 1967 war. This study will discuss the writing of four migrants from the first wave of migration which refers to those who migrated before 1948, primarily for economic reasons but also to escape Ottoman military service. These Palestinians migrated to the Americas and Europe, in particular.

In order to form a comprehensive picture of the characteristics of Palestinian identity, I will discuss the writings of Bendaly Jawzi in Russia, Aziz Doumet in Germany, Rawhi Khalidi in France, and Khalil Sakakini in the United States under three headings: political content, social content and cultural content.

Place	Writer	Period
Russia	*Bandaly Jawzi*	*Ottman & British Mandate*
Germany	*Aziz Doumet*	*Ottman & British Mandate*
France	*Rawhi Khalidi*	*Ottman & British Mandate*
United States	*Khalil Sakakini*	*Ottman & British Mandate*

1. The Political Content

At the beginning of the twentieth century Palestine was a province of the ailing Ottoman Empire, suffering from poor administration by the central government in Istanbul, and isolated from the intellectual and cultural movements taking place in the Arab world. Palestine was further stunted by a weak educational system, the replacement of Arabic by Turkish as the official language of the country and a sense of always living in the cultural past. These factors resulted in a general decline of cultural life. Many Palestinians left their homeland to escape political oppression, religious persecution, and for a better future. Many of these immigrants felt that in the Diaspora, they could think and express themselves freely in defense of their nation and could address its problems without fear of repercussion by the state. We will discuss this in particular in the writings of Bandaly Jawzi, an Arab Christian from Palestine, born in Bethlehem in 1871.

2. Bendaly Jawzi (1871-1942)

Bendaly Jawzi[2] represents an early model of the Palestinian migrant-author in the Diaspora. After completing his studies in Russia, Jawzi returned to Palestine in 1900 determined to remain. Faced with a deteriorating political, social and economic situation, resulting in poverty, ignorance and the infringement of civil liberties, he started alerting people through his writings : "Wake up from this hibernation, defend your rights and freedom." His liberal ideas, calling people to break restrictions and confront the unjust rule of reactionary forces prompted the Turkish authorities to force his departure from Jerusalem; subsequently he returned to Russia, where he spent more than forty years.

During his stay in the Diaspora, Jawzi wrote about the situation in his homeland and the Arab world. His research was published in leading magazines of the time: "al-Nafa'is" in Palestine, "al-Muktataf" in Lebanon, and "al-Hilal" in Egypt. At the same time Jawzi exchanged ideas with other Arab writers and intellectuals regarding various cultural, intellectual and political issues related to the Arab world.

Bandaly Jawzi made several trips back to Jerusalem, as well as to Syria, Iraq, and Iran and remained vitally concerned with the fate of his native land. During his visits to Jerusalem his brother's house became a popular center for literary and political discussions attended by members of the intellectual elite and leading families of Palestine. Discussions seem to have centered around questions of political consciousness, and the need to develop Palestinian solidarity on a new basis overcoming sectarian divisions, such as class and gender.

Jawzi was considered by his colleagues to be one of the leading intellectuals of his day and is still considered avant-garde in the history of Arab thought. Credited for his analysis of the history of Islam, he was the first scholar to employ a material interpretation of this history. His most famous book The History of Intellectual Movements in Islam (Min Tarikh al-Harakat al-Fikriyya fi al-Islam) in which he discusses social movements according to scientific and Marxist theories, was first published in Arabic in Jerusalem in 1928 to wide acclaim[3]. Jawzi's attempt to reinterpret Islamic principles in terms of modern science and technology was "based on recognition that all texts, including religious and historical documents, are the result of human interpretation, and that interpretations are inevitably influenced by the milieux in which they are produced". In a short introduction to his book, entitled The Unity of Social Laws, he refutes statements made by Western scholars about the East and its history, in response to French Orientalist, Ernest Renan, who said: "The development of religious nations was always based on other laws different from laws of Western nations." Jawzi responded that many Western historians believed that: "The factors affecting the history of European nations and the norms of public actors in their social lives are not the factors and dynamics operating in the Eastern nation's history, life and culture." Thus fifty years before Edward Said's landmark Orientalism, Bendali Jawzi analysed the same problematic construct of Oriental thought by which the West confronts the Near East and attempts to both exert control over it as well as to reproduce it politically, socially, ideologically, scientifically and in the imaginary realm. His analysis of Islamic intellectual movements is "offered not only as a corrective of Orientalism but also of Muslims' misapprehension of their own heritage." [4] With the best intentions, Tamara Sonn, in her analysis, Interpreting Islam, presents Jawzi as a forerunner of Edward Said with an affinity for postmodernist writers like Jacques Derrida and Michel Foucault. Thus, "Bendaly Jawzi and Edward Said were two wings of the same bird."

The continuing importance of his work lies in Jawzi's critical method of reevaluating both European "Orientalist" and classical Muslim accounts of Islamic history.

3. Social Content

From a sociological perspective, identity is formed through 'interaction' of the "self" with society. The writings and messages of Palestinian authors in the Diaspora to their families and friends are full of enthusiasm and optimism. The success of the first migrants and the money they were able to send home to their families, were among the primary factors contributing to the increase in Palestinian migration. The migration waves of Palestinians to the Americas were driven both by economic interests and a belief in the freedoms and opportunities presented by life there. The bulk of Palestinians migrating before 1914 worked in the fields of trade and sales, although, a small number were also highly successful in the fields of journalism and culture. Their writings were aimed at creating a stronger, freer and more sophisticated Arab society and were often critical of the difficulties encountered by expatriates in their new country of residence. We will now discuss the social content in Diaspora literature through the writings of Khalil Sakakini who wrote about his experience in the Diaspora.

4. Khalil Sakakini (1878 - 1953)

Sakakini[5] is one of the key prose writers in Palestinian literature. He distinguished himself as an essayist and developed an individual prose style characterized by its simplicity. Sakakini left Palestine in his twenties to escape the alienation and economic distress suffered by those living under the Ottoman regime, characterized by tyranny, corruption and absence of basic freedoms. He formed his ideas through exchanges with Syrian intellectuals (at this time greater Syria included Palestinians, Lebanese and Syrians) in New York, where he worked for the Literary Gazette.

Most of the letters he sent from New York to Jerusalem in this early period reflect his national consciousness, liberalism, and insurgent spirit regarding dependency on political and economic powers. The letters of Khalil al-Sakakini, sent from New York, where he stayed for a while before the First World War, should be considered part of Palestinian literature expressing, as they do, his longing for the motherland.[6]

Sakakini's social commentary is well expressed in the first book of his diary which covers the period from 1907 to 1912. He wrote in detail about his journey from Jerusalem to New York in 1907, and the nine month he spent in the Syrian district of Manhattan. This is a valuable historical resource which can be used to investigate and contextualize the character of the man behind the words. Sakakini's diary provides us with a lens to examine the ways Palestinians in the Diaspora looked at their homeland and allows us in the twenty-first century to examine some of the feelings and experiences of a man living during a formative period in Palestinian history.

Sakakini, however, did not like living in the Diaspora and upon discovering this bitter truth he reflected upon it in his diaries which were published in an eight-volume series, Hakatha Ana ya Donia (Such am I, Oh World).[7]

Sakakini wrote that he left his homeland due to political tyranny and lack of freedom, and that he would only return from exile when freedom had been achieved. Therefore, after the announcement of the new constitution in 1908 by the Turkish authorities, he said: "Now I can set up a school, establish a newspaper and an association for young people. Now we can raise our voices without embarrassment." Unfortunately, this new atmosphere of freedom and justice did not continue for long in Palestine.

While in New York Sakakini worked with the Lebanese writer, Farah Anton, editor of "al-Jamiah" magazine, who said to him once: "If you had consulted me before you came to this country, I would have advised you not to come." It is reported also that in one of the magazine's office meetings, Sakakini said to the brother of Farah Anton: "Many people consider migration to be a courageous act, and an ambition to glory, but in fact it is not. It is only a humiliation and demonization that kills independence and dignity, as immigrants are forced to be followers in the entire nation. And no matter how long the migrant stays in the Diaspora he will still be considered an outsider, and even if he becomes rich, gratitude will be bestowed upon the country and he might even be accused of having made his fortune in a despicable manner."

Khalil Sakakini said that the main motivation for his migration was the desire to gain knowledge, and that the outcome of his migration was knowledge: "My trip to Britain, and then my trip to America, and my assimilation of the principle of Nietzsche, the German philosopher, and other philosophers all contributed to changing my life."

Sakakini often expressed humanistic ideas, and had a business card on which he wrote: "Khalil Sakakini: Human Being, God willing." At the same time, he defined himself first and foremost as an Arab, and is hailed as one of the founding fathers of Arab nationalism in the region. He was an advocate of Pan-Arabism and envisaged Palestine united with Syria. He saw Zionism as a great threat and believed that Jewish right to the land had expired while the Arab right was "a living one."

While other writers in the Diaspora remained dependent on European references, Khalil Sakakini called for a national literature which would express Arab history and focus on the great values of the East. His call represented a desire for independence and profound awareness of his cultural heritage and civilization. We will explore how, via a different approach, the writings of other authors like Rawhi

Khalidi and Aziz Doumet interpreted and shaped Western ideas to be employed within a new and national cultural context. Sakakini's writings, in contrast, embodied his belief in the unity of human heritage, and the importance of the relationship between literature, art and nations.

5. The Cultural Content

The writings of Palestinians in the Diaspora made an important impact on the intellectual and social life of their country. A considerable percentage of what they wrote referred directly or indirectly to the problem of social reform known as "Islah". Scientific and literary advances of the West were disseminated by Palestinians living in the Diaspora through writings or translations, mainly from Russian, English and French. These translations had a major influence on the adoption of Arabic for the expression of modern ideas, and it may be said that translation was the most effective and consistent form of cultural interface with the West[8]. Nearly half of all printed Arabic texts between 1900 and 1950 were translations or adaptations of Western works of fiction, providing Palestinian readers with substantial information about intellectual life in the West. Rawhi Khalidi and Aziz Doumet were prominent representatives of this trend, introducing a wealth of Western thought into Arabic literature.

6. Rawhi Khalidi (1864 - 1913)

Khalidi, who was a student at the Sorbonne in Paris, immersed himself in French culture, working closely with French intellectuals

and writers. He was appointed an instructor in the Foreign Languages.
Association in Paris, and lived in the city of Bordeaux in southern France for ten years, during which time he published his research and studies in the Arab press.

Khalidi is generally considered to be pioneer of modern literary criticism in Palestine and the Arab World. Between 1902 and l904, he wrote a series of articles about the history of Arabic literature in the highly progressive magazine, al-Hilal in Egypt. These articles were collected and printed in 1904 in a book entitled: History of Arab and Western literatures and Victor Hugo (Tarikh `ilm al-Adab `ind al-Ifrang wa il-`arab wa Victor Hugo). Originally published under the pseudonym al-Maqdisi, these essays were written by al-Khalidi while he was the consul in Bordeaux in France. The work dealt with Victor Hugo and the literary connections between Arabic, French and English literature. He referred to Western models showing an impressive knowledge of French literature and literary theories. This book, reprinted in 1912, demonstrates Palestinian familiarity with Western literary criticism. Many critics view this work as the beginning of the modern critical movement in Palestine.

Khalidi was one of the most prominent advocates for the necessity of infusing Arabic literature with new forms of writing; however, he also struggled with the natural difficulties faced by those attempting to assimilate one culture to another. Khalidi's work was not an isolated phenomenon, as some critics believe. A few years later both Khalil Bayydas and Khalil Sakakini wrote essays about modern literature, which surpassed mere adaptations of European works.

7. Aziz Doumet
(1890-1943)

Living in Germany for many years, Doumet married there and worked for the German-Arab radio station. He mastered German, and had a passion for German literature. He also translated several German literary works and published them in Palestinian books and newspapers. In addition to various translations he wrote many plays and short stories in German, which were known throughout Germany and Austria. Doumet's objective was to make historical Arab themes known within German society, and his national cultural role and his commitment were manifested in his theatrical works which were performed in the most important theaters in Berlin. He was called by German critics the Faust of the East.

Doumet exerted great effort in the dissemination of Arabic literature throughout Germany, writing in German newspapers about Arab heritage and translating Arab poetry as well as reciting it in German clubs. In his lifetime he wrote a large number of plays some of which were presented in Germany, including "Governor of Acre", "Avicenna," "Last Umayyad," The Druze Mountain, "The Charm of the Snake," "Samiramis," "Beltnasser, Dancer of al-Fayoum," "Zubaydah," ,"Petra," and others.[9] In addition to being a playwright he was also a musician.

His early work shows an obvious openness to the "other," creating a positive climate for dialogue and intercourse between civilizations. Doumet's writing contributed to the objective of overcoming hostility and arrogance exhibited by white colonists towards peoples of the East, and confronted the ideas of Aryan superiority beginning to appear with the rise of Nazi ideology. This was negatively received by German journalists and critics of his theatrical work.

While in Germany, Doumet extended his support to Palestinian theatrical groups. He visited Palestine with his German wife many times to meet his family, his people, and fellow writers and authors and kept in contact with the most prominent writers in Palestine including Khalil Sakakini, Khalil Baydas, Nejati Sidky and others. Doumet wrote many articles in defense of Arab nationalism in German newspapers and numerous articles against Zionism during the Palestinian uprising of 1929.

A book recently published in Stockholm, about the secrets of the Nobel Prize, indicates that the Palestinian novelist and playwright Aziz Doumet was the first Arab nominated by the Swedish Academy for the Nobel Peace Prize in 1936. In 1936 Taha Hussein, the dean of Arabic literature was also nominated. Doumet's name, however, appeared before Taha Hussein's on the list of nominees. Aziz Doumet died in 1943 and his tomb is in a cemetery in Berlin.

8. Classification of the Writers

This brief presentation of four Palestinians writers in the Diaspora should help us to better understand their identities, and their political and social discourse. At the same time, their classification is important, because it determines the nature of the relationship between communities in the Diaspora and the motherland.[10]

There are many paradigms which dominate the field of migration studies. Since the relationship governing literary and intellectual production, is a sociological one, the most suitable approach for understanding the identity and relationships of Palestinians living abroad to their homeland and host societies is a taxonomy of four kinds: home, Diaspora, population in transit, and assimilated population[11]. This typology is intended to indicate a dynamic process rather than to describe a static position.

In Structural Semantics (1966) A.J. Greimas[12] suggests a formal procedure for the perception of meaning in a discourse, and provides a semiotic model designed to account for the articulation of meaning within a semantic universe. According to Greimas's model, the fundamental structure of Palestinian identity may be represented by two pairs of semantic classes. The classes in each oppose one another, while the pairs themselves are correlated in order to produce a thematic interdependence.

The different forms of expression, opinion articles, and books produced by the authors discussed above may be represented according to Greimas's model of four characteristics of Palestinian identity:

Sakakini & Khalidi

        Population in Transit   Home

        Diaspora   Assimilated population

                                      Jawzi & Domet

Relation of complementarily
Relation of contradiction
Relation of presupposition

The first paradigm, assimilation, is represented by Jawzi and Doumet who sought to fully acculturate and integrate in their host countries in Europe. The culture of these host countries is typically characterized as modern and universal, relative to that of Palestinian culture, which is often characterized as the opposite: traditional and local. These authors represent a cultural fusion and adaptation in the country of migration. The presence of similar Palestinian writers in Latin America can be noted. We must also clarify that assimilation does not imply that these individuals acculturated completely or lost their Palestinian identity.

Individuals like Khalil Sakakini fervently resisted these processes. Sakakini and Rawhi Khalidi were therefore people in transit. They were perceived as participating in the cultural, social, economic and political life of both countries: the country of origin, and the host country. They represent a class of multiculturalism in the country of migration. This category is characterized by its ability to participate in and contribute to the political, cultural and social development of their host and home countries.

9. Conclusion

The presence of Palestinian writers in the Diaspora influenced the development of their identity. However, the construction of this identity differs from one writer to another. A review of their writing shows that they became aware of their identity in the Diaspora. It also indicates a range of important aspects, namely:

1. A loss of enthusiasm for the public life of the Diaspora, and a keen awareness of a lack of harmony with the society, as seen in the case of Khalil Sakakini.

2. Friction with various styles of behavior in the communities of their homeland deepened their sense of freedom. They called for citizens in their homeland to revolt against injustice and tyranny in the defence of their country.
3. The intellectual and literary trends represented by the writings of those in the Diaspora were innovative, independent from schools of thought in the Arab world, and had their own objectives.
4. The emergence of a dedication to humanist values in their writings, such as love of homeland, the search for truth, longing for freedom, democracy, justice, brotherhood, equality, openness to the other, and respect for basic human rights.

In fact, a great source of inspiration in the evolution of Palestinian identity during the first half of the twentieth century did not originate solely from local factors, but also from contact with Palestinians in the Diaspora. Palestinian identity was a gradual product of this confrontation between local values and the dissemination of values introduced by Palestinian authors in the Diaspora.

5

The Impact of Place on Identity in the Works of Mahmoud Darwish

Liana Badr

The relationship between place- landscape and identity shows as clearly and powerfully as in the works of the Palestinian poet, Mahmoud Darwish. The lively relationship between both, which was lost due to political events, is regained through the purified aesthetics and the selective language of his poetry.

Before Darwish, Palestinians identified themselves with the then prevailing state of war and the enthusiastic slogans of the national struggle. Nobody paid attention to the fate of the identity of the Palestinian masses. On the other hand, Arab regimes manipulated the Palestine Question dubbing it a "sacred" cause to be dealt with according to their own interests. As a result, the question itself and Palestine as a place were transformed into a national intangible abstract.

Darwish's poetry regains and recreates that relationship between place and the people who belong to it, no matter where they are: at home or away. Living as refugees, in a most sensitive manner. The lost place emerges again, takes shape with a humanistic glow, and the abstract slogans of the 1948 Nakba, which decimated the Palestinian Cause into a general political slogan, retreat.

In general, Palestinian creative experiments have always been sensitive to the issue of place. Therefore, the creativity in Darwish's work lies in it's capacity to draw upon that delicate sensitivity towards the lost place. This feeling took on larger dimensions with the Nakba: the loss of land and displacement. The loss of original place has totally transformed the quality of life of Palestinians into a life filled with the feelings of loss, misery, need, and of suffering.

Displacement has become an imposed way of life for refugees who lost all their belongings and were driven out of Palestine to live in refugee camps. It is a way of life that gradually formed a new identity for the refugees, it is the refugee identity.

The Nakba not only changed the way a Palestinian identifies with his place of origin, but also formulated a new kind of identification with the "camp" as a transitional- permanent place- a new wounded identity that belongs to a new bitter reality that cannot be changed and overcome except when the existing geography, imposed by the colonizers, is changed. Palestinian Identity of the post 1948 Nakba is the result of the loss of land and the dispossession and displacement of the Palestinians in the wake of the withdrawal of Arab forces which were sent by the Arab regimes to Palestine.

The loss of land has become the equivalent of displacement and loss of the original identity. Since the Nakba, Palestinians have become defeated and poor, and have suddenly found themselves transformed from land owners to landless refugees.

The occupation of Palestine has been different from other cases of occupation elsewhere in the world. The occupiers in

Australia, for instance, tended to interbreed with the Aborigines. In Palestine, occupation meant the uprooting of the original people in a way similar to the extermination that took place in the U.S. against the Native Americans.

The Palestinians who managed to stay behind and are known as the Arabs of 1948 or the Interior Arabs, managed to maintain their Palestinian identity through a two pronged cultural process: rebelling against attempts to make them forget their Palestinianism, and the continuous enrichment of their alienated identity with renewable indicatives. Antoine Shalhat says: Palestinians rebelled against imposed attempts to forget the past and the continuous loading of the Palestinian collective memory with various historical and cultural indicatives of the Nakba, its results and the details of the past national identity of the Palestinians in Israel.[1]

The sudden disastrous conditions that engulfed the Palestinians, both those in Diaspora or within their occupied original homeland, could have lead to a total spiritual breakdown had it not been for poetry , which emerged as a savior of the national identity. Poetry was the first kind of literature, to play such a major role, because it was easier to absorb for the masses.[2]

The land of Palestine has been a target for confiscation since the beginning of the twentieth century. The British Mandate on Palestine, by the end of the First World War, played a major role in facilitating the transfer of land to the Jews to build settlements on, at the expense of the Palestinians. Since land has become a "motif" in Palestinian poetry and literature in general, the land, has become the equivalent of homeland:

"As Palestine fell victim to British colonial occupation, and with the crystallization of the Palestinian National

*Movement, land has become the material equivalent to
Home land. Any danger that threatens the one, threatens the other."*[3]

Since then, place has continued to press deep within culture. "Great importance has been attached to culture as the medium for the formulation of collective memory and nationhood, the same as that which happened with place.[4]

Palestinian identity which was meant to be broken and dispersed by the colonists, started to find itself in culture, "because identity is what personalizes the self and distinguishes oneself from another." [5]

Colonialism aims mostly at stifling the voices of people and destroying their capabilities. The effect of such behavior is usually the hardest on those who are deprived of the land they once owned. Carl Jespers describes such cases as "Cases-borderlines," which are cases that are distinguished by expressing themselves existentially in an extreme way. If we apply this to the Palestinians, this is manifested through a very strong and durable attachment which can barely be felt among peoples who haven't experienced such total loss and who feel that they have options for creativity. It is possible that the Palestinians who managed to develop certain customs such as making regular visits to their stolen land are those who suffered total loss and are the people whom Jespers describes as the cases of the border line.

In *Bab el Shams- The Sun's Gate*, a novel by Elias Khoory, we read about people expelled from their land, sneaking back home. In "Key" a documentary by actor and producer Salim Dao, as well as in other documentaries, the same theme is dwelt upon. Ahmad Darwish, a brother of Mahmoud Darwish, describes how the evacuated people of the village of Albarweh, go to their stolen village at every traditional festival and celebrate there. He describes the relationship that binds the Palestinian to his land and his identity. He says that those people are described as being present absentees. They cannot adopt their original identity or live on their land. In their memories, the village rises from under the ruins assuming its previous daily roles. Alleys and by-roads suddenly fill with playing children. The old gather in their "dawaween" to talk together, young girls carry their water jugs on their heads. Women gather under the unforgettable carob tree or by the well that reiterates the echoes of the past. They retell stories about the cruelties of human beings and enumerate the crimes that have been passed into laws to dispossess them.

Those Palestinians who managed to stay are called "present absentees." They are considered "citizens" but without enjoying most of their basic rights and are not allowed to inherit the property of their fathers and grandfathers. They are citizens without a future.[6]

In the present, refugees practice traditions that give priority to the restoration of the land. A Palestinian refugee considers his return to his place of origin, even for a visit, a principal duty. This is depicted in many literary works, including *Bab El Shams*.

As a result of the loss of land-place, Palestinian writers often use the text as a means to recreate lost land-place, with all its details. A writer treats the text as if it were new territory upon which he reinstates his loss paradise lost - homeland, and by so doing also restores his lost identity. This is a way to restore one's identity through writing. And in this way, literature has been transfigured as an expression of the identity of the Palestinian soul. Place becomes the equivalent of identity, and all its variations reflect themselves within the text. In this manner, place assumes a deeper and multiple existentialist meaning as long as the identity is threatened.

The text assumes the role of expressing the synchronized relationship between both of them. This applies to the Palestinian case in general , and to the poetry of Mahmoud Darwish in particular, where the indicatives of the Bashlarian place are reflected in: land, homeland, exile, home, repose, tranquility, lost paradise, space!

The relation of Mahmoud Darwish to poetry is best defined in the metaphorical way he defined it himself by comparing it to "being at home." He says: "The metaphorical home which the poet creates for himself is an internal home invented by the poet himself. It is a kind of a poetic verse. So, home becomes a poetic verse. A poetic verse changes into a home or a shelter. That's why I admire Arabic language. It selected one single word for home and for the poetic verse: "Bait". This is a beautiful conformity." [7]

Through poetic creativity, homeland becomes verse according to Darwish, while his likening refers the poetic verse to Bedouin life. This is a clever remark. For even if Darwish meant that the poetic verse is the tent which the Arabs took for a home, the tent still remains a home in the desert and not a shelter for refugees. This analysis confirms what Darwish meant when he said that poetry is the land of human beings and of history.

In an interview published in Al Safir newspaper in 2003 Darwish said, "In my poetry ..there are two things that support the poetic text: land and history. My poetic text has always been carried by them."[8] That's what explains why the beginning and end of each poem are about place, something similar to what is stated in the Old Testament, that in the beginning, there was the Word, that is, Creation. Creative poetry is, therefore, the home and the refuge for the preservation of life, no matter how the colonists destroy the homes of the Palestinians. As a result, the poet reinvents place in a literary manner as a means of reestablishing the identity of the

Palestinians lost by war. The poet works on the transformations that lead to uniting lost place with identity.

Place is of particular importance in the poetry of Mahmoud Darwish. Yet, a great deal of this particularity is derived from popular culture. That is why the poetry of Darwish represents the historical Palestinian popular spirit and its place in Palestinian history, both of which are the product of national achievements intertwined historically with the Arab world and the civilizations of humanity, old and new.[9]

The works of the poet contain very strong ties with Palestinian and Arab historical identity, as well as his preoccupation with emphasizing those ties and how to redefine them. This is evident in his saying: "Who has no place has no seasons".[10]

Darwish goes on to define the tragic effects of settlement activities on stolen Palestinian land; how they devour land and consume memory. He looks at the settlement of "Yesoor" built in place of his destroyed village, Albarweh. The question of place develops from the general to the personal, creating a particular value for the Darwishean place as a place which constitutes a process of movement between what is private and what is general.

It appears as though the poet returns here to the symbolism of home as a personal place for the individual, a place that is marked by its own colored grass and butterflies, which takes us back to Gaston Blashard and his description of the home- place duality with its walls "built with light shades that help the self feel safe and secure.. as long as the spiritual construction.. With all its pillars, corners, secretive and personal rooms, invite the outside world to the inside."[11]

The privacy of the Darwishean place is not restricted to the search for the first imagined home-place. It includes the challenge of preserving the memory, which is threatened by the colonialists. In his poem "A Cloud in my Hand," Darwish concentrates on the connection between the first place and language, as well as on the existential connection between them since birth:

"The Place was prepared for his birth:
His grandfathers, hill of sweet Basils
Looks east and west
And an Olive tree by another
Raise the roofs of language
In the Koran."[12]

This comment changes this intimate place to a cultural-linguistic- existential battlefield. Darwish says: "My feelings tell me that the battle between us is not only a military battle, we are driven towards a deep cultural struggle."[13]

There are many historical references describing this fight about place, according to the poet. Darwish also refers to symbols from the Torah (Old Testament) as will be shown elsewhere, or refers directly to history, as found in other poems.

6

Biblical Narrative and Palestinian Identity in Mahmoud Darwish's Writings

Mitri Raheb

So much has been said about this notable poet, and even more has been written about him that I will not try to add to that corpus. What I would like to do, however, is to bring forth a subject that may be worthy of your consideration; one that has not been – and will not be – written: Biblical Narrative and Palestinian Identity in Mahmoud Darwish's Writings.

I realize that this is no easy task. After all, the subject I am bringing to your attention today could be a theme for a doctoral thesis. Nevertheless, I have often felt spellbound by the symbols and allegories conjured up by our great poet. If his name had not been "Mahmoud," I would have thought him a Christian theologian, or a scholar able to decipher the biblical narrative, or even an Old Testament prophet who was able to express in poetic words the hopes and fears of his people helping them to hear God's words in their context. Indeed, our late poet was as versed in the biblical narrative as a well-informed theologian. In his poetry, he wrote about the Samaritan[1], Mary Magdalene[2], as well as the woman who poured scent on the feet of Jesus[3]. Moreover, he took examples from the Old Testament and mentioned Joseph and his brothers[4], Abraham[5], Ishmael[6], Joshua son of Nun[7], David and

Solomon[8], Song of Solomon[9], and Job[10]; as well as Cain and Abel[11], the land flowing with milk and honey[12], Sodom and Gomorrah[13], Lot[14], Noah[15], Isaiah[16], and Habakkuk[17]. His poetry also notes the birth of Jesus, his baptism, his transfiguration[18], his teachings, his first miracle in Cana when he turned water into wine[19], the parable of the Vineyard[20], his walking on water[21], his crucifixion, his resurrection, and his ascension[22]. Our renowned poet was conversant with the biblical narrative and knew countless themes and verses, some of which he incorporated in his poems, such as *"Hallelujah"*; *My God, my God, why have you forsaken me?; Love is strong as death; Vanity of vanities;* and his echoing of Jesus' words to the Greeks spoken of a grain of wheat; "If it die, it beareth much fruit."

In one of his last interviews with the newspaper, "Al Hayat" our great poet was asked:

> *"Speaking of religion, we notice that your poetry has some biblical influence, observed particularly in Nashīd al-Anshad (Song of Songs) in the lyrical content of Sareer al-Ghareeba (Bed of the Stranger), as well as others. Why has the biblical text interested you as a poet, and how has it affected you?"*

Darwish replied:

> *"First, I studied in Occupied Palestine. We were required to study some of the text of the Torah in Hebrew, and so I did. With that being said, I do not contemplate the Torah from a religious or historical perspective, but consider it rather as a work of literature."*

He was then asked the direct question: "Is the Bible one of your sources?" Darwish answered without hesitation:

> *"There is no doubt that it is one of my literary sources."*

This was followed by another question: "Have you re-read the Torah in Arabic?"

His answer was:

"Yes, I read several Arabic translations of it, including some recent ones of which I especially enjoy the plain ones. Such texts have to be translated in a very particular way. Nashīd al-Anāshīd (The Song of Songs) has been considered by some great universal poets as one of the most highly acclaimed pastoral songs in the history of poetry, despite its Pharaonic and Assyrian influences." [23]

Whoever reads this interview is certain to be surprised that Darwish was so well-acquainted with the biblical narrative that he had read it in several languages, several translations and several times! One might wonder: Did our poet under-estimate the value of the Bible? After all, he declared that he perceived the Bible strictly as a work of literature, and not as a religious or historical text. While this may seem to be the case at first glance, and on the surface, once we realize that in the mindset of the poet nothing but literature is immortal, we grasp that while describing the Bible as a "historical" or "religious" text may have sounded sophisticated, his portrayal of it as a work of literature renders it mighty and divine.

I have read all of Mahmoud Darwish's poems from the first to the last with the intention of seeing how and when Darwish quotes from the biblical narrative. I am able to depict four different stages in his life, indicating his context – whether Palestinian, international or his own personal context. There is no doubt that Darwish was one of our brilliant contextual "theologians." In each of these stages, specific literary texts dominate Darwish's thinking. Indeed, for every context there a text!

Let me briefly describe these four stages:

1. The First Stage (1964 – 1967)

The young Darwish, exiled from the village of Barwah, in his early twenties; lived in Haifa and felt oppressed, persecuted, imprisoned, yet he persisted. At this stage, he saw in the crucified Jesus a reflection of himself; a freedom fighter who endured suffering but who rose again. In three of his first four poems, the cross makes such a pronounced appearance that those who read Darwish's words will think they were written by a Latin American Liberation Theologian. Those of us who have memorized his poems in the lyrics of Marcel Khalife have perhaps not considered the considerable liberation theology emanating from them.

His poem "Ecce Homo" provides just such an example:

"They fettered his mouth with chains,
And tied his hands to the rock of the dead.
They said: You're a murderer.
They took his food, his clothes and his banners,
And threw him into the well of the dead.
They said: 'You're a thief.'
"You, with the bloody eyes and palms,
The night is soon to be gone,
The detention room won't last,
Nor will the chains,
Nero died, but Rome did not,
With her eyes, she fights.
A withered spike will die,
And will nourish the whole valley." [24]

And in the poem "The Singer Said" he recounts:

"The singer on the cross,
his wound glowing like a star
expressed everything to the people
around him, everything except regret:
This way I have died as I stand
and standing I die like a tree.
This way my cross becomes
a platform or a maestro's baton.
This way the nails of this cross
become musical chords.
This is how rain falls,
this is how trees grow."[25]

In this poem, the meaning of the cross is unmistakable: It stands for the path of redemption; the juncture of struggle; and the only way of salvation.

Another example of this stage is found in his poem "Nashīd (Anthem)":

"Hello?
I want Jesus
What! Who are you?
I am speaking from Israel
I have nails in my feet,
I carry a wreath of thorns
Which path do I choose
Oh man, which path?
Do I do penance for sweet salvation
Or do I walk on?
Do I walk on, or do I die?
I say to you: March on, men!"

Again in this poem, Darwish carries his cross. Feeling fatigued and doubtful, he hears the words of Jesus that give him the courage to continue his path and walk towards Golgotha. In this first stage, the last mention of the cross is found in the poem "A Love Song on the Cross," in which the crucified speaks to his lover: the city of Jerusalem.

> *"I love you Be my cross*
> *Be, as you wish, a dove tower*
> *If your hands were to dissolve me*
> *They would fill the desert with shroud"*

The cross is also significant here: it represents enduring love and serves as a message for goodness, tenderness and everlasting peace for humankind. Darwish wrote this poem the same year Jerusalem was captured and while was held under house arrest. Religious symbolism becomes dull in his poetry after the fall of Jerusalem, as though he had lost his speech and narrative due to the Naksah. At this stage, Darwish joined the Communist Party, left for Moscow, went to Egypt, and finally traveled to Beirut where he settled. In the period between the fall of Jerusalem in 1967 and up until the siege of Beirut in 1982, our poet avoided mentioning the biblical narrative and stayed away from religious metaphors. After all, he was now a Communist and unconcerned with parables. In those fifteen years, his inspiration derived from crucified was replaced by his socialist beliefs and connection with the Soviet Union. Nevertheless, the parable eventually outplayed communism, and divine influence took over once again. There was no way for him to escape the cross, which was present from the first moment ink touched paper and words were set in motion.

In this first stage (1964-1967) of Darwish's work, we can distinguish the liberation theologian who uses the image of the Crucified as a prototype to symbolize the Palestinian prisoner and martyr who stands against defeat and subjugation, carries his cross and sacrifices his own blood for a better future. There is no referral to the biblical narrative in his collections from 1967 to 1982, up until the siege of Beirut and the massacre of Sabra and Shatila in 1982 when suddenly, the poet's inspiration returned.

2. The Second Stage (1982 - 1993)

What the Palestinian people faced and endured in Beirut may be similar to the sense of abandonment that Jesus came up against from those closest to him:

> *"They reduced him, denounced him, they deserted him,*
> *they left him on the cross*
> *and placed him in the tomb,*
> *they besieged him between gravestones.*
> *They broke you, oh how they broke you,*
> *to make a throne out of your anguish,*
> *They split you, denounced you, they concealed you*
> *and made an army out of your distress,*
> *They put you in the gravestone and said: do not turn over*
> *They threw you in the well and said: do not turn over*
> *You greeted your battle, my mother's son*
> *A thousand years, a thousand years in the sun,*
> *They denounced you, for all they know is how to rattle and run*
> *They now rob you of your skin.*
> *Watch out from the likes of them, my mother's son*
> *You who are more than a father's son*
> *Oh how alone you are.."* [26]

In another example from this poem, Mahmoud writes:

"Allahu Akbar,
This verse is ours.
Read
In the name of the rebel who birthed sympathy
out of his pain
In the name of the rebel who withdraws
from your time
to follow his first call
the first and the first
We'll destroy the temple
In the name of the rebel who begins
Read
Our portrait is Beirut
Our Sura is Beirut..." [27]

In this poem, Darwish links the Quran and the Bible as if he were a prophet who received a *Sura* entitled "Beirut." He reads his poem as the rebel who gave birth to sympathy out of his pain, and who was called to destroy the temple in order to build it in three days.

Whoever reads "In Praise of the High Shadow" will find it filled with biblical metaphors related to Job[28], Adam – who was cast out of paradise like the Palestinians who left Beirut[29], Mary Magdalene[30], Isaiah – who lamented Jerusalem[31] and many other symbols and verses.

The second stage of Darwish's life starts with the siege of Beirut and continues until a little before the Oslo Accords. This is a pivotal stage. After Beirut, Palestinians felt abandoned by the other Arab nations. They felt alone: Palestine was sold by the Arabs like Yusuf had been sold by his brothers:

> "Oh my father, I am Yusuf
> Oh father, my brothers neither love me nor want me in their midst
> They assault me and cast stones and words at me
> They want me to die so they can eulogize me
> They closed the door of your house and left me outside
> They expelled me from the field
> Oh my father, they poisoned my grapes"...
> "What have I done, Oh my father?
> Why me?
> You named me Yusuf and they threw me into the well
> They accused the wolf
> The wolf is more merciful than my brothers
> Oh, my father
> Did I wrong anyone when I said that
> I saw eleven stars and the sun and the moon
> Saw them kneeling before me?"[32]

Another factor that made this a decisive stage in Darwish's life was the fall of the Soviet Union, which came as a shock for committed Communists who saw the world come crashing down before their eyes.

Faced with the betrayal of the Arab world on the one hand and the fall of the Soviet Union on the other, Darwish felt abandoned by everyone including God, yet it is at this stage particularly that he begins a conversation with God applying suggestive metaphors of prayer, such as the prayer in the Garden of Gethsemane before the Last Supper, and the prayer of Jesus on the Cross, as illustrated by two examples:

> "My God, my God, why have you forsaken me? Why did you wed Mary? [Mary here is a metaphor for Israel]

Why did you pledge my only tender to the army – Why?
I, the widow, the daughter of this stillness, the daughter of
your jilted word –
Why have you forsaken me?
My God, my God, why did you wed Mary?
You set down two nations from a spike
And wed me to a conception, and I complied;
complied with your forthcoming wisdom
Have you dismissed me, or have you set off to heal the other,
my enemy, from the guillotine?
Does she, she who is the same as I,
Does she have the right to ask to wed God?
and to ask God, my God, why have you forsaken me?
Why did you wed me, Lord? Why, why did you wed Mary?" [33]

"The Last Supper lingers, so do the Last Supper commandments,
Father, be full of grace with us,
Wait for us a little while, oh Lord!
Do not pull out the glass from us,
Take it slow, so that we may ask more than we have asked." [34]

At this stage, Jesus is no longer seen as the rebel in search of death, but rather as the son looking for another chance in life. The withering spikes that will nourish the whole valley are not what matter at this point. On the contrary, Darwish switches from a theology concerned with death to a witness of a theology that celebrates life. In this period before the first Intifada, we find him to be wary of speeches that might hail the victim:

"They'd love to see me dead, so they can say:
he was one of us, he belonged to us." [35]
It is also at this stage that he proclaims:
"We have on this earth what makes life worth living..." [36]

3. The Third Stage
(1993 - 1999)

The third stage which coincided along with the Oslo Accords, Darwish's rationale was the same as Edward Said's: He was opposed to the Accords. In this period, there is a great deal of symbolism alluding to Genesis, as Darwish draws metaphors from Oslo to the equality between Cain and Abel; the oppressor and the victim...[37] He also makes the comparison of self-sacrifice as drawn from the example of Abraham and his son (Ismail).[38]

4. The Fourth Stage
(1999 - 2008)

The fourth and final stage of Darwish's life began around 1999. The context changes just as Darwish's personal context also changed drastically. After undergoing open heart surgery in Paris, Darwish found himself in hospital, between life and death; between existence and nothingness; and in a battle between body and spirit. He was convinced that his death was still not imminent [39]. It was neither harvest time, nor the day of judgment.

At this stage, Darwish found himself battling with death. He ventured to understand the true meaning of life and speculated about whether he should follow Solomon's wise path, or Christ's rising from the dead. Darwish chose Solomon, the wise king, whose glory the poet identified with but whose path he nevertheless recognized as vain and ephemeral.

Darwish identifies with Solomon so much in this period that he almost seems to replicate Solomon's path, yet he finds it difficult to identify with Jesus when death advances him[40]:

> *"And wait*
> *A child will carry your soul in your place*
> *immortality is procreation nothing less*
> *everything is vain or ephemeral*
> *ephemeral or vain*
> *Who am I?*
> *The Song of Songs?*
> *or the wisdom of Ecclesiastics?*
> *You and I are me*
> *I'm poet*
> *and king*
> *and a wise man at the edge of the well*
> *No cloud in my open hand*
> *in my temple no eleven planets*
> *my body narrow*
> *my eternity narrow*
> *and my tomorrow sitting like a crown of dust on my throne*
> *Vain vanity of vanities ... vain*
> *Everything on earth is ephemeral*
> *The winds are north*
> *the winds are south*
> *The sun rises by itself and sets by itself*
> *nothing is new*
> *The past was yesterday*
> *futile in futility*
> *The temple is high*

and the wheat is high
If the sky comes down it rains
and if the land rises up it's destroyed
Anything that goes beyond its limits will become its
opposite one day
And life on earth is a shadow of something we can't see
Vanity vanity of vanities ... vain
Everything on earth is ephemeral
1,400 chariots
12,000 horses
Carry my gilded name from one age to another
I lived as no other poet
a king and sage
I grew old and bored with glory
I didn't lack for anything
Is this why the more my star rose the more my anxiety grew?
So what's Jerusalem and what's a throne
if nothing remains forever?
There's a time for birth
and a time for death
A time for silence
and a time for speech
A time for war
and a time for peace
and a time for time
nothing remains forever
Each river will be drunk by the sea
and the sea still is not full
Nothing remains forever
everything living will die
and death is still not full
Nothing will remain after me except a gilded name:
"Solomon was ..."

So what do the dead do with their names?
Is it the gold
or the song of songs
or the Ecclesiastes
who will illuminate the vastness of my gloom?
Vanity vanity of vanities ... vain
everything on earth is ephemeral
I saw myself walking like Christ on the lake
but I came down from the cross because of my fear of heights
and I don't preach the resurrection"[41]

Darwish did not in fact fear heights; he feared death. He had a hard time believing in the resurrection, yet with this lack of faith, life was deemed meaningless. In "Jidariyya (Mural)," Darwish discovers what man is able to keep in the face of death, and ends his poem by saying:

"This name is mine...
and also my friends' wherever they may be
And my temporary body is mine
present or absent...
Two metres of this earth will be enough for now
a metre and 75 centimetres for me
and the rest for flowers in a riot of colour
who will slowly drink me
And what was mine is mine: my yesterday
and what will be in the distant tomorrow in the return
of the fugitive soul
as if nothing has been
and as if nothing has been
A light wound on the arm of the absurd present
History taunting its victims
and its heroes...

> *throwing them a glance and passing on*
> *This sea is mine*
> *This sea air is mine*
> *And my name—if I mispronounce it on my coffin—is mine*
> *And as for me—full of all reasons for leaving—*
> *I am not mine*
> *I am not mine*
> *I am not mine"*[42]

When death drew near, Darwish realized that he did not have ownership of himself and he confessed that, after all, he had no control over his destiny.

While his proficiency in the Old Testament and the gospels is obvious to the reader, Darwish seems not to have been acquainted with Paul, whose name is nowhere mentioned in his poetry. Paul himself had a similar experience realizing that we do not live for ourselves, which is added to his faithful perception that "Whether we live or die, we belong to the Lord."

While Darwish stops at "I am not mine" and does not go further, Paul carries on: "None of us lives to himself alone… We belong to the Lord."

Darwish's poetry did not cease with *"Mural"* in 1999. He kept pondering the mysteries of life and death in his last eight years, as exemplified in his final collection of poetry: *"Almond Blossoms and Beyond"* in which he no longer fantasizes about his great hopes, but beginnings to grasp the meaning of life through its subtle nuances:

> *"It is said: Love is as strong as Death.*
> *I say: But lust for life, even with no satisfying proofs,*
> *is stronger than Life and Death.*

So let us end our private funeral rite
and share with our neighbors in song.
Life is axiomatic... and true as dust."[43]

In his last years, Darwish saw himself on a bridge swathed in dense fog. Similar to the Israelites, he would need to cross the river Jordan to end his exile and reach the Promised Land.[44] During his last days on this bridge, he witnessed with faithful eyes that which he had never seen before. Thus he resolved that: "Every place far from God and His earth is an exile," and "In a world that has no heaven, the earth becomes an abyss":[45]

"Shout so that you hear yourself, shout so that you know
that you are still alive, and you know that life is possible
on this earth.
Invent a hope for words, or an area, or a mirage,
to prolong hope.
And sing, for beauty is freedom.
I say: Life defined only as the opposite of death is not life."[46]

That was one of Darwish's last poems.

Those who read Darwish from start to finish will find a man who lived in the biblical narrative; a narrative which was not a fleeting phase in the poet's life, but a source of inspiration that influenced him so markedly that he used it at every juncture. For Darwish the biblical narrative of ancient times was but the metaphor of the Palestinian people today. Darwish, the Palestinian Muslim, was able to identify with the biblical narrative because he sensed that this narrative is the best expression of a people's identity. If Mahmoud Darwish had lived in Old Testament Palestine, his poetry would have been incorporated into the biblical corpus. As a biblical prophet, Darwish used biblical metaphors to reach his people with poetry that speaks to their hearts in a particular context. In doing so he showed that the biblical narrative is the best expression of the Palestinian narrative. Thus used the ancient biblical narrative to carve a contemporary Palestinian identity that is deeply rooted in Palestinian soil and experience.

7

Holy Places and the Formation of Identity:

The Case of Hebron / al-Khalīl

Ulrike Bechmann

1. Holy places from a perspective of the study of religion

Places that are considered "holy" by certain groups, very often have a long history. They are part of the space and landscape and therefore part of the history of the region. And they are part of the identity of the people living there. As such they may also become part of the identity of persons who belong to different related religious traditions and who venerate a place as "holy" through gifts and pilgrimage. "Holiness" is a mutual process between the history of a place, its religious traditions, various populations throughout the ages, religious leaders, and political contexts.[1]

A place is "holy" because of religious stories (mixed with history or entirely fictional stories) that are connected and bound to those places. These stories identify specific events or contents of beliefs with the places. They are expressed, remembered and reclaimed through the structure of the place or the buildings, the specific rituals and the way of conveying the religious tradition. These stories are also the basis for the veneration or a pilgrimage to a place from believers of the specific religion who are not living near the "holy place." Through the structure of the "holy place" and its rituals specific religious memory is conveyed.

A "holy place," its structure and its rituals, is part of the cultural memory of a story and/or an event, overlapping the living communicative memory of people, which ends with contemporary witnesses. In order to save a story or history for coming generations memory has to be saved by a cultural memory, be it text, architecture, rituals, narratives, structuring a landscape or any other cultural expression.[2] Cultural memory is no longer bound to the individual memory of people, quite the contrary; cultural memory reminds people of their belief and/or history. The structure of the place, the type of symbols, and the form of veneration[3] – all mark a place called "holy" or "sacred" in a certain way. The narrative and ritual memory establish a new kind of "memorialization" through a special "dialogue" with those who have died in order to discover the meaning of their experience for the living. The narrative of the memory and the ritual legitimize the places. Symbolic representations continue the narrative with different means and instruments. But memory is more than preserving or reconstructing the past. Cultural memory preserves the identity of the religious community and therefore serves the present community.

Holy places are additional to holy texts. Through a ritual or a pilgrimage a holy place and its veneration is consolidated and confidence in knowledge of the faith gains strength and renders a contribution for continuity and the identity of persons and the community.

In any age the community of a "holy place" has to decide if they wish to adhere cultural memory or if they want to add, remove or reconstruct the cultural memory according to their perspective of the memory. But this requires discourse about and with the "holy place" as memories and narratives are not easily changeable. "Holy places" often retain their holiness, even if religious, political or social transformations take place. Holy places can survive several transitions in terms of cultures and religions if they are not given up or destroyed. Perhaps a new memory dismantles the old one and serves the new community. Holy places do not only preserve identity. They also support transformations from the past to the present; they combine things that are originally different and they cause, secure, and bring about local symbolized continuity through history and tradition. Therefore a construction of different traditions that are present at the same place can be seen as a locally manifested "vertical ecumenism."[4]

Holy places are able to accumulate different rituals/rites and therefore even different religions, not only in a diachronic way (one after another) but also in a synchronic way and more. Throughout the history of the Middle East especially there are many holy places that are venerated because of their history from believers of different religions.[5] This is also the case for the tombs of Abraham/Ibrāhīm and other patriarchs and matriarchs in *Hebron/al-Khalīl.*[6]

2. Holy places and the hermeneutics of "The Other"

Holy places are distinctive indicators of identity and therefore distinctive indicators of the practical hermeneutics of "The Other" which is established through a holy place.

One indicator for the given hermeneutics is: Does the *present society* allow a holy place of a certain group to emerge? Or is it used by other religious identities? And is this "holy place" even supported and kept by the whole society for the sake of others? Even if the others are a minority, a political majority, or come from abroad?

A second indicator of the hermeneutics of "The Other," of the venerating group is: Does the *holy place* offer access not only to believers of its own religion, but also to people of other traditions or religions? Are they allowed to go there, are they allowed to pay respect to the place, can they be interested in the place or stay there for a while – within the frame of the ritual borders of the place? Is it even permitted to act religiously and with respect? This is not solely a question of interreligious encounters but also of the ecumenical encounter between branches of the same religion.

Of course it would be too simple to conclude that those communities whose holy places are open to "the Other" are also as a society open toward "The Other." And vice versa: Those who close their holy places for others are not necessarily rejecting "The Other." Still, there is a certain significance. In order, however, to draw final conclusions it is necessary to dig deeper and to analyze the political, social, and cultural context as it is the context that affects sacred spaces or "holy places."

Only by considering this contextuality is it possible to understand what kind of impact the construction of hermetic seclusion or open hospitality has on the hermeneutics of "The Other", on the holy place. The context of political or historical experiences, social, or culturally specific factors have an impact not only on the practical hermeneutics of "The Other" but also on their handling of their holy places and vice versa. This can be experienced for example in the highly competitive holy place of Hebron/al- Khalīl, the tombs of

Abraham, Sarah and other matriarchs and patriarchs, which we have visited. The case of Hebron/al- Khalīl is both historically and currently interesting as a study of the mutual influence of holy places and the building of identity. It is a place with longstanding and varying religious traditions as well as a political context with fierce conflicts. In Hebron/al-Khalīl there is an intersection of religious history and present political problems.

The philosopher Michel Foucault calls studies on these intersections an "archaeological" approach.[7] Archaeology not only means digging up a place but any access to the "archives" of the past on the background of their cultural system and thinking. This is combined with a genealogical approach which explores the meaning of these archives for the present. The current problems are a challenge for studying the holy place of Hebron/al- Khalīl from the beginning in order to see if analogies in its history are able to create a certain memory or a certain critique for the present. "The premise of the archaeological method is that systems of thought and knowledge (epistemic or discursive formations, in Foucault's terminology) are governed by rules, beyond those of grammar and logic, that operate beneath the consciousness of individual subjects and define a system of conceptual possibilities that determines the boundaries of thought in a given domain and period. So, for example, History of Madness should, Foucault maintained, be read as an intellectual excavation of the radically different discursive formations that governed talk and thought about madness from the 17th through the 19th centuries."[8] In investigating the archeology of a holy place this means analyzing the dynamics of excluding or including the foreign other and how they are erected and maintained or destructed by contemporary political powers.

3. Religious history of Hebron / al- Khalīl

Hebron/al-Khalīl is one of those places that has a longstanding, varying religious history and is a prominent example of an intersection of religious history and politics. Its history has to be considered together with the second holy place close to Hebron, the holy tree of Mamre, four kilometers from Hebron/al-Khalīl. Both places are bound to the biblical story of Abraham and Sarah (Gen 18; Gen 23; Gen 25), the announcement of a son born to Sarah and the tomb of Sarah and Abraham (the cave of Machpela). In the history of religion holy trees, holy stones (or altars), or holy waters such as springs are known as places of veneration for gods or goddesses.[9] The widespread tradition of a holy tree probably dates to the Middle or Late Bronze era (2nd millennium B.C. or even earlier) and the veneration of a goddess relevant (responsible) for fertility ("Zweiggöttin" or "twig-goddess").[10] The basis for the veneration of a tree is the narrative of the three angels visiting Abraham and Sarah; Gen18:1 identifies this tradition with Jahwe. The tomb and cave *Machpela* was also part of the biblical narrative about Abraham and Sarah (as narrative figures, not what is considered to be modern history) and was identified with Hebron.

Hebron (*Tel Rumeideh*) goes back to the 3rd Millenium B.C. and is one of the oldest towns of the region being the capital city of David (2 Sam 2-5). From the time of the Exile (587/6 B.C.) on Hebron was no longer part of Judah but belonged to the Edomites, to the Arabian part of Nabonid's Babylonian Kingdom (553 B.C,); Hebron was also part of the Arabian Qedrenes and part of the Persian empire. The narrative of Gen 23 was written at a time when Hebron was no longer part of Judah in order to claim once again that Hebron belonged to the province of Judah. Hebron and its surroundings are a geographical link between the southern Palestinian and the North Arabian population, as the four hundred ostraca found from the 4th century B.C. around Hebron demonstrate, they use Arab names and call upon the Qos, god of the Edomites.

Hebron[11] belonged to the province Idumaea under Roman rule. About 120 B.C. Hebron was re-conquered by the Maccabean Hyrkan I. According to Flavius Josephus Hyrkan I. forced the Idumaens to become Jews. Herod the Great, Idumaean himself, set up the tombs with a new structure and a wall around the tombs. During the first Jewish war Hebron was plundered by the Zealots and during that war (66-70 A.D.) was destroyed by the Romans as an important hindrance on their way to Jerusalem. Nevertheless a Jewish community must have stayed as can be seen the remains of synagogues dating from Byzantine times.

During the Byzantine era Mamre was venerated not only by Jews but also by Christians; the tradition of Gen 18 was venerated as a sacred place where God revealed himself and as a place to honor Abraham and Sarah. Reports of early pilgrims indicate a basilica in Mamre with a painting of the guests of Abraham that symbolized the meaning of the church. The guest in the middle of the group was drawn as Christ the redeemer. The holy tree probably stayed as part of the place beneath the basilica. The mosaic map of Madaba from the 6th century shows a basilica together with a tree. Yet not only Jews and Christians visited the place.

In the fifth century Bishop Sozomenos of Gaza complained that the market of Mamre was attractive for Palestinians, Phoenicians, Arabs, Jews, pagans and Christians. He wrote:

> *"Here the inhabitants of the country and of the regions round Palestine the Phoenicians, and the Arabians, assemble*

> *annually during the summer season to keep a brilliant feast; and many others, both buyers and sellers, resort thither on account of the fair. Indeed, this feast is diligently frequented by all nations: by the Jews, because they boast of their descent from the patriarch Abraham; by the Pagans, because angels there appeared to men; and by Christians, because He who for the salvation of mankind was born of a virgin, afterwards manifested Himself there to a godly man."* [12]

Sozomenos indicates various reasons different believers had for the veneration of Mamre. At that time Hebron and Mamre were part of the cultural memory of the Jewish, Christian and pagan peoples. Hebron and Mamre are, therefore, places with different religious rites both of which accumulated rites around the holy tree and the well. The basilica of Mamre was destroyed in the seventh century.

Finally, Islamic tradition was added to the place. It is difficult to reconstruct the early Islamic settlement of Hebron; but because of the role of Ibrāhīm in Islam, Muslims were able to connect and take part in the traditions of Hebron as a "holy place." Muslim traditions concerning Ibrāhīm are now located in Hebron and new narratives were established together with the tomb of the patriarchs and matriarchs. Those traditions make Hebron a holy place for Muslims. As prophets of Islamic history the patriarchs and matriarchs could easily be integrated. From then on Hebron developed from an agrarian center to a town that lived economically through its holy place while the city center slowly shifted from the settlement hills to the mosque with the holy places in the valley.[13]

The Crusaders didn't make too many changes in architecture but did change the mosque into a church. At that time the Faḍā'il literature elaborated the value of Hebron for the Islamic tradition. The Islamic rulers of the Ayyubides and the Mamluks invested in the construction and interior of the mosque. They closed the caves and put the cenotaphs that represented the caves below.

Abraham's title in the Qur'ān, Friend of God, was used as a name for Hebron, now called al-Khalīl. The tradition sees Ibrāhīm thrown into the fire (Q 21.69) and saved and Ibrāhīm's and Isma'īl's Hidschra to Mecca started in Mamre. Sarah's laughter (Q 11.71) was located there. Visiting the tombs people hoped for the intercession of Ibrāhīm by God and Ibrāhīm's hospitality is seen as his outstanding attribute. This motif of hospitality (Gen 18/Q 11.69-76) gained utmost importance and al-Muqqadasī, a tenth century author, *stated in connection with* the pilgrimage to al-Khalīl that Ibrāhīm was not able to eat without guests. From this tradition a *waqf* was founded in order to run an open guesthouse with free food for pilgrims. This tradition existed until modern times.

In sum, Hebron / al-Khalīl (together with Mamre) conveys several traditions of openness to others: the epiphany of God or angels, hospitality, intercessions for others, and the promise of a future through children. The traditions were not bound to a certain belief but were acceptable for different peoples and beliefs because of their semiotic openness and polysemy. They could be adopted from different religious traditions at this particular place throughout the ages. An increasing number of pilgrims felt the openness of the traditions: they received free food and hoped that Ibrāhīm's intercession for others could bring about an intercession for themselves. Women who were not able to conceive hoped for progeny. God's or an angel's revelation at the place supported the hope that wishes, hopes, and prayers would come true. Hebron/al-Khalīl served as a plurivalent holy place for many people. The veneration of forefathers and foremothers, and the transgressing of religious borders provoked skeptic commentary from orthodox Muslims. But the holy person who was venerated was Ibrahim – and therefore it was difficult to stop the cult of a central figure in the Qur'ān.

The cultural memory of Hebron/al-Khalīl includes different traditions up to the present and this combination of traditions makes it one the most remarkable cultic places in the region. An overview of the development of the religious traditions indicates that the significance of the holy place relied not only on religious traditions but also on the political context, which tradition was present or dominant and how this tradition dealt with the others.

Hebron / al-Khalīl has a longstanding and varying function in the formation of different identities which also includes a history of conflicts.

5. Hebron / al-Khalīl in political turmoils in the twentieth century

This holy place is also an example of how religion and religious identity was and is used and misused for political interests through the centuries including the present. In times of conflicts, holy places intensify the fight between different identities. In the fierce conflicts of the twentieth century by Israeli settlers and some Muslim groups Hebron/al-Khalīl is claimed by and bound to one identity only. Analyzing the conflicting situation in the light of the Bible without a concise and differentiated analysis of the political context deepens the conflict and hinders finding a political way of living together based on justice for both.

In 1967 the West-Bank was conquered and occupied by the Israeli military and settlements have been erected ever since. In Hebron settlers live in the midst of the town among the Palestinian population and in 1968 founded the settlement of Kiryat Arba. Access to the mosque and the tombs of the patriarchs and matriarchs were split, and a synagogue was erected within the mosque. Today, Muslims only have access to the mosque by a checkpoint manned by soldiers. The "empire" destroys free access by controlling it.

The settlers of Hebron are one of the fiercest extremist settler groups in the West-Bank with a nationalistic-religious attitude.[14] Hebron is a symbol for settlers to return to primarily Jewish property. They combine the military occupation with religious-Jewish claims on the holy places. Baruch Goldstein's attack in 1994 on the mosque of Hebron killing nearly thirty Muslims at prayer before he was killed was a sad culmination of the settlement movement. Part of the settlement movement sees Goldstein as a martyr and as such his tomb is visited as a "holy place," The text at his tomb says:

"Here lies the saint, Dr. Baruch Kappel Goldstein, blessed be the memory of the righteous and holy man, may the Lord avenge his blood, who devoted his soul to the Jews, Jewish religion and Jewish land. His hands are innocent and his heart is pure. He was killed as a martyr of God on the 14th of Adar, Purim, in the year 5754 (1994)."

Goldstein's deadly violence not only killed people but also violated the inner structure of the holy place of Hebron/al-Khalīl. His tomb does not allow access for people other than settlers and their followers. It will never carry a message like the tomb of Ibrahīm and his family. It does not represent plurality but rather dominance bought dearly by the death of others. The voice of this tomb contradicts the voice of the tombs of its forefathers and foremothers. It may currently be venerated by settlers but it is neither important for the Jewish people of Israel in general nor for all those living in the settlements. Goldstein's tomb will never have a message stressing other people via hospitality, intercession or promise of a future; it will only communicate a message of violence and self-interest at the expense of others. This "holy place" probably cannot survive transformations of the political context. It may be "holy" for some time and some people, but it is dependent on a military force to exist.

The past rests in itself like the dead rest in their tombs. In the sight of dead humans all differences are silent. A tomb is a place where differences can be settled without the necessity of being dissolved. Whoever excludes, degrades, kills or destroys at such a place is misusing the central meaning of the place: the capability to accept and to live in plurality. If people do not visit a "holy place" longing for this message it is not possible to hear it. The place itself objects and is no longer able to unfold its might and power but is misused for exclusion and destruction.

A joint commemoration of victims of violence, however, enables people to end an attitude of violence and to support the identity and the right to exist of "The Other." The *parents circle*[15] is an organization of Israelis and Palestinians who have lost a family member in the conflict. They meet and try to work toward this attitude despite or because of their personal sorrow and loss. It is necessary to have the same reference point; a common goal of reciprocity and justice.

6. Identity building in Hebron / al-Khalīl in times of conflict

Hebron/al-Khalīl has the ability to unfurl such a power. But this holy place is an example of how religion and religious identity was and is used and misused for political interests throughout the centuries as well as today. I don't for see that Hebron/al-Khalīl will send a different message in the near future. The conflict is about politics and as long as there is no political solution, it doesn't seem possible to handle a holy site differently. Religion and politics are closely connected. As long as holy places are in the grip of political interests they cannot speak out of their own, deeply rooted identity of freedom and openness.

If we think ahead to a time when an agreement between Israel and Palestinians might exist it will be interesting what message and image of identity comes from Hebron/al-Khalīl. What new tradition at the core of the place will be taken up for the formation of Palestinian identity? Will it be the tradition of hospitality and openness to foreigners, believers of all traditions, especially for Jewish, Christian and Muslim believers, and be a welcoming place like Ibrahīm welcomed strangers? Or will it be a place that harks back to the memory of being excluded and living through oppression so that a revived openness is simply not possible? It will also depend on the Palestinian political context itself. Will it be an open, plural civil society with different religious identities or will it be a society that chooses to close? If we visit Hebron/al-Khalīl in that future we will know.

8

Land of Sprouting Twigs

Vertical Ecumenism in Palestinian Art and Culture

Thomas Staubli

The southern Levant is a small strip of fertile land between the sea to the west and the desert to the east. Fertile land means crop, trees, animals, food, life – while sea (Canaan. *yam*) and desert (Canaan. *mot*) are symbols of chaos and danger of death. This geographic grouping has formed the minds of the people living in the area for thousands of years who have a profound awareness of the blessings of the earth. The famous biblical myth even says that we are taken from the earth, formed by God, and enlivened by his breath (Gen 2:7) Adam is part of *adamah*. The earth nourishes, it spends gifts as does Eve, the mother of all living (Gen 3:20), and at the end it takes the body. No wonder that the earth has been understood as the living body of woman as it is expressed by Job (1:21): "Naked I came from my mother's womb, and naked shall I return there." Both fertile ground and the birthing woman's womb are identified. During the Chalcolithic period, a time when important fundamentals of southern Levantine civilization were laid, people made boxes of clay with an anthropomorphic front for a second burial of human bones to emphasize magically the idea of returning to the womb, to a place with the power to bring the body back to life.

1. Woman, twig and tree symbolism for the land in modern Palestinian art

It is precisely this regenerative force of the earth that has become so important for the Palestinians in the last few decades as a symbol of resistance and hope for the ending of the occupation, expressed in the image of a woman in traditional Palestinian clothes decorated with twigs or holding a branch, as we can be seen on a mural from Gaza (**fig. 1**). Typical of the national impact of such symbolism today is the Palestinian flag on the sleeves of the woman's abbaya. The same mix of traditional floral symbolism and modern elements of identity can be found on the *qabeh*, the embroidered breast panel of the traditional *thob*, as shown in the published works of the collector Widad Kawar (**fig. 2**), where traditional stylized twigs are added to flags, Dome-of-the-Rock-emblems and PLO-characters. The autodidact, Zuhdi al-Adawi, today living in a Syrian refugee camp, reflects in his work, inspired by the art of social realism and smuggled out of the Ashkelon prison, the forces of resistance of Palestinian prisoners. Again the power for vegetal regeneration is crucial in his art. The pictured example (**fig. 3**) is of a branch held in the fist of a prisoner but also the roots of a burning candle with the eye of a woman, illuminating the prisoner's darkness. In "Ismael" (**fig. 4**), one of his "emblems of decay," Suleiman Mansour, a major figure in Palestinian art, reminds Ismael, son of Abraham and Hagar, the ancestor of the Arab people. Below the figures, on a broken slab, roses symbolize the martyrs of the Intifada. Mansour also uses vegetation symbolism to express the forces of resurrection. But at the end of the twentieth century the rose connoted different elements than the olive branch. It is impossible not to link it with James Oppenheim's famous poem "Bread and Roses" (1911) and, therefore, with the idea of solidarity beyond religious and national boundaries: »As we come marching, marching, we battle, too, for men – for they are women's children, and we mother them again." At the other end of the spectrum of vegetation symbolism, very close to the signifier of the symbol, Vera Tamari's installation »Tale of a tree« (**fig. 5**) reflects the hundreds of olive trees destroyed by Israeli settlers and the military. Is a tree with roots dating to the time when the Judean highlands were cultivated during the Chalcolithic period (4500-3600 BC), nothing more than an electric bulb which can be clicked off? The tree, even more than the twig, represents continuity of civilization and life. A final example of modern Palestinian art shows, that sometimes the connection between Canaanite culture and modern Palestinian art is not an element of unconscious tradition in the histoire du longue durée (Braudel), but of a very conscious quotation of an-up-to date awareness of culture as part of the political struggle. Abdel Rahmen Al Muzayen (born 1943 in Qubeibeh, now living in Gaza), a former general in the Palestinian Liberation Organization, a master of ink drawings, reflects the destruction of the city of Jenin in the figure of Anat, the ancient goddess of the Canaanites, symbolizing the soul and the strength of Palestine (**fig. 6**). Indeed in his painting we find not only the twig as an emblematic shield of the goddess, but also an uprooted palm tree, saved by the woman, flowers on the qabeh and doves, one of the animals of the ancient goddess, and at the same time, a modern symbol of peace.

2. Witnesses of "Vertical Ecumenism"

The last four examples were part of the first comprehensive Palestinian Art Exhibition in the United States entitled, "Made in Palestine", in Houston Texas in 2003, organized by the Ineri Foundation.

The total of six images taken from Palestinian art and folk art demonstrating the importance of twigs as symbols of regeneration and life are, of course, only the tip of an iceberg. But as such they are the last witnesses of an important "Vertical Ecumenism."

The category of "Vertical Ecumenism" has been developed in the BIBLE + ORIENT Museum of the University of Fribourg (Switzerland) to help understand the basal elements of continuity in a context of clash-rhetoric and conflict-politics as a background for a more fair and complete dialogue between religions and cultures. The information in our media is dominated by violent events, terroristic activism, and the horror vision of a clash of civilizations. Evidently, identity is mainly constructed of differences, expressed in violent acts and repeated in a brainwashing manner in the daily news. But what we urgently need for a horizontal dialogue between religious, ethnic or political groups is a deep awareness of "vertical", and historical connections and developments- an awareness of the genetic codes of our cultures which are part of our collective memory, partly conscious and partly unconscious.

If the historian is "the medic of the memory," as Eugen Rosenstock-Huessy said, then it is the duty of the historian to bring the essential heritage of different groups (religious, ethnic, political) which they have in common back to memory. For some decades in Europe we have experienced the denial of Christian roots by those who emphasize the tradition of Enlightenment against ecclesiastic institutions. Christianity has a long and bloody history of denial of its Jewish roots and Islam and Judaism have, in common, a violent ideology towards their pagan roots, the Canaanites, and the time of ignorance (*jahiliyya*). The – sometimes justified – critique of the parents by their children became in many cases a self-righteous dogma which hindered a happy development in coexistence or even a mutual joy of differences.

With the example of sprouting twigs as one of the oldest and most important symbols of heritage of Canaanite culture I'd like to illustrate the potential of "Vertical Ecumenism" (advancing two studies published in German: Staubli 2005 and 2013).

3. Twigs as symbol of the blessings of the goddess

One of the oldest figurative decorations from the southern Levant, on a late Neolithic bone from HaGosherim (northern Galilee, around 6000 BC; **fig 7**), shows a twig in a telling way, namely coming out of the vulva of the anthropomorphized and, therefore, godly earth, feeding a capride. In the early Chalcolithic period the twig-capride combination appears on one of the famous bronze scepters from Nahal Mishmar (**fig. 8**). In the first phase of the Early Bronze Age the motif of dancing or mourning women is evident for the first time in the southern Levant on a clay pot (**fig. 9**).

In the Canaanite art of the Middle Bronze Age II (1750-1550 BC) twigs are nearly omnipresent. With striking frequency they are combined with a naked woman; sometimes they are flanking her or held by her. They may even sprout from her vulva or from her navel (**fig. 10**). The godly character of the mostly frontal depicted goddess can be emphasized by a neb-sign (master/mistress) under her feet. Sometimes she has big ears referring to her acceptance of human prayers or she wears godly signs on her head like horns or crowns or she appears with risen arms in the epiphany-gesture. She can be represented by a so-called Hathor fetish, combined with a twig (**fig. 11**), and she can be venerated by women in one of her forms as an anthropomorphic goddess, as a fetish, or as a twig (**fig.

12). Sometimes the woman is depicted dancing with twigs in her hands (**fig. 13**).

The motif of this special kind of goddess during the Middle Bronze IIB has been named "twig-goddess" (Schroer 1987). She is the Levantine variant of the ancient Near eastern goddess of the earth, representing the regenerating powers of the earth, when fertilized by the winter rains. It is noteworthy in this context to remember, that Elohim was not creating plants according to the myth of Gen 1:11 but only said: "Let the earth put forth vegetation: plants yielding seed, and fruit trees of every kind on earth that bear fruit with the seed in it." Even for Elohim it was not possible to replace the regenerating power of the earth (Keel/Schroer 22008: 52 with fig. 18).

The realm of the goddess is filled with a series of animals, which can be combined with the twig. They do not represent a biotope. Rather they represent conceptual aspects of the goddess, which we today would call, with our lingual tendency to abstraction: regeneration, refreshment, fertility, power, defense of life, etc. The oldest animal in the sphere of the goddess is – as we have seen already (**fig. 7-8**) – the capride (which means animals similar to a goat, an ibex or a gazelle; **fig. 14**). Other animals are the lion, the vulture, different kind of serpents (**fig. 15**), the crocodile, the hippopotamus, the velvet monkey and the tilapia fish.

5. The twig as an attribute of a god

Twigs also appear in combination with the falcon-headed god, a Levantine variant of the weather god, inspired by the Egyptian Horus (**fig. 16**) who often holds twigs as a kind of scepter. In a local Levantine the veneration of the Egyptian creation-god, Ptah, is combined with a twig (**fig. 17**). From here it is a small step to the combination of twigs with human beings, animals or hybrids, representing royal authority and power. This is especially true for the symbols of the pharaoh like the red crown of Lower Egypt, the Sphinx, but also for the highly typical Canaanite motif of the city-ruler in his robe with a broad hem (**fig. 18**) and for the prince on a donkey. Twigs too are held by the venerators of the weather god (**fig. 19**), possibly representing princes.

6. The twig as autonomous code for regeneration

Twigs are not only attributes of the earth goddess, her partner or her venerators, but symbols of the adorable holiness of the cosmos-regenerating powers of vegetation.

We may deduce this from pictures where the twig forms the center of a composition, sometimes in a series as a kind of *pluralis maiestatis* (**fig. 20**), sometimes in splendid isolation (**fig. 21**). In such a position the iconem of the twig converges syntactically with a holy or stylized tree.

7. Further development of the twig and the twig-cult

In the Late Bronze Age the twig was also combined with the name of Amun (**fig. 22**). That motif was now found more rarely in Levantine iconography. During the Iron Age the (stylized) tree was more common. But the limits between twig and tree are fluent as may be seen from the fragments of a painted jar, where the twig or tree bears the explicit legend elat, "goddess" and is flanked by caprids (**fig. 23**; cf. fig. 4-5; 11). On a Late Bronze cylinder seal from Amman (**fig. 24**) two human figures hold batons which are very similar to the later Greek *thyrsoi* (cf. fig. 2), giving further support to the above mentioned thesis, that Dionysus is a God of Levantine origins.

Throughout the Iron Age the twig motif was still present, but sometimes in new ways. A singular stamp seal from Akko provides insight to a cult scene, most probably during a *rosh khodesh* rite (**fig.25**). We see a man praying between a twig and a cult stand with a twig motif.

Indeed twig motifs on cult stands are not rare as can be seen from the recently published Yabne stands (Kletter/Ziffer/Zwickel 2010). An anthropomorphic goddess from Lakhish, this time presenting her breasts – a gesture rooted in the Near east and not in Egypt (cf. with fig. 7) – is associated with the twig (**fig. 26**). As well both new and characteristic for the late Iron Age, there is the combination of the name of the seal owner with a twig (**fig. 27**). The veneration of the moon as a regeneration symbol in combination with such symbols from the realm of animals and vegetation remains important (**fig.28**; cf. fig. 22).

During the Persian era twigs were prominent on coins, the new mass medium. In the same manner as twigs flanking the naked goddess, they now flanked the owl of Athena (**fig. 29**; around 400 BC). This motif of the owl became one of the most important symbols of valuable money in the southern Levant. But instead of adapting the correct Athenian iconography of the olive twig Levantine designers integrated it in their own traditional concept of the flanking twigs. At the end of the Persian period Hellenistic forms in art were more and more visible in the Levant, but often the motifs were not new as is the case for a venerator with a twig on a Samarian bullae (**fig. 30**; 375-335 BC; cf. fig. 15-16).

8. Twigs on local coins

It is indeed amazing to see, and today is also a reason for hope, that the ongoing political changes in the Levant, from the Babylonians to the Persians, from the Persians to the Macedonians did not harm the Levantine piety expressed by the twig. An illustrative scene from literature shows how the victory of Judith over Holofernes was been celebrated (Judith 16,12-13): "Then all the women of Israel ran together to see her, and blessed her, and made a dance among them for her: and she took branches (gr. *thyrsous*) in her hand, and gave also to the women that were with her. And they crowned themselves with olive wreaths (gr. *tên elaian*), she and those (women; Karrer/Kraus 2011: 1314) who were with her, and she went before all the people in the dance, leading all the women: and all the men of Israel followed in their armor and wearing garlands (*stephánôn*), and with songs on their lips."

From Hellenistic times onwards plants are the most important icons on Judean coins. Apart from the laurel and olive wreath, palm trees, ears, reeds, pomegranates, grapes and grape leaves is the simple, botanically indefinable twig (sometimes a palm twig) which appears often and in the most symbolically relevant contexts. On a coin of Alexander Yannai (**fig. 31**) the inscription "Jonathan, the King" is written to the left and to the right side of a twig and may be an allusion to Zech 4,1-4 (cf. also Sir 50,10) where the prince and the high priest are represented by two olive trees flanking the menorah, representing God. In the same line stands is a coin of Herod Antipas (**fig. 32**) whose title, "Herod, the Tetrarch" is surrounded by a twig. Another variant is the coin of Shimon bar Gamaliel with the inscription "Shimon (Prince) of Israel" (**fig. 33**). Still closer to the vision of Zecharja is a coin of Herod the Great on which, over the plumed helmet, a star is flanked by a pair of twigs (**fig. 34**). The star would replace the menorah of Zecharjas's vision. But it is also possible that Herod saw himself as the messianic star (Numb 24:17; Küchler 1989). In a variation of Herod's coins the twigs flank a tripod, maybe perhaps pointing to libations poured via twigs during the festival of Sukkot(**fig. 35**; cf. 37). Even on local coins of Roman Caesars, twigs are found as an example of Claudius shows (**fig. 36**). On the coins of the first and the second revolt the twig is sometimes combined with a vessel (**fig. 37**). The setting probably refers to a rite of Sukkot. During the ceremony water was spattered by a twig in order to animate God to send rain. Especially noteworthy for the ongoing symbolic importance of the twig are the coins of Eleasar and Shimon bar Giora, minted during the first revolt (**fig. 38**) which show a lulav and an etrog together with the words "Year xy of the liberation of Israel". Lulav means nothing more than a sprout (of a tree). According to their interpretations of Lev 23:40, for the rabbis this was an elaborate bouquet of a palm branch, a myrtle twig and a willow twig. Together with the etrog, a citrus fruit (originally from China: *Citrus medica cedra*), the bouquet was swung during the ceremony. The lulav was evidently the rabbinic version of the age-old Levantine tradition of concretizing godly blessings with a twig. Even on Hadrianic coins, minted in Rome, celebrating the victory over the second Jewish revolt, twigs are prominent. (**fig. 39**) Showing the children of Juda paying homage to Caesar with twigs in their hands. The first Islamic coin of Jerusalem, minted by Caliph Abd el-Malik, pursues the old tradition in a more abstract form, showing a menorah with five arms, which can be read also as a stylized tree or twig (**fig. 40**).

At the same time the Canaanite twig tradition not only continues on the coinage of the city state of Jerusalem, but also on those of other centers in the southern Levant. It is worth mentioning the coinage of Ashkelon, where we find the iconography of Phanebal (the face, *pnei*, of Baal; **fig. 41**). A coin from the times of Julia Domna shows a juvenile god with a weapon in the right and a twig in his left hand. In this cult image the age-old myth of Baal continues, after which a hero pacifies the country by force, dominating the chaotic powers, so that new life may sprout from its earth. An example of how the local twig tradition continues in the hand of a goddess is exemplified by a terracotta figure from Petra, which is a variant of Isis. She appears in the role of a mourner, sitting, her right hand on her cheek, while in her left hand a twig points to the earth (**fig. 42**). This goddess was very important in Petra. Even a rock sculpture from Wadi Abu Olleqa shows the prominent combination of twigs and most likely mourning women in the local Transjordan art of the Early Bronze Age (cf. fig. 9; Is 66:14 and below fig. 51), and also on twigs on local Byzantine coffins of the Byzantine period (**fig. 43**).

9. Twigs in Palestinian folk culture

It would be of great interest to follow the use and development of the twig symbol during the epochs dominated by Islamic cultures in the Near East. Not being a specialist in those periods I have to jump over several centuries now, hoping that this conference encourages an enthusiast to do the job. Let us take a final look at Palestinian folk culture of the last decades. Normally, on Arab amulets, beside texts only abstract signs are to be found. In Palestine, however, the twig is the exception to this rule (**fig. 44**). Still, on amulets of the present era, the olive branch is sometimes combined with the Bismillah (**fig. 45**).

On the intimate medium of the amulet a twig may connote prosperity, wealth and life in a broad sense. On storage facilities, the meaning of the symbol is more concise. It recalls the real presence of godly blessing in the form of barley or wheat grains (**fig. 46**), oil or water (**fig. 47**) in containers, made of adobe or burnt clay. The twigs in this context sometimes tend to look like an ear or a palm tree, but they never have a truly realistic shape. The vegetative elements in Palestinian embroidery are manifold as may be seen from a tobacco bag (**fig. 48**) or from the detail of a shawl (**fig. 49**). Twigs – even in a very abstract form - are also the basic motif of the rich décor of the Palestinian thob, the traditional female robe, and even more on the *sarma* (wedding dress; **fig. 50**; for many other examples see Kawar 2011 and Munayyer 2011) so women may appear as a living tree or – in more Canaanite or biblical language – as the above mentioned *'em kol-ḥai*, "the mother of all living" (Gen 3:20). Margarita Skinner and Widad Kamel Kawar in their *Treasury of Stitches from 1850 to 1950* list thirteen different branch types, not to mention other floral motifs such as trees or fruits: *'īrq al-nafnuf* "airy fairy branch", *'īrq al-nafnūf məkabbas* "double ariy fairy branch", *'īrq al-lōz* "almond branch", *'īrq al-tuffah* "apple branch", *'īrq al-qrunfūl* "carnation branch", *'īrq al-quwār* "flower pot branch" of the Gaza area, *'īrq al-'īnab* "grape's Branch" of the Jaffa area, *'īrq al-turmus* "lupine branch" of the Beersheba area, *'īrq alinjāssah* "pear branch" of the Negev area, *'īrq al-lāff* "rolling branch" of the Ramallah area and most important *'īrq al-zeytūn* "olive branch" of all areas *'arnūs durah* "ears of corn" in the Hebron area and *jadāyel sabel* "ears of wheat plait" in the Negev area. Finally the twig as a symbol of life beyond the limits of earthly life (cf. fig. 9; 42) is still present today in Palestinian mourning rites. After a Muslim burial – here in the main cemetery of Jerusalem – palm branches are stuck in the earth or put on the grave (**fig. 51**). Last but not least the global Christian celebration of Palm Sunday with its twig procession of olive branches has its roots in the southern Levant, namely in the already mentioned victory ceremonies of Hellenistic times.

10. Twigs in the state emblems of modern Israel and Palestine

More astonishing than the survival of the twig as a main symbol and, therefore, decorative element in Palestinian folk culture is perhaps the prominent place of the twig in the iconography of the modern, secular State of Israel (**fig. 52**). While the Lebanon did honor to the old Canaanite tradition against the holiness of the plants by putting the cedar in the white middle field of the flag (since the eighteenth century in the white flag of the Maronites, because according to Ps 92:12 the just will grow like a cedar on the Lebanon, from 1920 to 1943 in the white field of the French tricolor and now in the white strip of the flag of the Habsburgian monarchy, admired by the Lebanese banker Henry Pharaon who suggested this design), the young Israeli state honored the Canaanite tradition by flanking a menorah on its official state seal. The reference to Canaan however is not explicit and the interpretation of the composition is rather of a political nature. Olive branches are interpreted as symbols of the democratic and secular state, while the menorah is thought to be a sign of the religious traditions of the people. On a deeper level the picture of course is a quotation of Zecharja's vision (4,1-14) of God, the royal and the priestly authority, anointed by olive oil. But, on an even deeper level of the tradition, Zecharja's vision turns out to be an allegory of the old constellation of twigs, flanking a main symbol of the goddess. As we have seen, in his days, *the (Iron Age IIC)*, the blessing of the goddess was especially depicted in the picture of twigs flanking the new moon (fig. 25; 28).

From the start of this year 2013 Palestine also has a proper state seal (**fig. 53**), developed some years ago by Khaled Jarrar as a provocative-prophetic image. It shows the Palestinian sun bird, a popular small Nectariniidae bird. More important than the bird in my opinion is the twig with the flowers which feed the bird. Iconems on a state emblem are few, and selected carefully. On the background of the visualized tradition I argue that it is hardly a coincidence that we find in the emblems of both states – Israel and Palestine – a twig. Even if the style of the twigs and their iconographic syntax is quite different it seems to be clear that the affinity of both cultures – Jewish and Arab – for twigs is an expression of their deepest common Canaanite grounds.

9

Reading Palestine Realities with American Indian eyes

Robert O. Smith

"Oh my name it is nothin' / My age it means less
The country I come from / Is called the Midwest
I's taught and brought up there / The laws to abide
And that the land that I live in / Has God on its side

Oh the history books tell it / They tell it so well
The cavalries charged / The Indians fell
The cavalries charged / The Indians died
Oh the country was young / With God on its side"

Bob Dylan, "With God On Our Side" (1963)[1]

Recently, for a conference focused on the interplay between biblical interpretation and contemporary politics, I was invited to present a paper on the foundation of American religious ideology and the Israeli-Palestinian conflict. The conference organizers knew that the topic was of great interest to me. When I saw the program, I was surprised, though, to see the title they had chosen for me: "How the West Was Won."

I immediately saw that my German hosts were making a joke. They probably expected that I would suggest an alternative title. But instead I turned the tables and decided to rise to the occasion. Here's how I began:

> *"How the West was Won." The phrase conjures a variety of romantic images of the Lone Ranger and his nearly mute Indian sidekick, Tonto, or a seemingly endless stream of Hollywood movies. Images of the so-called Wild West still inform American icons like the Marlboro Man, informing for Americans and others the proper sense of American masculinity and national identity. The most common tropes in stories of 'how the West was won' are the struggles between outlaws and lawmen (with most of the attention being paid to the outlaws) and, of course, the archetypal relationship between 'cowboys and Indians.' Like so many of us in Oklahoma—the U.S. state founded on top of what had once been designated as "Indian Territory"—I am both a cowboy and an Indian. One of my grandfathers on my father's side, Jonathan T. Smith, was a horseman in Kentucky who, for a variety of circumstances that involved jail time for killing a man, found himself in Indian Territory. From my mother's side, I receive the heritage of being a citizen of the Chickasaw Nation, one of the so-called Five Civilized Tribes that, after 1830, walked on the Trail of Tears from our homeland in the southeastern United States to what is now south-central Oklahoma... [M]y contribution focuses on how the narrative of conquest was performed in the territorial expansion of the United States. Thus, I speak as both a cowboy and an Indian, a person committed to both dialogue with Jews and accompaniment of Palestinians who is also implicated by the injustices perpetuated in the name of U.S. national interest.*

I was glad to have a bit more control over the title of this presentation. As we together reflect on identity in relation to space and time, I am struck by how my engagement with Palestine has brought me into richer, deeper relationship with my Chickasaw identity. In this chapter, I will explore some ways different American Indians have reflected on their relationship with Palestinian experience and offer some ideas on deepening American Indian contributions toward strengthening trans-indigenous solidarity between themselves and Palestinians.

1. Is Palestine Read? Is Palestine Red?

There are 565 federally-recognized tribes, or American Indian nations, in the United States. Throughout the country, Indians, including those of mixed heritage, now comprise less than 2% of the overall population. In census data collected between 2007 and 2011, nine of the fifty states had poverty rates of about 30 percent or more for American Indians and Alaska Natives. In that period, five major cities had American Indian poverty rates of about 30 percent, while American Indians in Rapid City, S. Dakota, had a poverty rate of over 50 percent.[2] Average American Indian household income is significantly lower than the national average ($33,300 compared to $46,200). Nearly a quarter of American Indians lack health insurance, leading to "major health disparities" within the population: "alcoholism mortality rates are 514 percent higher than the general population" and "suicide rates are more than double; Native teens experience the highest rate of suicide of any population group in the United States."[3] Diabetes and tuberculosis are also major health problems. All of this points to a situation in which most American Indians are focused on their own situation—in their nation or in their immediate communities—rather than on the plight of other groups.

Nevertheless, the topic of Palestine crops up occasionally in American Indian media, especially newspapers. *Indian Country Today* is one of the leading national publications carrying news and opinion relevant to American Indian concerns. On some occasions, the newspaper's editor has offered thoughts on U.S. foreign policy, including U.S. engagement with the Israeli-Palestinian conflict. The record of discussions on Palestine in *Indian Country Today* reveals an ongoing debate about how American Indians read Palestine.

The editorial board of *Indian Country Today* addressed Palestine in April 2002, in the midst of the Second Intifada. The editors referred to the Israeli-Palestinian conflict as "the oldest of tribal conflicts." Noting "the ills created by an imperial Europe," the editorial asserted that "Israelis and Palestinians are cousins—Semitic relatives—at war all of these decades over a land they both would occupy." The editors sought to strike a balance between concerns for Israelis and Palestinians. While "the continuous imposition of more and more Israeli settlements on Palestinian land... is reminiscent of the conscious 'checker-boarding' of reservations with non-Indian homesteads," they claimed that "Equally, American Indians intimately understand the plight of the Jewish people, who have suffered so much throughout history."[4]

Individual American Indian voices have been less concerned about striking such "balance" in their discussion of the Israeli-Palestinian conflict. In February 2006, Robert Robideau, at the time serving as co-director of the Leonard Peltier Defense Committee, published an article titled "God Given Right: Palestine and Native America" in the online forum *Counterpunch*. Detailing the religious justifications of land theft and writing after the January 2006 election victories by Hamas, Robideau expressed solidarity with interwoven comparisons between Hamas and the American Indian Movement, with which he and Peltier were associated. "The Palestinian people continue to struggle through various groups like Hamas in self defense of their sovereignty and to keep their remaining lands," he wrote. "So too, have north American Indian people continued to struggle to keep what is left of their lands and recover stolen lands. The Federal Government offers the Lakota Nations 100's of millions for their sacred Black Hills, but the Lakota people have refused the federal paper dollars, firmly stating, 'Our sacred land is not for sale!'" Calling for continued resistance, Robideau concluded by saying, "The 'Gods' must be crazy to think that their programs of racism and genocide will stop freedom fighters around the world from carrying on with their struggles for liberation and self defense."[5]

When U.S. President George W. Bush addressed the Israeli Knesset in May 2008, Steven Newcomb, Director of the Indigenous Law Institute, published an article in *Indian Country Today* suggesting that Bush's use of the Old Testament constituted a form of American Zionism. Newcomb linked Bush's use of the Old Testament to the kind of thinking that has played such a prominent role in the historic treatment of American Indians by the United States, and in the callous and often brutal mistreatment of Palestinian people by the State of Israel. The mental model of a chosen people and a promised land provides a convenient rationalization whereby one people feels entitled and justified, by divine right, to take over, possess, and profit from the lands of other peoples.

After explicating the use of the Doctrine of Discovery within U.S. Supreme Court Jurisprudence, especially in the 1823 case *Johnson v. M'Intosh*, Newcomb suggested that this "mental framework has greatly contributed to the intractable aspects of U.S. policy toward American Indians and Israel's policy toward the Palestinian people."[6]

Newcomb's article drew a response from the Anti-Defamation League, claiming that "Steven Newcomb is wrong to compare the mistreatment of American Indians by the United States to the historic plight of the Palestinian people as a result of the founding of the state of Israel in 1948." The ADL representative insisted, instead, that "Israel... continues to embrace every opportunity to resolve the conflict," which began when "the Arab nations rejected the [1947 UN partition] plan and waged war on the nascent Israeli state." Since then, "Israel's many overtures for peace have been met with threats, wars and terrorist attacks against civilians."[7] Pro-Israeli interests, it seems, have a motivation not only to present their version of history but to diminish any possible identification between Palestinians and American Indians.

After the events of September 11, 2001, the administration of George W. Bush began waging what it called a "War on Terror" against parts of the Muslim world, including Afghanistan and Iraq. In 2006, the editors of *Indian Country Today* took stock of the various ways conflicts in the Middle East were being compared with American Indian history and experience, only to find them wanting: "Bad analogies from American Indian history are becoming the fad among pundits on the Middle East," they wrote. "We wish they would cut it out." In addition to criticizing two authors who were, at the time, offering "the increasingly popular modeling of American Middle East strategy on the so-called 'Indian wars.'" Describing "this pseudo-analysis" as "a mishmash of superficial history and offensive cliché," they cite a former U.S. Foreign Service officer claiming that "the area outside of the Green Zone in Baghdad is now referred to as the Red Zone—terrorist-infested territory as dangers to non-native as the lands inhabited by the Redskins were to whites during the Indian wars."[8]

The most egregious analysis critiqued in this editorial, however, is from Israeli historian Benny Morris. The editors take issue with Morris's comments, published that year in *Ha'aretz*, that "Even the great American democracy could not have been created without the annihilation of the Indians. There are cases in which the overall, final good justifies harsh and cruel acts that are committed in the course of history." When the editors of *Indian Country Today* spoke in person with Morris, "he apologized for appearing indifferent to the 'extermination' of the Indians," he said. "I feel bad about what happened to the Indians, although it was probably more from germs than the 7th Cavalry." From the editors' perspective, "his apology... only made things worse." Rather than the continued callousness of his analysis, the editors were critical of this historian's bad history: "As every Native person in this country has probably had to explain at some point or another, Indians are not extinct." The editors' conclusion is clear: "The Middle Eastern experts don't seem to have much knowledge of the tribal treaties, if they are even aware that Indians still exist. Until they learn a bit more of this history, they should leave Indian country alone."[9]

In their critique of Benny Morris, the editors of *Indian Country Today* make the claim that "the expulsion of the Eastern tribes is a separate history and it does no good to anyone to drag it into a Middle East crossfire." I humbly disagree. As a citizen of the Chickasaw Nation, recognizing that those events did indeed come "late in the game," those events and the structures of settler-colonial power that enabled them provide perhaps the most important analogs between American Indian and Palestinian experience.

The removal of the Cherokee, Chickasaw, Choctaw, Muscogee Creek, and Seminole nations from the southeastern United States to "Indian Territory" in what is now the State of Oklahoma constitutes a compelling precursor to Palestinian narratives of Palestinian experience. These tribes were designated as "civilized" by the surrounding Euro-American powers. Anthony Wallace describes the aftermath of Indian Removal as "an immediate disaster, costly in lives and wealth" as well as "a disaster that never ended" in which "Indian territory... became a vast, poverty-stricken concentration camp for dispossessed Native Americans" in which the Bureau of Indian Affairs controlled all aspects of life. Palestinians may well be reminded of their narratives of al-Nakba, their own national catastrophe experienced in 1948. Likewise, Palestinians might recognize elements of their experience in Wallace's observation that while President Jackson "never proposed exterminating the Indians or, at least in public rhetoric, removing by force of arms those who wished to remain... he was adept at devising conditions that would make those who chose not to remove so miserable that they would emigrate eventually anyway." The experience of the Five Civilized Tribes provides a cautionary tale to Palestinians who trust implicitly that their efforts to comply with Israeli demands will eventually or inevitably result in the gaining of Palestinian sovereignty. While some, like Jedediah Morse, sought the "complete civilization of the Indians," for most white people, "the threat was not so much the savage, drunken Indian as the civilized one, who if left in place to govern himself in his own territory would beat the white man at his own game—raising cotton—and prevent forever the further acquisition of Indian land."[10]

In addition to this record of cultural continuity between the settler-colonial societies of nineteenth-century North America and twentieth-century Israel, the analogy is further strengthened in the comparative legal frameworks for indigenous dispossession. As can be seen throughout the history of Israeli administration of the Palestinian territories occupied in 1967, the final justification for U.S. treatment of its indigenous population was not proven at the barrel of a rifle but with the legal creativity of the American courts.

Lindsay Robertson's *Conquest by Law: How the Discovery of America Dispossessed Indigenous Peoples of Their Lands* provides the most comprehensive history and interpretation of *Johnson v. M'Intosh*, the Supreme Court case in which Chief Justice John Marshall outlined the first articulation of the "Discovery Doctrine" by which Western powers assumed legal possession of Indian lands. The true tragedy of the decision came in its aftermath. Georgia immediately seized upon the doctrine to justify its threat to evict the Cherokee Nation from the state's presumed boundaries. While Marshall would later seek to repudiate his own legal doctrine, President Andrew Jackson reinstated and reinforced the ruling to continue the policy of Indian Removal.

In a later paraphrase of *Johnson v. M'Intosh*, Jackson's Secretary of War, Lewis Cass, argued that "When the Europeans landed upon this continent... they found it inhabited by numerous tribes of savages, independent of one another, and generally engaged in hostilities." "Under such circumstances," he continued, "jurisdiction [was] well assumed, and its extend must depend upon the opinion of the dominant party." Discovery, as Marshall had held, "'gave an exclusive right to extinguish the Indian title of occupancy, either by purchase or conquest; and gave them also a right to such a degree of sovereignty, as the circumstances of the people would allow them to exercise.'"[11] The logic of this presentation is clear: force determines the right of the dominant power against the interests of the savages. This presumption of white privilege for land rights has become enshrined in American law and thus embedded in American legal and popular culture.

This preservation of white privilege is recapitulated in American official support for Israeli claims to Palestinian land, and respect for the legal systems, structures, and interpretations that most often uphold those claims. Even if the legal regimes are not identical, American popular opinion and official policy is canted in such a way that it grants the "civilized" power the benefit of the doubt, whether the land was acquired "either by purchase or conquest." As a Chickasaw, if not as a citizen of the United States, I recognize the story of my people in the experiences of the Palestinian people, even this "late in the game."

As I write in August 2013, in a context shaped by another round of U.S.-sponsored peace talks between Palestinians and the State of Israel, the next chapter of comparison between Palestinian and American Indian experience is being written. In September 2011, the Israeli Knesset approved a plan regulating the Bedouin "settlements" in the Negev desert. If implemented, the "Prawer Plan" will result in the displacement of around 40,000 Bedouin from their present locations. When approached for comment on this issue, the Assistant to The Director of Public Affairs for the Embassy of Israel in Washington, DC, suggested an article published on the "Israel Hayom" website, calling the Prawer Plan a "win-win for Bedouin and the Negev." The article helpfully demonstrates that support for the plan traverses Israeli political lines and is endorsed by at least one Bedouin:

> *"Hassan Kaabia, a Bedouin officer in the Israel Defense Forces from the village of Kaabia who now works for the Foreign Ministry, says that the sedentarization of the Bedouin people is necessary and inevitable, and the alternative is poverty, crime and illness. The state also has to protect its most limited natural resource – land – through organized planning. ' This transition, difficult as it may be, is fascinating and another piece in the cosmopolitan mosaic that is the modern State of Israel,' he says."*[12]

The Prawer Plan's claim to be an expression of charity to Israel's less fortunate citizens, an effort to bring Bedouin "into 'the 21st century" by significantly improving their standard of living," brings it into clear dialogue with the rhetoric surrounding U.S. Indian Removal in the 1830s. Many Indians originally from the southeast United States might recognize the memories of their own experience when Abu al-Kian, who lives in Atir, says with his voice shaking, "For 41 years I worked on this land, in the fresh air, for the Ministry of Agriculture and the Jewish National Fund, planting trees and putting out forest fires... I have citizenship, but they still destroyed my house. Now I have only the shirt on my back. It's like they're saying to me, 'Just leave and go to hell.'"[13]

2. The Politics of Tribal Identification

Not every American Indian aware of the Israeli-Palestinian situation identifies with Palestinian history and experience. In 2002, some Jewish news sources buzzed with reports on Santos Hawk's Blood Suarez, an Apache from Texas living in New Jersey, who proclaimed solidarity with the Jewish people and, by extension, the State of Israel. "We were highly offended when things came out in the media comparing Native Americans to Palestinians," one story quoted him as saying. "I admire the people of Israel: They're people who stand up to defend their homeland. We are not with the Palestinian people."[14]

Suarez's perspective stands in sharp contrast to that of Robert Allen Warrior (Osage), whose essay, "Canaanites, Cowboys, and Indians," presented a case for American Indian identification with Palestinian concerns. Observing that most "liberation theologies... are preoccupied with the Exodus story... as the fundamental model for liberation," Warrior saw that just after the Exodus, "Yahweh the deliverer became Yahweh the conqueror." If they identify with a character in this narrative, Native Americans are more likely to identify with the Canaanites, the people who already lived in the

Promised Land." As Warrior puts it:

> *"As a member of the Osage Nation of American Indians who stands in solidarity with other tribal people around the world, I read the Exodus stories with Canaanite eyes. And, it is the Canaanite side of the story that has been overlooked by those seeking to articulate theologies of liberation. Especially ignored are those parts of the story that describe Yahweh's command to mercilessly annihilate the indigenous population."*

For Warrior, these orders of annihilation are not just elements in an ancient biblical text, but a mythos pervading the contemporary condition of his people. "We can understand," he says, "how America's self-image as a 'chosen people' has provided a rhetoric to mystify domination." This domination continues unchallenged and unabated to this day.[15]

In December 2012, Ben Shelly, President of the Navajo Nation, visited Israel to learn about Israeli strategies for tourism and agricultural development. The visit included meetings with Knesset leaders, including the head of the Knesset Christian Allies Caucus. "I want to work with your people—I know that Israel is self-sufficient, what we need is your expertise, what can we share," Shelly said during his visit to the Knesset. "What I read of you—you were no different than we are," he said, "how did you survive while moving forward in technology, greenhouses—I am interested in that and becoming partners."[16] In February 2013, Shelly met in Scotsdale with Israeli diplomats and the Arizona Israel Business Council. That March, Shelly opened a conference with the title "Navajo and Israel Agricultural Gathering for First Nations."[17]

Shelly's visit was highly controversial among some Navajo and other American Indian activists and intellectuals. Navajo activist Janene Yazzie criticized President Shelly for visiting Israel to learn about chemical irrigation techniques and genetically-modified produce at a time when Native communities were returning to sustainability through traditional farming techniques.[18] In April 2013, a group of American Indian scholars, including Robert Allen Warrior, published an open letter to President Shelly, challenging his cooperation with the State of Israel. The letter read, in part:

> *"As indigenous educators, we find your support for the state of Israel to be in complete contradiction to our values and sense of justice. Israel has illegally occupied Palestine for decades. Your public and political engagement with [Israeli] Prime Minister Benjamin Netanyahu and other Israeli officials sends a message that you endorse the continued occupation of the West Bank, including construction of new Jewish settlements there, as well as the ongoing settler colonial situation for Palestinians residing within the 1948 boundaries asserted by the Israeli state, and exclusion of Palestinian refugees from reclaiming their homes and homeland after being violently expelled during the nakba (catastrophe) when Israel was founded."*

The authors of the letter took issue with Shelly's statement to Israelis: "you were no different than we are." They instead offered a strong counter-identification with Palestinian experience:

> *"Thanks to the wisdom of our ancestors, we have persisted. But our prospects as peoples will never be as full or complete as they might have been had those who colonized us been just and honest in their dealings with us. A similar process has unfolded for Palestinian people over the past half-century. Indeed, Israeli demolition of the homes of Palestinian families is not all that different than the Long Walk your people endured in 1864. Your collusion with the Israeli government*

is a betrayal of that shared history and of the wisdom that has helped all Indigenous Peoples survive for centuries."

J. Kehaulani Kauanui (Kanaka Maoli), another of the letter's authors, suggested that "the Israeli government's courting of Shelley is a form of 'Redwashing'—the promotion of Indigenous Peoples of the Americas as a deliberate strategy to conceal the continuing violations of the Palestinian people." She was openly suspicious about how this relationship came about: "Why any tribal leader would want to partner-up with Netanyahu is beyond curious; it is morally repugnant."[19]

3. Concluding Reflections

Steven Salaita, a young Palestinian-American scholar, sees a fundamental connection between Palestinian and Native American experience. "The issue of Manifest Destiny in Palestine warrants interrogation," he says, "because the notion that one people's scriptural prophecies override the rights of another people's very existence is, in fact, the theological foundation of New World conquest. The covenantal aspect of settler colonialism has bound Natives and Palestinians to the same class of resistance despite the great differences in their cultures."[20]

Salaita offers a series of quotations in American and Israeli rhetoric regarding their respective indigenous populations. He counterposes, for instance, the nineteenth U.S. military order to ""[K]ill and scalp all, little and big [because] nits make lice" with Avraham Stern's suggestion that Palestinians are "beasts of the desert, not a legitimate people." Reflecting on the judgment of "savagism" imparted to American Indians for their resistance to colonization,

Salaita reports Zeev Jabotinsky's dictum that "Zionist colonization, even the most restricted, must either be terminated or carried out in defiance of the will of the native population." Zionist recapitulations of American expansionist rhetoric are, Salaita says, "not merely parallel, but confederated. Zionists drew inspiration from American history in colonizing Palestine, and American history also shaped the outlook of American leaders toward the Near East." From these and many other confederated parallels, Salaita concludes that "the comparative foundation of New World and Holy Land conquest offers us an aperture to the past that exerts influence on the present. If we are truly to understand the conquest of modern Palestine, then it would benefit Palestine scholars to first turn a critical eye toward the conquest of the Americas."[21]

As one who is both a Cowboy and an Indian, my engagement over several years with Israel and Palestine has kindled visceral reflections on all aspects of my own cultural and hereditary identity. Living within that complexity has allowed me to more fully engage the narratives, identities, tastes and aromas overlapping one another in this land called holy. As a light-skinned American male, I carry within me the confederated ideologies of conquest that dispossessed the peoples whose heritage flows in my veins. Although I recognize parts of myself in both the Israeli soldier manning a checkpoint and the Palestinian worker being herded through under the barrel of their gun, the call to resistance sounds louder in me than the will to power.

10

Exile as Identity:

African Americans, Palestinians, and the Book of Ezekiel

Dexter Callender, Jr.

Introduction

The Bible has played a significant role in reinforcing value systems that lead to policies of alienation and disenfranchisement. Many have pointed out the problematic nature of the text and have questioned whether it can provide the resources to resolve such situations or is it part of the problem. Who represents whom in its broad strokes of good and evil? Who speaks for God? Such familiar questions are fraught with unexamined modernist presuppositions regarding identity, subjectivity, self, and society. The Book of Ezekiel presents imagery in which the Levites are identified as transgressors responsible for bringing harm to the nation and therefore marginalized—physically separated within the cosmic geography of the book's concluding vision. The precise nature of this marginalization and the identity of the Levites as the marginalized have posed problems for readers of the text. Many of the interpretive difficulties recognized by biblical scholars are the product of approaches that are based on modernist assumptions concerning the self. Taking such presuppositions into account allows us to see the biblical text in new ways and to find within it resources to engage issues that have manifested in a variety of ways over time. To draw parallels between African-Americans and Palestinians is not novel. To do so is to explore two unique configurations of human experience through the similarities and differences that define their individual and shared identities.[1] In this paper, I approach the prophet's rhetoric concerning exile and identity in light of postmodern conceptions of the self that render identity in terms of complex subjectivity. This paper reads Ezekiel's account of the reasons necessitating exile against socio-political realities facing African Americans and Palestinians, whose identity is marked by marginalization that assumes material form in the prison industrial complex in the U.S. and the wall separating the West Bank from Israel. Reading along these lines reveals how the Book of Ezekiel provides resources to reflect upon the challenges of identity and action facing African Americans and Palestinians. The biblical image of the Levite as presented in the Book of Ezekiel as a teaching for the exiles reveals a logic that informs experiences of disenfranchisement shared by African-Americans and Palestinians.

A curious homology between Palestinians and African-Americans has become startlingly apparent in recent years. According to legal scholar Michelle Alexander, a recent estimate suggests that in the poorest neighborhoods of the United States three out of four young black men can expect to serve time in prison.[2] Presently no other country in the world incarcerates such an astonishing percentage of its racial or ethnic minorities.[3] The situation pertaining to Palestinians both in refugee camps and behind the wall around the West Bank underscores how for both groups, the reality of physical marginalization within society, this state of exile becomes an increasingly dominant marker of identity. In both cases, the physical margin is established on the rationale of the interest of safety from those set on the other side. In both cases the nature of the marginalization and the identity of the marginalized are highly problematic. Aspects of this comparison calls to mind the biblical portrayal of the Levites, a group that is both central to society and marginalized within it.

1. The Levites in Ezekiel 44

The walled alienation shared by African Americans and Palestinians recalls the image of the Levites in Ezekiel 44, who, having been blamed for the present ills of society, were physically separated within society. The Book of Ezekiel presents the situation of the exile in terms that describe it as the result of cultic abuses. In simple terms, the cultic abuses of the people, worshipping idols and following other gods, resulted in God abandoning the people and the land, leaving the land open to destruction and its people to dispersion. One group that is placed at the center is the Levites. In chapter 44:9-10 we read:[4]

> "Thus says the Lord GOD: No foreigner (בן־נכר), uncircumcised in heart (ערל לב) and flesh, of all the foreigners who are among the people of Israel, shall enter my sanctuary. But the Levites who went far (רחקו) from me when Israel went astray (בתעות) who went astray from me after their idols, shall bear their punishment (נשאו עונם)."

He goes on later to write (v. 13):

> "They shall not come near to me, to serve me as priest, nor come near any of my sacred offerings, the things that are most sacred; but they shall bear their shame (נשאו כלמתם), and the abominations that they have committed."

Modern biblical scholars have taken note of the restrictions placed upon the Levites as marking a significant moment in the history of ancient Israel. According to this account, the Levites designate a priestly order that by the neo-Babylonian period came to be displaced by those who identified with the house of Aaron.[5] But the identity of the Levites remains largely obscure. The folk etymology of the name of the eponymous ancestor in Gen 29:34 provides insight into a conception that was popular at some point in time. An alternative possible etymology derives the name from "lend" or "pledge." Texts present them as landless or itinerant, as *gerim*, "resident aliens" (Judges 17:7-9, 19:1). In laws they are paired with *gerim* (Deut 12:12; 14:29; 26:12), who more broadly speaking were the disenfranchised and poor who possessed limited rights.[6] The very presence of the *gerim* also stood as a reminder of oppression endured by the Israelites (Exod 22:20, 23:9; Deut 24:18, 22). Moreover, the *ger*, as the symbol of vulnerability with widows and orphans, is the special concern of justice (Deut 10:12-22). Elsewhere also as possessing cities and surrounding lands is a concern of justice.

2. Exile, Language and Identity

The theme of exile provides a fundamental framework for understanding Ezekiel's appropriation of the image of the Levites. It is worth observing at the outset that Ezekiel as intermediary is invested in helping the community cope with the trauma of exile. The Book of Ezekiel presents itself within the exilic period and exile is its basic theme. It opens with the prophet describing his location among the exiles. The vision that closes the book places the people back in the land, with the temple restored and Yahweh once again present. Beyond being physically uprooted from home, exile is fundamentally a relational matter of self and other. In Lacanian terms, self and other are defined around language. Alongside what we recognize as the 'concrete' historical realities that gave rise to the received text lies the aspect of reality in language and the symbolic register. That is to say, the meaning of the physical displacement resides in the symbolic order where self and other are defined. Reflection on this dimension was not lost to the prophet and his editors. Language has long been seen as playing an alienating role in human subjectivity.[7] Where is the speaking "I"? To what precisely do we attach the pronoun? Where exactly *is* the human subject? Such questions address the mystery of human subjectivity as it pertains to language. Ezekiel and his editors present the identity of Yahweh as a matter of complex subjectivity that comes together as an "I" in the symbolic order, and that as such is inseparable from human subjectivity.

For Jacques Lacan, the emergence of the ego is at once the disruption of the primordial sense of essential unity.[8] With the acquisition of language, human subjectivity is irreparably severed, the gap unbridgeable.[9] Lacan's structuralist reading of the unconscious understood the body to be in effect "at the mercy of language, at the mercy of the symbolic order."[10] The unconscious is not the privileged seat of subjectivity but is itself an *other*. Our spoken language represents at the most basic level an incursion of the other. As Bruce Fink explains, "the Other seems then to slip in the back door while children are learning a language that is virtually indispensable to their survival in the world as we know it. Though widely considered innocuous and purely utilitarian in nature, language brings with it a fundamental form of alienation that is part and parcel of learning *one's mother tongue*."[11] Further, the language we consider "ours" is, in fact, an internalization of the desires and discourses of others and constitutes a foreign presence within us.[12] For Lacan, strictly speaking, desire does not exist apart from language, rather it inhabits language.[13] This has immediate implications for agency, freedom, and responsibility.[14] The subject's entry into language also correspondingly and necessarily entails, according to Lacan, a negation of the real. The symbol is the murder of the thing. Alienated humanity is cut off from the realm of the real – the realm of what comes to language as "God." The models of Lacan and his followers, for whatever they lack in immediate transparency, offer a tool to reflect upon Ezekiel's often less than transparent use of language in conveying his conception of Yahweh, the human self and society.[15]

The logic of exile that Ezekiel draws upon is not only material but existential. Given that exile is a matter of identity and self and that generally speaking, the Book of Ezekiel is widely recognized as presenting problems with respect to the self.

The logic of exile that Ezekiel draws upon is a logic predicated upon fear of the Other — that is on fear of foreignness and its proximity. It sources lie close to the wisdom tradition in ancient Near Eastern literature in what is commonly referred to as "the doctrine of reward." According to it, an individual's proper conduct carries the prospect of prosperity, progeny, longevity and possession of the land. It is presented most fully in the Book of Deuteronomy which incorporates these as rewards for faithfulness to Yahweh and, unlike the broader wisdom tradition, expresses it in nationalistic terms.[16] The notion of connection to land as expressing home and safety appears frequently. In Psalm 37 the meek and the righteous will 'possess the land' (vv. 11, 22, 29, 34; cf. 25:13).[17] Comparable expressions include dwelling in the land (Ps. 37:3, 27, 29; Prov 2:21-22; 10:30), and "to lengthen (or multiply) one's days upon the land" (Deut 4:25 and 40; 5:30; 11:9 and 21), which also embodies the wisdom tradition's concept of 'possessing the land' with the exception that Deuteronomy relates it to the entire nation as opposed to the individual.[18] Conversely, the doctrine of reward marks out punishment in terms opposite to those of the reward. Thus, failure to uphold the tenets of the Torah results in "perishing from" the land (4:26; 11:17; cf. Josh.

23:13 and 16) or being "plucked" or uprooted from it (Deut 28:63; cf. Prov. 2:22; cf. 15:25; cf. Ps. 52:7).[19]

Although Deuteronomy applies this imagery directly to the nation as opposed to the individual, it nonetheless establishes a strong tie to the person through what some have termed "the principle of individual retribution." According to Deuteronomy 7:10 God "repays directly those who reject him" (cf. Exod. 20:5b-6 = Deut. 5:9b-10; Exod. 34:6-7; Num. 14:18). In this we find a connection to imagery found in Ezekiel (Ezek.14:12-23; 18; 33:1-20) and notably in Jeremiah as well (31:29-30).[20] Thus we find a tension between individual and community where the two cannot be easily separated.

At the same time, the doctrine of rewards in wisdom literature and its motif of land for the righteous and loss of land and exile for the wicked may be seen as *ironic*. That is, life seems marked by the opposite. It is in fact not deeds of piety that procure wealth, but acts of cunning and power. Even the very act of Yahweh "giving" the land to Israel is not presented as a peaceful transaction, but a violent seizure, dispossessing groups who are not faceless, but named. The historical flux is no illusion – its violence is real and its pain palpable. Thus, in an external sense, an ethical mandate is established on the reality of the human inclination to the aggression that arises from envy. The activity of Yahweh in the text is in fact the activity of humanity. We see this clearly in Ezekiel in many ways. To be cut off from one's people is to be torn from the symbolic world or home, from the familiar patterns that make up 'home' within the order of the symbolic.[21]

3. The Paradoxical Alienation of the Levites

To return to Ezek 44, Ezekiel presents the image of the Levite as alienated yet paradoxically close to God. Ezekiel is among the literati and his images draw from tradition, appropriating it in various ways to present teachings. Despite the editorial history of the book, there is much to commend the idea of taking Ezekiel and his editors as representing a school or tradition. In this sense, apparent contradictory assertions need not be dismissed simply as two separate hands.[22] We must note that the Levites were also among the literati.[23] They are presented as scribes and teachers. Moreover, we are inclined to wonder whether the Levites were writing about themselves.

For many biblical scholars this text marks an historical event, the decline of a particular priestly house.[24] Inasmuch as the Book of Ezekiel is a book reflecting priestly concerns and interests, in many respects, the Levites represent both the human condition and the scapegoated outgroup. Ezekiel places the blame for the situation of exile in its entirety on the Levites. As direct consequence, the Levites are demoted to a lower priestly order and as such are alienated and disenfranchised. It is worth noticing that the image of the Levite outside of Ezekiel presents them as alienated and disenfranchised. The crime is idolatry. For this, the Levites bear the iniquity of the people.

The Levitical bearing of iniquity in Ezek 44:10 must also be seen in the light of priestly function.[25] Bearing iniquity is associated with the mediating role of priesthood, which by virtue of certain cultic acts symbolically bore the consequences of iniquity for the people. That what we encounter is not limited to the sacrificial cult is evident elsewhere in Ezekiel, where it applies to prophetic activity. Ezekiel himself "bears iniquity" symbolically in 4:4-6.

In Ezekiel 14 a similar image of bearing iniquity as consequence is used of the prophet who leads people to stumble. In Ezek 14 it applies to prophet and people who receive his messages. Further, in Numbers 16-18 *"bearing responsibility for offenses,* i.e., suffering the consequences for any offense, is tied to the fear of a more general human reality of being apart from God's presence. In Num17:12-13, the people, arguing that all should have access to the divine presence, say to Moses "We are perishing; we are lost, all of us are lost! ¹Everyone who approaches the tabernacle of the Lord will die. Are we all to perish?" Here, the context is the curious "rebellion" of Korah, Dathan, and Abiram, about whom we read in Num 16, "They assembled against Moses and against Aaron, and said to them, 'You have gone too far! All the congregation are holy, every one of them, and the Lord is among them. So why then do you exalt yourselves above the assembly of the Lord?"

Unlike Ezekiel 14 where the stated consequence is death, in Ezekiel 44 the consequence is manifested in the physical separation from the 'good' Levites.[26] Moreover in Ezekiel 44 the Levites retain access to God. Finally, in the background of our discussion lies a connection between the Levites and violence.[27] The danger in a paradoxical way relates to the presentation in Exodus 32 in the golden calf episode.

4. Conclusion

As a teaching aimed at people in physical exile, the image of the Levite in Ezekiel engages disenfranchisement as a real condition of separation and points beyond it to its situatedness in the symbolic order as a relational matter of identity. As presented by Ezekiel and his editors, the Levites occupy a position in the symbolic order which invites comparison with Palestinians and African Americans. They are on the margins of society. They are viewed from other positions in the symbolic order as a danger. What seems less immediately apparent is the intermediary aspect through the bearing of iniquity. The identity of the Levites begins in one sense with the birth narrative in which they are given their name "joined". In view of complex subjectivity, in which the self emerges around language and the symbolic order, the notion of proximity to God is seen as privilege and responsibility. The particularism of Israel and the nations that is normally considered in terms of concrete fixed identities is instead revealed as a teaching that occupies a universal frame in which self and other are constantly negotiated. Different figurations appear outside of Ezekiel in texts such as Isaiah 56, in which deliverance is tied to justice and is announced as arriving soon. Identity as fixed and static is challenged in the foreigner in language that resonates with the imagery that Ezekiel draws from. Here, individual well-being is described in the "foreigner *joined* to the Lord" who is exhorted *not* to say "the Lord will separate me from his people" (v. 3).

Rather, we read in vv. 6-7:

"The foreigners (בני הנכר) who join themselves to the LORD, to minister to him, to love the name of the LORD, and to be his servants, all who keep the sabbath, and do not profane it, and hold fast my covenant-- [7] *these I will bring to my holy mountain, and make them joyful in my house of prayer; their burnt offerings and their sacrifices will be accepted on my altar; for my house shall be called a house of prayer for all peoples."*

Here too emphasis upon the dimension of self and other is made clear: "Thus says the Lord GOD, who gathers the outcasts of Israel, I will gather others to them besides those already gathered" (v. 8).

If Ezek 44 represents the rhetoric of an historical ingroup aimed at securing a hierarchy of privilege that restricts one group for the sake of empowering another or that scapegoats a group on the basis of a phenomenal identity that is fixed, it also contains the seeds of its own subversion. Communities become empowered when the conditions that constitute them as a particular other (and therefore subject to treatment as such) are bracketed and not permitted to inscribe an absolute individual identity. A condition of freedom exists despite the conditions of subjugation. This condition of freedom, when realized in the individual, establishes both the foundation for hope and the foundation for the possibility of the kind of selfless act necessary for the survival of those within the group.

11

The text as a landscape and the landscape as a text:

Reading Jeremiah 32 through Palestinian and Israeli eyes

Janneke Stegeman

> *As part of my PhD research on Jeremiah 32 and its reception which I hope to finish in the autumn of 2013, I read the chapter with groups of Palestinian Christians and Israeli Jews in 2008/2009. In this paper, I present part of those findings.[1]*

The Book of Jeremiah is written by people under the hegemony of first the Babylonians and later the Persians. The book was composed, redacted and rewritten over a long period before, during and after the Babylonian exile and is, therefore, interpreted tradition.

During the period of the development of the book, highly diverse, conflicting groups identified with the prophet Jeremiah and Judean society became divided as a result of Babylonian and Persian politics. The book, thus, contains (traces of) a variety of perspectives, consisting of appropriations of the figure of Jeremiah and the themes the book contains. In this paper I do not discuss Jeremiah, but rather the imaginations built around the prophet and the themes present in the book, from a critical, post-colonial perspective.[2] In my view, that does not take away the value or authority of the text. Rather this is how it needs to be read. The book contains a move from flesh to word, and the development of that word. I will conclude this paper with some remarks on how to read the Book of Jeremiah.

1. Successful appropriation

To Palestinian Christian readers, Jeremiah 32 is a problematic text in the first place because the Zionist narrative identifies exclusively with the text, or better with the layer in which returning exiles claim to be the people of God and the heirs of the land. In my view, the problem Palestinians have with this text is not just a Palestinian problem. It is relevant for all, both religious and non-religious readers, who recognize that the set of texts we call the Old Testament continues to influence our world.

Palestinian appropriations of this text can succeed if Palestinian readers arrive at an interpretation that enables them to be Palestinian, which means a reading that does not surrender to occupation, but counters the Zionist claim of the text, while claiming a cultural, historical link with the Old Testament.

The central question in this paper is: *How can Palestinians, both as Palestinians and as Christians, identify themselves as heirs to Jeremiah 32?*

First, I wish to present briefly the different layers that can be reconstructed within the text, and then reflect on what this means to readers who are heirs of this text and committed to peace and justice.

2. Identity-space constructions in Jeremiah 32

I argue that relations to space are crucial in understanding Jeremiah 32. Both text and landscape are layered. These layers testify to different groups influencing the text/the tradition. When new layers are added, often traces are left of older layers. Both text and landscape, therefore, are ambiguous and fluid entities: traces of older layers can always be discovered. In addition, connections to land and imaginations of landscape are crucial to understanding Jeremiah 32. Palestinian identity is connected both to the text of Jeremiah and to the landscape present (and disputed) in it.

Images of place, in connection to time, which are central in the text, the city of Jerusalem and the land of Judah:

> *v., 7:* "*Behold, Chanamel, the sun of Shallum your uncle will come to you, saying:*
> *'Buy for you my field that is at Anatoth, because to you is the right of redemption to buy.'*"

[Jeremiah buys the land]

> *v., 14* "*Thus has spoken Adonai of Hosts, the Lord of Israel:*
> *'Take these documents, this document of purchase, the sealed one and this open one, and put them in an earthenware jar so that they last a long time.'*"
> *v., 15:* "*For thus says the Lord of Hosts, the God of Israel:*
> *'Houses and fields and vineyards will continually be bought in this land (= Benjamin).'*"

Vs. 6-15 describe how Jeremiah purchases a plot of land from his cousin in Anathot, in the land of Benjamin. Vs. 14 and 15 interpret this purchase in terms of continuity in the area of Benjamin, from an economic point of view. The exile is not part of the narrative of purchase in vs. 6-15. The introduction does put the text in the context of the siege of Jerusalem by the Babylonians, while vs. 43-44 interpret the narrative from a (post-) exilic perspective:

> *v. 43:* "*Fields will be bought in this land of which you say: 'It is a desolation without men or beast. It is given into the hands of the Chaldeans.'*"

> *v. 44:* "*Fields will be bought with money and deeds written and sealed and witnesses will witness in the land of Benjamin, and in the places around Jerusalem, and in the towns of Judah, the towns of the hill country, the towns of the Shephelah, and the towns of the Negev, because I will restore their fortunes.*"

The statement of the you (plural) group in v. 43 can be understand as the perspective of those exiled Judeans who argue for return; in their view the land is empty (which fits the Zionist perspective). The geographical area is expanded, compared to vs. 14, 15. Hope for the future now concerns not only Benjamin, but also the areas around Jerusalem. The city itself, however, is not mentioned. As in vs. 14, 15 restoration is understood in economic terms.

Vs. 36-41 present a totally different perspective on restoration. Here, restoration is spiritual, described as an unprecedented situation of harmony between people and God. In addition, the city of Jerusalem is in focus.

3. The evil city versus the good land

How can these diverse imaginations of space be perceived? I will now look at imaginations of city and land in the text:

v. 31: "For to my anger and to my wrath this city has been from the day on which I built her until this day so that I will remove it from my sight."

v. 22: "And you have given them this land which you swore to their fathers to give to them, a land flowing with milk and honey."

The city is presented as bad, and the land as the good land. Connecting this to the focus on Benjamin in vs. 6-15 and the presentation of return presented in v. 44 as a return to the land (not the city), both in economic terms, I offer the following reconstruction: We know that after 586, when the upper layer of Judah was exiled, some Judeans remained in the land. Jerusalem was no longer the center, but Mizpah, in Benjamin. In my view, to these people of the land, Jerusalem was the evil city, and the future lay in the area of Benjamin. When some of the exiles returned, Jerusalem was still devastated. To them too, the future may have been in the land, not yet in the city, but in a larger area: v. 44. Here exile and return are absolute categories, as they are in the Zionist narrative. The narrative of the people in the land and those who 'return' are mutually exclusive.

Again later, the dispute between "returning exiles"[3] and people of the land became less important. Other disputes arose. Jerusalem was rebuilt. However, this did not bring the hoped for 'redemption'. Exile was reinterpreted and it became a more spiritual category (it is possible to be in exile while being in the land). This narrative steps over the controversies between returning exiles and people of the land. And thus the last layer transforms concepts of time and place.

I do not understand this more inclusive voice as a 'solution' to the problematic character of this text. This is not an inclusive text. The narratives of those who sought refuge in Egypt, or those who remained in Babylon are not present. Of the narrative of the people of the land, only traces are present. The text thus is not inherently capable of effecting conflict resolution. However, it does have the rather unique quality of having been shaped and understood by centuries of appropriation and re-appropriation. It continues to be authoritative to readers. The text as a shared heritage is a potentially rich space: the act of *tradere* requires openness to be criticized, changed and transformed by the text. At the same time, there are many factors limiting the space in which transformation can take place, most importantly an understanding of religious and national narratives as fixed and unchanging, and a lack of awareness of the way in which they interact and are fluid. Jeremiah 32 provides both the means for the encounter to take place and serves as a very troubling stumbling block in the meetings.

I see it as a responsibility of scholars to delve into voices in the text that are hidden and covered under dominant voices. This is a crucial task of biblical scholars, both with respect to the biblical text, and with respect to later interpretations. In can lead to a new perspective on biblical texts, that is mindful of the tendency of narratives of identity to be exclusive, and strives to build more inclusive narratives.

4. Some examples of Palestinian and Israeli appropriations

Palestinian readers

Many readers feel that the text does not acknowledge Palestinian experiences:

> *"We did just like Jeremiah. We kept the documents. But we do not get our homes back."*

Some readers point out that the text is exclusive, and therefore reject it from a desire to construct an inclusive Palestinian theology:

> *"My notion of God is all-embracing, for all nations, whether they come from Abrahamic religions or not. I have a problem with how the term for God is narrowed to be a God of a group of people."*
> *There are many narratives not found here. For instance that of the people who decided to stay in Babylon."*

Sometimes, Palestinian readers reject the text from an exclusive, Palestinian perspective:

> *"If you believe in Jesus, there shouldn't be Jews anymore. As a result, the Old Testament is 'a word for Christians, not for Jews."*

Although some readers identify with elements in the text, most Palestinian readers reject the text either from a religious perspective, or from a Palestinian perspective. The tendency of readers to identify the text with the Zionist narrative leaves no room for alternative approaches to the text. As a result, a contextual Palestinian reading hardly develops.

Israeli readers

Some Israeli readers identify with the text from a national-religious perspective:

> *"As I read it, I became excited. [..] I feel it talks about me. I am the fulfilling.*
> *This chapter for me is very private, it is about my people. It is about our dirty laundry. It is difficult to discuss it with people who are not from my nation, because to be honest it is like cleaning our dirty laundry outside."*

Some Israeli readers find the text problematic because it is claimed by Zionism:

> *"Texts like this are part of our problem as Israelis. They create a reality.*
> *Maybe I am living in a dream. More than I acknowledged in the beginning. [..] But I am surprised at how much it [Jer. 32] is in our lives. [...] If we like it or not. Ignoring it might even be a bigger problem."*

Many Israeli readers fail to distinguish between religious identity and national identity. They experience no distance from the text and do not recognize the harm the Zionist narrative does to Palestinians. Some readers do attempt to deconstruct the Zionist narrative, but this is a challenging and fear-laden process. Such fixed views on identity, narratives and religious tradition leave very little space for transformation to occur. Retreating to exclusivist, fixed understandings of national and/or religious identity is a frequent but hopeless strategy.

I would argue that recognizing the layeredness of the Jeremianic tradition can stimulate recognition of the layeredness and ambiguity of one's own narratives. This requires enormous commitment for both Israeli and Palestinian readers. From Israeli participants it requires the courage to acknowledge the oppressive politics of their state. From the Palestinians it requires the courage to meet what they view as representatives of their oppressors. An encounter requires transformation in the way conflict and identity are perceived.

5. Negotiating narratives

The Jeremianic tradition can be of value in this process of opening up more or less fixed positions, but it needs a very careful approach, a considerable amount of time, highly dedicated participants and group leaders capable of hosting such a complex process. I want to focus here on the role of exegetes in this process. Exegetes need to create space between the text and its readers in which transformation can take place. The Jeremianic tradition needs to be rediscovered as living tradition that is ambiguous and layered, and cannot be claimed exclusively. The tradition needs to be freed from readers' desires to read an internally coherent text containing beautiful religious truths, or meeting other assumptions. A more flexible approach to religious tradition is necessary, which takes into account the way the text is shaped in processes of identity formation, in which conflict usually plays a role. As is clear from the above, many religious readers object to such a view, which in their eyes does not fit the quality of the text. As a scholar of the Old Testament, I argue that this is how the text presents itself and wants to be understood. Recognition of the different voices in the text, and therefore of the important role of the community of readers to find their own voice requires a new hermeneutics. This requires from readers a readiness to live with ambiguity. It requires the same readiness with respect to the narratives functioning in one's society.

I argue for an approach to the text that recognizes the way it is shaped through historical processes – even though not all of these can be reconstructed, and that recognizes that we too as readers are continually negotiating our identity, and need to do so. In the Dutch context, I think it is necessary to re-appropriate our history of slavery and apartheid, that are barely present in our narrative.

When biblical scholars help readers to discover the text with its layeredness and ambiguity, they provide the reader with a framework to connect to their own narratives. In that case, both the ambiguity of the Jeremianic narrative, of the Israeli and Palestinian narratives (and those of many others), can come to the fore. People who dare to delve into hidden aspects of identity, uncovering new parts of the self and the biblical narrative are capable of finding ways out of the conflict. I have to stress that this is necessary particularly in the case of Israeli readers, who are less aware of the existence of the Palestinian narrative and the devastating effects of Israeli hegemony.[4] What is needed is for people, not only Israelis and Palestinians but all of us, to look beyond conflict, beyond the ordinary ways that we have learned to view and subdivide the world. I am advocating neither a reading that ignores the political, conflicting contexts of a religious tradition, nor one that denies that many narratives are so hidden from us that they have become lost. Rather, I am arguing for a reading that acknowledges power negotiations both within the text and in present-day contexts. This perspective also acknowledges the harm that the conflict does to both Palestinian and Israeli society today, and attempts to imagine overcoming historical injustice by reformulating narratives, and continuing injustices by criticizing misuse of power.

As readers, we are invited to connect our narratives to the narratives of the text, to become part of the negotiation of identity taking place there. When we recognize the ambiguity and complexity of the text, it is easier also to recognize the ambiguity in our own narratives, and the ongoing need to be more inclusive. I argue then, with Martha Nussbaum, that 'we must go beyond judging texts according to prescribed ethical standards'. Thinking of ethical judgment 'as consisting simply in the application of antecedently formulated rules' prepares readers badly for 'the actual flow of life and for the necessary resourcefulness in confronting its surprises.'[5]

12

Religious Identity as Gift and Task

A Christian Perspective

Ottmar Fuchs, Tübingen

Everyone receives his or her life without doing anything for it. Birth, as the fundamental basis of identity is free, it is given unconditionally. In a Christian context we say: birth is pure grace. What does this mean, this fact that life and identity are first *given*, for the personal and political responsibility of and for human beings? Many people find themselves in families or sociopolitical conditions, in which they cannot experience life as a gift and in which they are hindered by merciless structures, from developing their personal and cultural identities in justice and freedom. And in spite of these structures, how can this original experience, that life is *given*, *give* strength and hope, to retain and to develop one's identity in difficult situations and to fight for better conditions?

Introduction

I would like to outline in the following text, how religious identity can be a gift for life and for solidarity both to the inside and to the outside. What are the criteria of such a religious identity, in whatever time and space it may occur? How can religious identity experienced as a resource which gives strength and power for living, endure what cannot be changed, or fight against the power and violence of oppression and iniquity? We will see that this is not only a religious question, but a political one, too. Because religious attitudes can sharpen political and social situations, sometimes they are the most effective elicitors and instigators of violence and actions of terror, because they are able to legitimize everything. This refers to non-religious belief systems as well.

There is no need to decide the argument of whether sociopolitical or religious motivations lead to oppressing or revolting violence and in both cases for killing others. But sometimes religious influence is the deepest and most effective one, epecially if the people concerned are not necessarily poor as in the case of militant Jewish settlers and some Palestinians. There are examples showing the religious effect even if there are no social problems. Numerous people are willing to use violence, for whatever purpose, for example terrorists, from different areas, often come and do come from well-to-do families. In that case naked religious ideology shapes their motives.

But in most cases religious fundamentalism hails from the roots of social problems, and is sharpened by religious attitude, or vice versa, or simultaneously. Here the danger of fundamntalistic reactions touches the Palestinans, too. Most Palestinians are socially deprived of their rights, and many of them are, therefore, disadvantaged and unemployed. This depends largely on the situation and on what kind of religious identity has been shaped in their respective religious communities. My question is: What role does religious identity play in shaping the identities of individuals and their collectives in different times and spaces?

As the mayor at our meeting in Hebron said: If there are political differences, then there is generally a possibility of discussion. But if there are religious questions involved, especially fundamentalist attitudes, then there is usually no possibility of discussing anything. Therefore it is important to concentrate on the issue, and what kind of religious identity we have and need to foster.

For the sake of the future of Palestine and of all countries in the world, we have to ask the question: How do we deal with religious tradition and heritage? How do we transform religious identity, individually and collectively, into dimensions and motivations which do not exclude and degrade others, who are in certain respects different from us, to a faith which includes everybody in universal salvation and solidarity? This question of our own and others' religious identity is both crucial and important: Can people everywhere experience that they are desired, accepted and loved by other people so that they are able to accept others and campaign for their welfare, too? This is a great religious hope. Namely, that if people realize the unending, inexhaustible love of God, then they are gifted with a strength which we need so badly, with the power of solidarity for all.

I would guess that quite a few of you will be surprised and perhaps astonished by what I have to say. I do not want to diminish religious faith. Instead my aim is to deepen the Christian or Islamic faith (in which religion always takes place) to the heart of each belief, not to make God vulnerable but to give Him the greatness and magnanimity He *is* Himself and for which He is to be praised, for His inexhaustible mercy. I am sure that this deepening of our faith will bring the Christian faith to its core and heart of identity. Tolerance will overtake difficulties only if it is rooted in a certain realisation of the Christian faith itself. I believe every religion has its own possibilities and resources for similar transformation and to take responsibility for avoiding fundamentalism in one's own complex identity.

1. Love as a given?

The sociologist, Hartmut Rosa, distinguishes between two different maps or profiles of human beings in the world[1]: a map of judgements and a map of desires. Desiring and being desired are more profound and have to do with the area of emotional affection (or aversion), while judgements relate to moral and ethical attitudes and lead to fixed principles.

Love can be that which connects the two: it extends to the depths of desiring and of being desired, and grounds corresponding attitudes and judgements therein. The most profound human experience is to be wanted and welcomed in love – either by other *people* or, in the area of religion, by a *god*. The Bible contains powerful texts in which God encounters humans on the level of passionate desire, for example in Hosea 11.

People who have been loved and are able to love, who have thus received the gift of love in both ways, share a profound experience: the experience of being desired and welcomed unconditionally. The person who loves wants their loved one to *be*, to be there, to live, to exist. To be wanted from birth, even from conception, is a gift; a person's very existence becomes a gift because he/she is wanted. Rich findings surely await those who search in poems and stories and in poetry and prose, for the traces of this connection between infinity and love, between love and an existence that is desired and wanted, between love and the pain of death. "It is what it is, says love," writes the German poet Erich Fried in one of his poems. This is a brilliant insight: love desires being and protects that which is.

To love a person means to say: You must not die. This assertion of Gabriel Marcel highlights an experience which the Christian faith extends to include the love of *God*. To be loved by God means that God says to us: once born nobody must die. Are humans permitted to hold these ideas and hopes even in relation to all humanity, of the world, and the universe? Asking the questions: What is the motive the existence of everything? Why is there not merely nothing? "Is it love?" In the musical "Fiddler on the Roof," Tevye the milkman puts this question, repeatedly to his wife, Golde. The quality of their life together allows him to answer yes to it; and we may put the same question to the creator. In asking 'Why?' and 'What for?' we are not simply asking whether there is a God who made everything; we are also asking *why* God made all of this. What is His/Her motive? Is it God's amusement to witness the blossoming and destruction of life – similar to the way, in ancient empires, gladiators were fed well and kept healthy to enable them to butcher each other? This kind of God would not add anything to atheist evolution: for in the end there is no difference between believing in a cold God (even if cold 'merely' towards others) and believing in a cold universe.

2. Love enhances and encompasses everything

It is the quality of such experiences that touches the membrane of the world beyond and of infinity. Most religions hold to the faith that God is merciful. It is precisely because God created humans out of love that we may hold onto the hope that God will not let humans perish. The hope is that divine love will not allow human existence to fall into emptiness at the point of death, but to embrace it. When my father died in 1987, my mother insisted that the inscription on the gravestone should include his name as well as the sentence: "God is *love* and *life*."

If an unending God is love, then His or Her love is unending. That which is loved is saved, and if love really is God – that is, if love is limitless and infinite – everything is loved and everything is saved. As the First Letter to the Corinthians says in chapter 15, the key question is ultimately: Is the wholly impossible possible for us – is life saved beyond death and calamity?

Is it saved just as though all evil and suffering had not happened had not been experienced? On what conditions? Or is it unconditional? And what impact does this unconditionality have on people with their respective memories and experiences of life? Because if every loveless action is not negated, ignored and considered undone even in eternity, that would be a contradiction to universal love. In the last judgement nothing that has happened must or will be lost. Everything re-appears and is elevated into a state of being infinitely loved, in the horror that was experienced or in the joy of what happened.[2]

From the vantage point of this inexhaustible love which can be fully experienced in the last jugdement, all lovelessness is condemned even more sharply and all pain and suffering inflicted on others is extended into divine infinity. Because God never withdraws his love as a punishment, we will be able to experience deep remorse – not as a condition of reconciling grace but as its consequence. The pain of any punishment inflicted outside the scope of this love would never reach the human heart, it would always fall short and would itself be exclusive.

This judgement of grace applies to all humans, and the same criterion applies to believers. Different options of religious commitment are judged by the "fruits" (see also Matthew 7:16) they produce following Matthew 25: "For I was hungry and you gave me food" (Matthew 25:34). That is, by the motives on the basis of which people in need were welcomed. Nothing is said about faith in the last judgement.

3. Political implications

The German philosopher Theodor W. Adorno states precisely what the problem is with "love": "Everyone today, without exception, feels insufficiently loved, because no-one is able to love sufficiently." This sort of love cannot be preached and prescribed, because to do so "already presupposes in those to whom one appeals a character structure different from the one that needs to be changed." Demands are pointless here: "The exhortation to give more warmth to children amounts to pumping out warmth artificially, thereby negating it. The exhortation to love – possibly even in its imperative form, that one should do it — is itself part of the ideology coldness perpetuates. It bears the compulsive, oppressive quality that counteracts the ability to love." Adorno senses that one of the incisive and "greatest impulses of Christianity ...was to eradicate the coldness that permeates everything. But this attempt failed; surely because it did not reach into the societal order that produces and reproduces that coldness."[3] In theological terms: the real lives of people have not been sufficiently sustained, reached and changed by the message of the universal and unlimited love of God, which first gives in order to enable, and which is not given only after conditions have been met. Over the centuries this love has been tied closely much with all-too-human and inhumane conditions.

This leads to the political implications of my reflections. There is a spiritual provocation here which poses an enormous challenge to social policy and global politics. We urgently need both: ways in which we can imagine our identities as being loved – as a source of a solidarity that transcends personal benefit. The global financial crisis highlighted how unscrupulous investors find themselves in a system which allows them to gamble away hundreds of billions of dollars or euros: money which over decades could have been used to help effectively stem the exponentially growing poverty and oppression of human beings. A similar point applies with regard to the ecological survival of humanity and planet earth.

We need models and discourses of solidarity that make an impossible possibility into both a practical desire and an element of our discourse regarding accountability and responsibility[4]: that of extending to the children of the world as much solidarity as to one's own children, beyond one's immediate social ties and beyond personal benefit. Those who refuse to share now are already engaged in killing and will have to kill a millionfold later in wars of distribution. Horst-Eberhard Richter's title "Those who refuse to suffer will have to hate!" has achieved acute global significance.[5] Those who refuse to share will have to hurt, disadvantage and, ultimately, exterminate others.

Those who do not experience love are unable to love. As an inexhaustible grace, "impossible" religious faith might be able to enhance "being loved" as a resource for humans to draw on. Individuals receive this message against the background of their varying psychological constitutions. Although allowing oneself to be loved unconditionally is encouraging news, for many it also amounts to a difficult challenge. Because of deficiencies in their experiences with other people, many people are, in fact, unable to open themselves up to unconditionally. This leads to a search for safety and redemption by meeting conditions rather than through letting go within an honest, unconditionally loving relationship. In this world, unconditionality works in a strangely paradoxical way: in order to make itself experienced at all, it must grasp and transform these circumstances. A key tenet of the theology of grace is borne out here: neither physical and mental "health" nor sinlessness are necessary for experiencing the loyalty of God's love. In this regard, the Bible presents a flexible God.[6]

This world always requires adjustments and compromises that involve if-then arrangements depending on the social circumstances. The more conditional and thus the more uncertain these circumstances are, the more individuals feel compelled to prioritize their own safety, even in imaginary ways, in order to find some sort of firm ground to stand on. What individuals achieve here, they project onto the divine and experience as acceptance by God. This is the basic issue of any fundamentalism. Nor can the problem be resolved by postulating that one has to be able to allow oneself to be loved in this way. This apparent solution only exacerbates the problem. The sole way forward consists in an acceptance that can actually be experienced.

4. From the very beginning: theological equality

For Hannah Arendt, birth is the event "through which every human being once appears in the world as something uniquely new." [7] All life is preceded by the gift of being created that is, being born. Thus birth is already the grace of being wanted and loved unconditionally by God and having been brought into existence for this reason. Birth is free just as one's lifetime is free. This grace does not represent arbitrariness but total unconditionality. Birth makes grace experienceable within creation. Josef Wohlmuth uses the metaphor of a "non-determinable beginning" to characterise the nature of birth. [8] This refers not only to individuals, but analogically also to different groups of individuals, cultures, peoples and societies.

Being chosen to be loved is thus not identical with the biblical notion of being chosen to believe. Being loved coincides with creation or, on the individual level, with birth. God's love is shown, not only at the point of being chosen for faith, but at the moment of creation and through everything that is created. To restrict God's love to those who have been chosen is one of the most fatal mistakes religions make, both because this diminishes God and because of the consequences for those who do not belong to the chosen. Birth is the primordial justification in the sense of St. Paul's explicit theology of justification, according to which all are loved by God, as they are, without any conditions so that they are free to change out of this love. All of us are desired by God whoever we are and whatever we are going to become. Therapists say that for humans the most important thing is to be and feel desired.

To be sure, Christians continue to be chosen in a special way: through faith they *know* of this infinite love of God, may trust in it and live life out of such faith. God alone gives the gift of faith, far from the fateful exclusivism of fatalist ideas about predestination in which God predetermines who receives the gift of faith and who does not and is therefore condemned. This is not the remit of chosenness: its remit is vicarious reception on behalf of all.[9]

What is the difference then between the faithful and others? Simply put, whether I do or do not know that someone loves me makes a huge difference. And this is the great gift we have received in terms of the love of God. Therefore, faith is itself the gift of being chosen and nothing else. For faith involves believing that God loves even without this faith, unconditionally, and regardless of what people do with it. Where God's unlimited grace, in the form of infinite love for all people, is part of the experience of faith, it mobilises the human heart as a powerful source of good and engenders universal solidarity with others (even those who are completely different), especially with oppressed peoples, faith communities, cultures, and ethnicities.

Thus the notion has to be abandoned that those who do not believe in the Christian way lack something: they already have "everything" – life and, in it, they realize the love of God. To impute some sort of deficiency to those who believe differently or not at all undermines their status as children and (following the pastoral constitution of Vatican II) as people of God, which everyone is given through birth. It also undermines the radical love given through the radical gift of birth. Simone Weil offers a fascinating insight here: "One of the most precious delights of earthly love that of serving the loved one unknown to him or her, is possible in the case of God only by being an atheist."[10]

Every human being has been called into life. But not everyone is able, within the context of their lives and socialisation, to experience the givenness of birth for what it is, a blessing.[11] The conditions of this world may run counter to the unconditionality of birth, or they may support its realisation. Faith as well as the churches, in their message, hopefully support and facilitate blessings and celebrate the explicitness of the universal grace of birth which, however, occurs and exists without them. The German theologian Karl Rahner reminds us that, through sacraments and preaching, the language of the Church presents and makes conscious that which is the case in all places and can occur in all places: "Did I not bring Israel up from Egypt, the Philistines from Caphtor and the Aramits from Kir?" (Amos 9:7), and, hopefully, the Palestinians from Israel's oppression!

5. Mission from a Christian perspective: a liberating release

To burden each other with if-then demands is the first sign that friendship or love are receding. Those who cling to others do not understand the balance between love and freedom. The same applies, but even more so, to our relationship to transcendence, to God. Faith is not the condition of this love, but the space where it is experienced explicitly.

Everyone can love and be loved. Believers may add – in a low-key way – that this love is to do with God, and that their faith includes the experience of God's inexhaustible love which gives strength to do good. And they will be even more credible to the extent to which they exemplify this acceptance of others in their lives. This faith makes it possible to understand that which is other but can also surpass it insofar as that which is other must be protected simply because of its birth, i.e., unconditionally. All people are loved by God, unconditionally. There is no need to believe in order to be loved. This happens in any case.

And this is where Christianity's truth lies: in telling all who are born that they are wanted by God and helping them to realise this fact, without conditions, following the theology of justification 'Just as people who are sinful and far from faith, are loved infinitely by God even before they have changed. This remains the case even if someone never changes. Not because God is indifferent to how we live; but because God's response is different, not in terms of the intensity of His love, but in terms of the difference between joy and pain within love, based on God's substantial empathy in Christ; in terms of solidarity with victims and in terms of accusation of and reconciliation for the perpetrators. To suggest an anthropological analogy (familiar to parents who do not withdraw their love from sons and daughters who may have made questionable choices, or may have gone the wrong way in their eyes) the intensity of God's love always remains the same; the difference is that love given to sinful people becomes painful – a "cross to bear," as it were – whereas love given to good people is a joy.

Whether individuals turn to the churches, saying "Here is where we wish to be and stay," or whether they remain in their own life spaces, religions and cultures, is out of anyone's control. From this perspective, "mission" is already successful when individuals discover the depth of this unconditional love in their own religions: the mercy of God features in every surah of the Qur'an. When, for example, inspired by the way Christians believe in and live the unconditionality of God's love, Muslims deepen their own corresponding traditions and trust in their own faith's ability to remove any limits to God's love, all has been achieved.

Years ago I was told about two families, one Muslim, the other Christian, who were neighbours and got along together very well; both being helpful and friendly towards each other. One day the Muslim lady said to her Christian neighbour: "I cannot go on believing that you don't go to heaven." Where people, through their own faith, allow themselves to be redeemed from a fearsome and exclusive God, in this way, Christian mission has been successful. In Christianity we have traditions, in which believers do not wish to be in heaven, if there is even one human being who is not saved, whoever he or she may have been; a sinner or an unbeliever. I mention for example Theresa of Avila and Charles Peguy.

6. A profligate approach:

unchained and unchaining

So I plead for a "light" or "weak" faith, a parallel thought to the notion of "weak reason" espoused by the philosopher Gianni Vattimo means a deliberation which does not want to be superior, which refuses to play the platonistic emperor over life counting abstract victories against realities. This is a light faith, not because it contains light things (the cross is certainly not light) but in the way we live it as an undeserved gift, which we do not "possess". According to St. Paul in 1 Cor 7, 29-31: to have it as if not having it. Faith and God are not possessions. This is a faith which loosens and throws away the chains of enforcing people inside and outside communities, by unchaining faith and unchaining believers from fear and oppression. This is the future of religions. Otherwise they will make everything worse and should disappear.

Belief in God is a bonus; it is neither necessary for living a good life, nor for living a good life which benefits others. For this, only one thing is necessary: the human experience of tenderness and acceptance. No one has to explore God through religious language games. Christians demonstrate that being chosen to believe in such a God is good and beneficial, that it makes both resources available and strength to show solidarity beyond personal boundaries. But there are no necessary and compelling reasons for having to believe in order to achieve salvation.

In this sense, faith is as overflowing and superfluous as the miracle of profligacy at the wedding at Cana (see John 2:1-12). It is interesting and surprising to note that in John, Jesus' first miracle is not a miracle of healing, and there is no shortage or deficiency to address. The people have already had enough food and drink. And now they are being given more, even better wine. No one is in need, at least not in this particular situation. And what's more, no less than six water jugs holding a hundred liters each are filled to overflowing. Everything is turned into wine. Isn't this wasting a miracle on lavishness? Of course it is wonderful to see and celebrate life delighting in wine, that is, faith. And it is in this sense experienced as indispensable because in many situations faith is experienced as a powerful sustaining force in life.

Faith is free, it is "gratis", it is not necessary, but it is precious, inexhaustibly precious, simply because it is not necessary. The perspective of faith makes many things in life appear even more precious than they already are, but also more painful than they are, and both already exist anyway.

Similar to art, music and poetry, faith is an overflowing luxury: no one has to visit the opera to be able to live. And yet, a beautiful concert casts a glow, as it were, onto all life. And people choose to "waste" money on such experiences. Hence, according to the French philosopher George Bataille, faith is correlated more with the anti-economy of profligacy than the economy of purpose.[12] With our sensitivity enhanced on the basis of this love relationship, life resonates in empathy with the sorrow of those who are sad and the joy of those who are happy. And this is done, not in return for what has been received, not out of obedience, but from empowerment.

How special it is to be allowed to fall in love. How lucky one is to have good friends. Neither of these can be produced or even enforced. They are examples of those extraordinary experiences of love that do not diminish everyday experiences of loyalty and mutual solidarity, yet are more than those. They are not necesary for living a valuable human life, but they have the power to deepen the experience of life enormously.

Praise and worship of God demarcate the spiritual space where a "useless" God is experienced – "useless" in the sense that he is never fully identical with any experience, purpose or intention.[13] And this dynamic of continual growth extends into eternity, and is forever open-ended. The realm of faith is a heterotopia in the sense of the French philosopher Michel Foucault, a place of otherness within the world "governed by wholly different laws and visions, where things follow an altogether different order."[14] Whoever believes in God in such a way will never be tempted to deify him- or herself.

7. Religious identity without Self deifiention

In 1939 the German Protestant theologian Dietrich Bonhoeffer experienced great tension while living in New York. Without being able to explain to his friends or even to himself, from an existential yet ultimately unfathomable feeling which stemmed from the depth of his faith he felt compelled to leave America and return to Nazi-Germany and to the very real danger of being killed, although his earlier plans had been quite different. After having refused to stay on in New York, Dietrich Bonhoeffer wrote on 20 July 1939: "For me this has probably more meaning at the moment than what I am able to see clearly. God alone knows. It is strange, in all my decisions I am not really clear about the motives. Is this a sign of lack of clarity, inner untruthfulness or is it a sign of the fact that we are led beyond our knowledge or is it both? In the end one is more likely to act from a level which remains hidden... At the end of the day I can only pray that God judges this day and all decisions mercifully. It is now in his hand."[15]

Because one could also find good ethical arguments, justifiable in Christian faith, for remaining in New York, an existential decision was needed which reached beyond all arguments and which did not brush aside the rational – but which finally stood, not because it was able to justify itself but because it put its appreciation of the truth confidently into God's hand.

Something peculiar and totally anti fundamentalist presents itself in this case: namely the strict connection between absolute self-devotion and non-claimed absolute truth regarding such a decision which totally affected Bonhoeffer totally. Bonhoeffer was imprisoned and murdered by the Nazis. Bonhoeffer hoped that his decision was the right one, but did not know if it was, neither as regards mental capacity nor his relationship with God. He put the validity of the truth of his ultimate decision in God's hand. Such a relationship with God leaves it to God to judge the validity of one's decision even if the decision is ultimately for one's own existence. It prevents that fatalism and fanaticism which often appear in very radical self-abandon as temptation, namely to claim for oneself and against others God's ultimate truth in the quality of the finality of a decision which affects one's existence. Bonhoeffer made it very clear: In no decision, even one of deadly consequence, regarding his own Christian identity, did he claim God's absolute truth.

8. For the sake of identities

The more people and cultures are allowed to develop their own identities, the more they are able, with this self-respect, to also open themselves to self-limitation and self-relativization with regard to other areas of life and people. What is valid for people is also valid for cultures: where an individual is able to experience the importance of his own existence, in a situation of social recognition and acceptance, which is maintained despite its inconsistency, he can dispense with having to borrow his identity from the collective identity of a larger "community" for the sake of his feeling of self-esteem. Where the ego is allowed to develop, one does not need to instrumentalise others to compensate for one's own weak ego. The more one enters the depths of life, the less one needs expansion in the breadth. The more one is allowed to learn to love and accept oneself, the more one is able to grant this to others.

This is an eminently important connection which is also applicable to cultural units. Where they are allowed to find their strength in themselves, they do not need any hegemony over others. It is then possible to dispense with only being interested in the maintenance of conventions instead of being interested in living one's life intensively. Singular wholeness leads to the removal of power over the whole. It is possible then too, to look at oneself from the outside, because there is an outside (and not claimed as an area which should not be outside but should be integrated into one's identity): for example if somebody judges his/her own context from the foreign perspective of another culture or if he/she lets oneself be criticised by members of another religion. It is an integrated part of every living identity, not to remain always in one's own context but to look at one's identity with the eyes of other identities: to take on the perspectives of others, especially of those whose viewpoint discovers themselves as rather limited or as people who are not in solidarity with them or who even cause injustice and poverty among them.

Those who can accept, value, and criticise their own limitations do not need any colonial limitlessness to experience themselves as important. It is exactly this equal openness towards all beings which is the test of authenticity for the difference between genuine and fascistic entirety. Fascistic entirety is namely in a position to activate, in a highly cunning manner, emotional levels in a mass of ego-weak people to an extent that they believe that chauvinistic and extensive claims to power over others are actually their own deepest desires. But this is a manipulated effect in which the pathos for the power over others prevents genuine self-realisation in realistic self-moderation.

9. The universalisation of Christian and Churchian solidarity

Christianity can refer to its own long history of misinterpreting God's universality which has cost millions of people the possibilities of living, freedom and finally life itself. Religion inhibits solidarity whenever it restricts God's love to its own area and considers all those, who don't belong to its faith, hardly or not at all worthy of solidarity. That is a *heavy* faith, such as having a possession to defend, including God. But God needs no defense. In the Bible God allows Himself to be accused as in the Psalms and in the Book of Job. On the other hand, religion always accelerates solidarity if it grants God's love to all people and experiences its own limited area as a learning field where inward turning solidarity reaches for the outside.

Every religious chauvinism applies God's mercy only *to itself*, and thus renders itself universal in relation to others, completely losing sight of God's mercy for all his creatures. Universal and thus integral strategies form the sharpest contradictions to removing the borders of self against the background of the only existing universality, namely God himself. The issue of "inward- outward" has never ceased to be a problem. From the Israeli-Palestinian conflict we know that the letter of the Bible alone does not save people from a religiously entitled withdrawal of solidarity; this is only done by the the Spirit and the intention respectively with which the Bible is read, namely that dynamism expressed in the Bible towards a more merciful God and a more universal inter-human solidarity. The Christian creed thus coincides with human rights. Everything depends on a "globalised" understanding of grace within the horizon of a radical solidarity with all people.

In our world-historical context it is absolutely necessary to promote this dynamism as a globalisation of solidarity. The neo-liberal and capitalistic globalisation which has already pushed more than one billion people below the poverty line and into abject misery, and which has sharpened the gulf between the North and the South and also crosswise between the poorest and the richest, has to be countered by all powers of goodwill, namely the globalisation of a solidarity which embraces all people and all nations. It needs to be a solidarity which is not based on egotism but also includes the renunciation of advantages to oneself. This global solidarity has to be implemented before wars of thirst and hunger will force rich countries to do so, or, respectively, and more probable, before countries with military and economic strength fall into the terrible temptation of closing their borders exposing millions and most likely billions of people to death from thirst and hunger.

In order to motivate this type of behaviour and to open people's views one needs relevant fields where solidarity is experienced within the more comprehensible area of our own social forms and societal life. What is not learnt there cannot be realized on the outside and the future. But the opposite is also valid. Where people in partnerships care for the poor and oppressed, they learn to consider also more critically their own social areas and to meet the local victims of a situation with greater solidarity. For the sake of the universal option for the poor and oppressed a mutual global network of solidarity is needed between inside and outside and between near and far. The center, in which our conference is taking place, and this conference itself are an impressing example for such a networking. This mirrors the future of our Christian and, at the same time, interreligiously constructive identity.

I close with the hope-giving sentence, which Mitri Raheb sometimes uses when speaking: "Believe it or not!" In Raheb's words this expression is not an alternative but a statement that an issue that seems impossible has already become reality. Indeed, Rev. Raheb often uses this phrase after something unbelievable has been achieved.

I hope that my plea for a religious faith which opens the mental ideological prison of religion, which enhances solidarity to all people as well as confidence in a God whom we do have to excuse or defend, whom we must not use as a legitimatization for our own wicked purposes against others, who gives liberty and love to everybody - will be and will become a reality everywhere: Believe it or not!

13

Infiltrators or Next of Kin

Identity Negotiations around the Label 'Mistanenim' of African Migrants in Israel and its Connection to the Von Palestinians[1]

Mirjam van Reisen

Erik Borgman

1. Bone of my bone, flesh of my flesh

In the opening stories of the Bible exploring what it means that we, along with the rest of the cosmos, are not gods but creatures, the suggestion is that human beings participate in their environment by exchanging gifts. We receive food, shelter and especially company, and in return we name the givers of these gifts. As it is written: 'whatever Adam called every living creature, that was its name' (Gn. 2:19). When Adam, as the prototypical human being, finally sees Havva (Eve, the 'life-giver'), he exclaims: 'This at last is bone of my bones and flesh of my flesh' (Gn. 2:22). Here the name expresses the closeness of the relationship: the woman is called *isha* (אישה) in Hebrew to show her closeness to the man, *ish* (איש). Clearly, naming and stories about naming are not simply about identity, but about who we are. They are about relations: who are we in our connections to these others?

This is not to say that naming *constitutes* the relations. The suggestion in the early stories of the Bible is that to really discover another creature, especially another human being, means meeting 'a helper as our partner' with whom we are called to build a community of equals. The question is how we respond to this discovery. The biblical tradition projects that we should allow other human beings to name us as much as we name them. It is written: "You shall love your neighbor as yourself" (Lv. 19:18) not "You can treat your neighbor as you see fit". In South African culture this idea is expressed as *ubuntu:* "I exist because of you" or "A person is a person through other persons."[2] In a process of reciprocal naming of our respective worlds we create a common world in which we live as part of a whole.[3]

However, as we know only too well, human history is in fact full of rivalry and conflict, violence and war. Usually this is not between total strangers, but between next of kin. And this has been so from the beginning: 'Cain rose up against his brother Abel, and killed him' (Gen. 4:8). Because of this we know that potential helpers and partners can turn out to be rivals and even enemies. Therefore, when we do recognize a fellow human being, we will be tempted to treat him/her as Adam treated the animals: he gave them names, but he did not find a helper and a partner among those to whom he gave a name. He labeled and he ordered, and thus he controlled and he mastered. It may be the melancholia of the modern human condition: craving for the company of other beings who are our equals and whom we can trust. And whilst we are aware that it is impossible for human beings to be alone (cf. Gen. 2:18), we tend to become afraid once we meet a being that seems to be 'bone of my bones and flesh of my flesh'. Who knows what it might imply to depend on him or her and what he or she might do to us?

2. The Anxiety of the Nation State

Modern nation states are founded on the fiction that we are able to solve the question of who is to be trusted, and who does and who does not belong in the community of those with whom we will share our destiny. To fight the existential anxiety that results from recognizing the possibility that others may cause harm, we invent and label enemies so as to define and localize the threat. Safety then becomes synonymous with controlling the enemy, barring him from the neighborhood, even getting rid of him, or at least not allowing his presence to be unobserved and on his own terms. Naturally, this does not provide more safety, as the anxiety routinely returns and even doubles or triples in intensity. Having defined the enemy, there is the uncertainty of being able to control him compounded by the difficulty of recognizing and localizing him/her.

The growing vulnerability of nation states, the increasing permeability of borders and the globalization and integration in economic and financial networks, leads governments to be concerned with the fluidity of citizenship. They focus on migrants, refugees and asylum seekers as a means of sustaining their definition of what a citizen is and hence their long-term survival. Are these migrants really who they claim to be, people under threat, or are they in fact enemies of our prosperity, and of our peace and our culture of freedom and equality? As the nation state seeks to define its community of citizens, it is especially disconcerting and uncomfortable that many refugees by definition do not have a clear identity of their own in the prevailing system of national and racial labels, and it is precisely this non-identity that may indeed have provoked them into fleeing or moving. In the context of the growing fragility of the current nation state, it is increasingly regarded as imperative that migrants are unequivocally labeled and named. Without such labels they cannot be controlled and distinguished from 'true' and 'normal' citizens in order to avoid the nation state losing its definition and its 'raison d'être' of separating 'us' from 'them'.

In the European Union it is clear that migration and asylum policies are usually not intended to deal with the situation of those seeking a safer home, or a place that seems more promising to facilitate a decent life. These policies first and foremost aim at the proper labeling of migrants and the positions they are entitled to in society, to avoid blurring categories that are supposed to be essential for the definition of the composition of citizenship of the nation state. Hence the issue of 'foreigners' is at the basis of the very survival of the state conceptualized as the primary keeper of security for its citizens. Within the context of protection offered by the state, citizens prove to be easily convinced of the need to accept clear categories to determine who belongs and who does not.

Nonetheless, we do not live in a world of merely categories. We know that we cannot live in such a world. Among us there will always be individuals and groups who see the humanity of the people we try to classify in clear-cut categories, thus crossing the abstract delineations that have been invented. In the biblical story at the beginning of Exodus, Moses is rescued by the daughter of the very Pharaoh who had ordered the killing of all newborn Hebrew boys, because she sees in him a human child, not the potential enemy her father projected (Ex. 2:5-10).

How do we in Europe make sense of centuries of colonization and the two world wars in the twentieth century? How do we make sense of a history in which civilians were excluded from the protection of their community and country without access to a rule of law? Millions of Africans were displaced all over the world, sold and kept in slavery – if not killed. Millions of Jews were excluded from citizenship, a history that finally culminated in the Nazi extermination camps. But ultimately the dehumanization which is at the basis of these horrors always crumbles and fails. Anne Frank is a young sister to all of us when she observes in the midst of misery:

> *"The best remedy for those who are afraid, lonely or unhappy is definitely to go outside, somewhere where they can be alone, alone with the heavens, nature and God. Because just then, only then does one feel that all is as it should be and God wants to see human beings happy within the simple, but beautiful nature."*[4]

Apparently even in the most improbable of circumstances people can discover that they are provided for and have the task of providing for others.

Thus Europe's history brings home the fact that human beings *have* fundamental rights even when no system or law recognizes them.[5] They are bone of our bones and flesh of our flesh, which obliges us to treat them as we would desire to be treated ourselves; with dignity and respect. Each of us knows anxiety, has experienced what it means to be threatened, has felt how it is to not be tolerated, or to be in a position where we cannot make demands. 'You shall… love the stranger', it is said in the Book of Deuteronomy, 'for you were strangers in the land of Egypt' (10:21). Our anxiety, which may lead us to prosecute others, because we see them as potential threats, can also bring us to recognize anxiety in others and to act in their support. Jesus seems to have repeated this command in a different context as he said that we should love our enemies (Mt. 5:44;

Lc. 6:27). We have all been enemies ourselves, or felt that we were treated as such when we in fact needed love and compassion.

It is probably fair to say that Israel is a country born from extreme anxiety. That anxiety did not come out of nowhere. It resulted from the almost successful attempt to exterminate the Jewish population of Europe by the Nazis and its collaborators. Some survivors tried to move as far away geographically as possible from that history of pogroms and persecution, attempting to forget their Jewishness or quietly keeping it in the background of their new lives. Desiring to live safely as modern people in a modern society, many who were able moved to the U.S. Others vowed to themselves and to coming generations that the future would never again be like the recent past. Having experienced that ultimately nobody could be trusted –as seen by the way the Allies had not come to their rescue when the Nazi's tried to 'solve' definitively the question the Jews allegedly embodied, by not even tying to bomb the railroads to and from the gas chambers in the extermination camps – they established Israel as a Jewish state in the country of Palestine in 1948. For them, recent history gave ultimate credibility to the Zionist narrative of the Jewish people, expelled from their homeland and scattered over the Gentile world, waiting for the right moment to return home to their country of origin. Israel should be safely Jewish, imagined as a place where every Jew in the world should be able to flee when in danger, and to be secure against any foreign threat.[6]

In real life, the establishment of Israel was a much more complicated and paradoxical affair than that for which the Zionist narrative accounted.[7] As a variant of nineteenth century nationalism, Zionism presupposed a homogenous Jewish people as a given. The assumption was that it was somehow unambiguously clear who belonged and who did not. Zionism conceived of a homeland whose people had the moral, if not yet legal right to it.[8] Nevertheless, as the

Israeli historian Shlomo Sand has argued convincingly, the notion of a Jewish people as clearly defined, the claim as a people on Israel as its original inhabitants, the base within a framework of rights of the claim to the land of Israel, and the demarcation of Israel as a land with natural boundaries, inherently lacks the precision that was imagined.[9]

Once that is clear, once cannot escape dealing with some hard questions. Why would the land not belong to the people who had lived on it and cultivated it for centuries before the State of Israel was established in 1948? What could justify the expulsion of the original Palestinians from their homes and communities through a combination of pressure, intimidation and terrorist violence? What are the foundations for the claim to belong to the Jewish people and to benefit from the right of immigration from every country in the world to Israel? And perhaps the hardest question of all: how can sovereignty be established with so many conflicting claims?

In actual fact, these questions were not answered through philosophical debate, but by concrete praxes of removal and incorporation, inclusion and exclusion, of remembering and forgetting. The Separation Wall for instance literally provides a definition of inclusion and exclusion by creating a fixed frontier separating Israelis and Palestinians. The battles, the injustices and the contestation are made invisible. For instance, the University of Tel Aviv erected four places of memory to commemorate Jewish history. However, the centuries old history of the village al-Shaykh Muwannis, on whose ground the University was built, is not mentioned and thus the history of the expulsion of the villagers, whose homes were torn down and whose land was taken away from them, remains virtually hidden.[10]

3. Inflitrators or Mistanenim

This brings us to the issue we want to explore further in this paper. When Palestinians whose ancestral lands where taken returned to places where they had lived, they were called 'infiltrators'. Even if they simply returned to collect a few belongings, or visit their fields and perhaps revive some memories.[11]

The Hebrew word 'mistanenim' translates as 'infiltrators' (one mistanen / mistanenet (pl)), in Hebrew: מסתננים, מסתנן מסתננת. Based on the Hebrew root "S-N-N," the words for both "filter" (masnen) and "sieve" (mesanenet) are formed.[12] The term 'infiltrators' is associated with Palestinian refugees who were driven or fled from their villages during the 1948 Arab – Israeli War and later found themselves on the other side of a hostile border. Israeli actions to establish the State of Israel included the uprooting of 700,000 Palestinians, described by historian Benny Morris as 'transfers' without which the establishment of the State of Israel would not have been possible. This is an uncomfortable conclusion as *Haaretz* interviewer Ari Shavit describes:

> *"[Morris] gives the observer the feeling that this agitated individual, who with his own hands opened the Zionist Pandora's box, is still having difficulty coping with what he found in it, still finding it hard to deal with the internal contradictions that are his lot and the lot of us all."*[13]

Today the sons and daughters of the Palestinians who were 'transfered' sometimes seek to visit their ancestral homes, but are equally labelled with the term 'infiltrator'. In an article entitled "It was always my dream to reach Jaffa, Syrian infiltrator says", the newspaper *Haaretz* reported on August 17, 2013 the story of 28 year old Hijazi, who was raised in Syria, and who hitchhiked "to Jaffa in search of what had been his parents' home before they [were] driven away during a war over Israel's founding in 1948."[14] Hijazi was arrested on a charge of 'infiltration'. In his comments to the media he portrayed his desire as simply a personal motive: "I imagine there are many Palestinians who don't want to come back here, just like there are many Jews who also don't want to stay.'"

The term 'infiltrator' is associated with military (command driven) action. It is also associated with secretive operations against authorities while remaining invisible. In 1948 Witold Pilecky, a native of Poland, was executed after he had allegedly 'infiltrated' Communist Poland from the West. Pilecky has since become known as the Auschwitz Infiltrator and has recently received posthumous fame. The story is that he, being from non-Jewish descent, volunteered in 1940 to infiltrate Auschwitz and thus allowed himself to be rounded up by the Gestapo. Pilecki spent thirty-one months in the notorious concentration camp, organizing an inmate resistance network and shipping intelligence about the camp's operations to the Polish resistance and the Western Allies.[15] The Jewish Library records that:

> "He began sending information... confirming that the Nazis were seeking the extermination of the Jews to Britain and the United States as early as 1941. [...] Documents released from the Polish Archives... raised questions as to why the Allies ... never did anything to put an end to the atrocities being committed that they learned of so early in the war."[16]

The dictionary defines an 'infiltrator' as someone who takes up a position surreptitiously for the purpose of espionage, as a spy, undercover agent - (military) a secret agent hired by a state to obtain information about its enemies or by a business to obtain industrial secrets from competitors or an intruder (as troops) with hostile intent.[17] A Hebrew dictionary provides the meaning "entered in secret/hidden and without permission; broke through (penetrated)."[18]

Indeed, the flight of Palestinians displaced by the 1948 Arab-Israeli War gave Israel the possibility of inserting agents as spies into neighbouring countries, where they were disguised as refugees.[19] These infiltrating operations meant that identities crossed and double crossed, as the following story from the internet newspaper *The Times of Israel* relates:

> *"At the moment of Israel's creation 65 years ago, Isaac was a Jewish refugee from an Arab country who was in a different Arab country pretending to be an Arab refugee from a Jewish country. The multiplicity of lost homes and the layers of displacement in his story contain something essential about the country he helped found — a home for homeless people — and about the wars and loss among Jews and Arabs that have been part of its existence since then."*

Matti Friedman, the journalist recording the story of Isaac Shushan, concludes: 'one can also discern the idea that perhaps the easy division between Jews and Arabs might not be as firm as we tend to think.'[20]

For Israelis the term infiltrator has long been largely associated with security threats. A current Jewish resident of Jerusalem remembers:

> *"People my age (60) do remember fear of infiltrators that might be terrorists. Some of them were, but with time we learnt that most were only farmers trying to get some of their crops."*[21]

Despite recognition in hindsight of the reasons why Palestinian villagers might try to reach their former land, the term remains associated with danger: "During the '50s and the '60s, until the '67 war," she states; "after that, borders became somewhat less of a problem."[22]

In 1954 the term 'infiltrator' was for the first time defined officially in Israeli law. An 'infiltrator' was considered to be a person:

> *"Who has entered Israel knowingly and unlawfully and who at any time between the 16th Kislev, 3708 (29th November, 1947) and his entry was - (1) a national or citizen of the Lebanon, Egypt, Syria, Saudi-Arabia, Trans-Jordan, Iraq or the Yemen ; or (2) a resident or visitor in one of those countries or in any part of Palestine outside Israel; or (3) a Palestinian citizen or a Palestinian resident without nationality or citizenship or whose nationality or citizenship was doubtful and who, during the said period, left his ordinary place of residence in an area which has become a part of Israel for a place outside Israel."*[23]

The law stipulates severe sentencing, which was increased in subsequent amendments. The law also affected those who help 'infiltrators':

> *"Where a person has sheltered an infiltrator or has otherwise aided an infiltrator in order to facilitate his infiltration or his unlawful presence in Israel, and the Court is satisfied that he has given such shelter or aid before, that person is liable to imprisonment for a term of fifteen years or to a fine of ten thousand pounds or to both such penalties."*[24]

An order that amended the law in 1969 explicitly connected 'infiltrators' to deportation:

"The military commander may order, in writing, the deportation of an infiltrator from the Area, whether charged with an offence under this order or whether not charged and the deportation order shall serve as the legal source for holding such infiltrator in custody pending his deportation."[25]

The context of the 1954 law and subsequent amendments was highly specific. In an analysis of the word 'infiltrator' in *Haaretz* in 2012, journalist Michael Handelzalts gives this background to the term:

"The Hebrew word is loaded with very specific historical meaning. It brings us back to the 1950s, the first years of the recently established State of Israel following the bloody period of the War of Independence, ... what is referred to today by the Palestinians as the 'Nakba' (catastrophe). [...] The broader context of those incidents were the efforts of the Palestinian refugees to return to the places they had left – voluntarily or unwillingly – within the borders of Israel, or in other words to realize their 'right of return'. The young State of Israel was adamant about thwarting any such attempt, even in the case of Palestinians who remained within the country's borders – i.e., not 'infiltrators' – and wanted to return to the villages they had left during the war."[26]

Originally a word for people threatening stability or security by inimical intent, the 1954 law associated an 'infiltrator' with arrangements as to who belonged where, which people belonged in which country or region. Those who had formerly lived in Palestine were now of 'doubtful' citizenship and for this reason alone they were perceived as risks to what was experienced as 'security'. It was not so much their real threat in terms of military danger, but their subversion of the standard narrative of what Israel was and how it became a

Jewish state that made them into unwanted persons. The Palestinian Human Rights organisation Al-Haq notes how the 1969 military order defines 'unlawful' entry into an area "by reference to the opposite term 'lawful', which means 'as per permit by the military commander'"[27] Thus not just the possible criminal intent of the persons, but the mere *presence* of Palestinians on Israeli territory was criminalized.

In 2010 Israel adopted two new military orders, the1649 'Order regarding Security Provisions' and the 1650 'Order regarding Prevention of Infiltration', issued by the Israeli Defence Force.[28] The adoption of the orders has raised great concern among the Palestinian community and international human rights organisations. It widens the use of the label 'infiltrator' to within the Occupied Palestinian Territories (OPT). Lawful presence for Palestinians in the OPTs requires formal authorisation by Israeli authorities, even though the OPT provides IDs and, Israel for its part, has no updated ID records since 2000. This, combined with the presence of Palestinians from Gaza on the West Bank, has raised fears that the order will allow for large-scale deportations of Palestinians from the West Bank to Gaza or elsewhere. Al Haq also expresses concern that the order further criminalises people charged as 'infiltrators', as they may not only face deportation, but can also be sentenced to up to seven years of imprisonment. Given the difficult situation of many Palestinians, 'lawful' mobility is in reality hardly feasible and will leave many vulnerable to such charges, and therefore to possible imprisonment.

All of this could of course be interpreted in terms of the ongoing struggle between Israelis and Palestinians over the control and moral ownership of land. And indeed, these new orders enable the Israeli occupying forces to control and illegally dislocate large groups of people.[29] It has been concluded that this new order is part of an overarching policy that has been in crescendo since 1967: maximizing Israeli control of (Palestinian) land and minimizing the number of

(Palestinian) people. The fact that this policy is targeting a specific national group and the fact that it is accompanied by a persistent settlement policy in the occupied Palestinian territories renders these policies, not only discriminatory, but also racist and colonial.[30]

Clearly the new orders have extended the issue of 'infiltrators' from control over Israeli territory to the OPT. The orders further undermine the idea of the OPT as a sovereign state, thus increasingly corroding the idea of a Two State Solution for Israel / Palestine.

One could argue that the broadening of the label 'infiltrators' through the law in this way, defines the Palestinians as de facto subjects of the state of Israel, perhaps under a colonial type structure. By extension the identity of the State of Israel reveals itself as in a relationship with the Palestinian people, unless it fundamentally denies the Palestinians their humanity. "Flesh of our flesh and bone of our bone"– the recognition of shared humanity then has to be brought into the discourse of Israeli – Palestinians relations.

Infiltrators from the Horn of Africa

The new orders, however, do not just target Palestinians. The definition of 'infiltrators' was extended from applying to Palestinians and other 'Arabs' – seen as the 'enemy' who embodies the threat to the state of Israel – to an undefined open category. The orders created fear that internationals who may be 'undesirable' by the Israeli Defence Forces are no longer secure in terms of their presence in the West Bank under the authority of the OPT. Moreover, these 'infiltrators' can now comprise any non-Israeli foreigners, in the OPT or in Israel: peace activists in Ramallah, or desperate refugees from Eritrea and the Sudan in Tel Aviv, fleeing desolate situations back home and hoping to find a save heaven. Thus Israel's alleged 'infiltrators' of old, dare we say its next-of-kin Palestinians, are joined by new old family members entering their Holy Land. They are labelled as 'infiltrators' as well, and treated as such.

Father Mussie Zerai, an Eritrean Roman Catholic priest based in Rome, was the first to be confronted with increasing numbers of desperate calls for help from fellow Eritreans in the Sinai and Israel. The crisis that was revealed emerged as a part of a broader crisis. Refugees trying to cross the Mediterranean to Europe had Fr. Mussie's telephone number in the event that something happened during the crossing. Fr. Mussie has been trusted to intervene with the authorities as groups of Eritreans increasingly become stuck. Crossings have become more and more hazardous and. Fr. Mussie's appeals often fall on deaf ears.

In 2011 alone, 1500 people were known to have lost their lives in the Mediterranean, states the European Council.[31] Its report suggests that the authorities, rescue workers and other ships knowingly turned away from saving refugees in difficulty. Analyzing a particular incident in which seventy-two people lost their life, it states:

> *"From this story, a catalogue of failures became apparent: [...] the Italian and Maltese Maritime Rescue Coordination Centres failed to launch any search and rescue operation, and NATO failed to react to the distress calls, even though there were military vessels under its control in the boat's vicinity when the distress call was sent. The Flag States of vessels close to the boat also failed to rescue the people in distress. Furthermore, two unidentified fishing vessels also failed to respond to the direct calls for assistance from the boat in distress. [...] Perhaps of most concern... is the alleged failure of the helicopter and the military vessel to go to the aid of the boat in distress [...] [M]any opportunities for saving the lives of the people on board the boat were lost."*[32]

On 8 July 2013 Pope Francis made his first pastoral visit to Lampedusa, the Italian island which provides the first soil for many who do make the crossing. Pope Francis threw a wreath of flowers into the sea in memory of refugees who have perished. The BBC reported that "a small boat carrying 166 Africans – reportedly Eritreans – arrived at Lampedusa's port just hours before the Pope's plane touched down."[33] Using a small painted boat as an altar for Mass, in honour of the rickety boats that refugees use to make the hazardous journey, Pope Francis condemned 'global indifference' to their plight. Referring to the parable of the Good Samaritan, he said: "We see our brother half dead on the side of the road, and perhaps we say to ourselves: 'poor soul...!', and then go on our way. It's not our responsibility, and with that we feel reassured".[34] His spokesperson explained to the BBC that:

> *"Pope Francis is showing that when the Christian faith says 'love your neighbour,' it doesn't just mean the person next door. This tiny island shows the incredible contrast between the global North and South, between the 'haves' of the world and the 'have nots.'"*[35]

Pope Francis expresses concern not only that people should be helped, if possible. They should of course. But the main issue is the growing incapacity of the world to see them as human beings, "bone of my bones and flesh of my flesh." In his homily the Pope said: "We are a society which has forgotten how to weep, how to experience compassion – 'suffering with' others" and his question was: "Has any one wept?" over "the cruelty of our world, of our own hearts, and of all those who in anonymity make social and economic decisions which open the door to tragic situations like this."

In 2007 and 2008 the Italian government concluded agreements with the Khadafi administration to return migrants from Italy to

Libya. Eritreans, persecuted, facing execution or detention at home, and fearful of being returned by the Libyan authorities, looked for alternative safe routes. In 2009 Fr. Mussie Zerai started to receive calls from the Sinai desert concerning Eritean refugees who were held captive by Bedouins in torture houses against ransom. This crisis rapidly deepened as ransoms increased to the sum of USD 40,000. Research based on more than a hundred interviews has revealed the extensive use of torture on the hostages.[36] The hostages include children, infants and babies. Women and girls are routinely raped and have given birth to babies conceived in detention. Hostages may be held over a period of months, even years, and once released are invariably injured and severely weakened by malnutrition. The hostages refer to Sinai as "hell". Their story has been told over and over. But has compassion been shown? Does anyone care? Has anyone wept?

The houses of the kidnappers are located close to the Israeli border. While many of the hostages have died as a result of torture, or are killed when they are unlikely to produce ransom, those who have been released have sought to find safety by crossing the border to Israel. In Tel Aviv the Israeli relief groups Hotline for Migrant Workers and Physicians for Human Rights try to support the increasing numbers of refugees. Among these thousands are former hostages held in Sinai. The traumatized Sinai hostages sleep in the open air, in Levinsky Park in south Tel Aviv. Interviews with the Sinai hostages show that Israel was not intended as a destination for many, prior to their ordeal in the Sinai.[37] Eritreans have been taken by force and against their will from refugee camps in Sudan, as confirmed by the UN High Commissioner for Refugees, Gutteres, in 2012, when he visited the refugee camp of Kassala.[38] The UN has described in detail the involvement of the Eritrean administration in the trafficking.[39]

In Israel, the Sinai hostages are routinely jumbled together with other African migrants who have entered Israel in recent years:

foreign workers legally brought by the Israeli government, some of whose visas have expired; foreign migrants entering Israel illegally to find work; asylum seekers and refugees from countries other than Eritrea, such as Sudan. Many of these – even if illegal – find work with municipalities in Israel as street cleaners, or as manual workers or in other low paid jobs. Hotline for Migrant Workers reported that by April 2012 at least 58,088 asylum seekers had entered Israel. According to Hotline most refugees originated from Eritrea (56.46%) and Sudan (25.91%).[40]

In January 2012 the prevention of Infiltration law in Israel was once again amended to – in the words of Human Rights Watch –:

"Define all irregular border-crossers as 'infiltrators'. The law permits Israeli authorities to detain all irregular border-crossers, including asylum seekers and their children, for three years or more before their deportation. The law also allows officials to detain some people indefinitely, even if border control officials recognize they might face persecution if returned to their country."[41]

From July 2012 refugees and asylum seekers have been detained, with women and children separated from their husbands and fathers, even though almost all Eritreans and most Sudanese would qualify for asylum if given the chance to apply – a right they are routinely denied, despite Israel's ratification of Refugee Conventions.[42] Recently, Israel has also started to deport both Sudanese and Eritrean refugees under dubious 'voluntary' schemes.

Haaretz journalist Michael Handelzalts has commented on the unfolding situation:

"What piqued my curiosity was the fact that suddenly [...] the rhetoric changed. The 70-odd thousand foreigners originating

from several African countries, hitherto referred to by Israeli official spokesman as 'economic migrants'... and 'refugees'... became 'infiltrators.'"[43]

Handelszalts' article was entitled: "Word for word: By renaming migrants 'infiltrators', Israel is forging a new reality". As a so called 'streamer' to the article, *Haaretz* printed: "As they juggle terminology, Israeli politicians can paint migrants as a menace – not unlike Palestinian refugees."[44] Linking Africans to Palestinians through the use of the word 'infiltrators' is interpreted here as a way of spreading anxiety. Handelzalts expresses the concern that the use of the term changes the way in which African migrants are perceived:

"We Israelis should know better than all people that words forge our relations with reality. After all, it was by uttering words that God created the world we live in. And we know from our bloody recent past and present that one side's 'terrorist' is another side's 'freedom fighter'. Similarly, the seemingly objective term 'foreign worker' [...] differs vastly from the term 'refugee', which refers to someone who deserves compassion and mercy and possibly asylum, and that is [...] diametrically opposed to 'infiltrator', which denotes something sinister and downright dangerous."

As experts tell us, the word *mestanen* has a clear link with the related Semitic language of the Horn of Africa region, called Ge'ez. The equivalent term to *mestanen* in Amharic, which evolved from the classic Ge'ez, is *ser-go ge'b*. It refers to unauthorised entry, but reflects intent to enter. The term is made up of two words. The root of the first word is *mes'reg,* which is used to describe water seeping through a narrow opening. The second word refers to 'entrant', and used together with the first associates with the word *mestanen.*[45] It has a similar etymological root as the Arabic متسلل, *mutasallil* (s.) and *mutasallilien* (pl.). This term is currently used in Egypt to describe refugees detained for deportation or already deported, among which are many Eritreans.[46]

The meaning of the word 'infiltrator' is derived from its etymology, its current use as well as its memory: "words, apart from their sway over our perception of reality, have a memory as well, which can permeate the discourse even when the speakers are not aware of it."[47] Israeli journalist Shoshana Kordova reports how Yaakov Katz, Knesset member for the right-wing National Union Party stated that there are so many illegal African immigrants living in Tel Aviv, that Tel Avivians will soon be "moving to the West Bank" as their city "becomes African":

> *"The word Katz used to describe the immigrants was 'mistanenim', or 'infiltrators'. It is a word that seems particularly well-suited to scaremongering, since it conjures the other kind of mistanenim: Palestinians from the West Bank who lack permits but sneak into Israel to work."*[48]

Referring to the Book of Exodus and its command "You shall not wrong or oppress a resident alien, for you were aliens in the land of Egypt" (Ex. 22:21), Kordova notes: "In modern Israel, though, that injunction often collides with the goal of retaining the state's Jewish character, causing religious public figures to advocate kicking the strangers out."[49]

While Palestinians associate the term 'infiltrators' with themselves, it seems that Israelis associate the term nowadays more with 'illegal Africans.' For instance, a young Israeli student, asked what the term means, responded via e-mail:

> *"In recent years, there is a problem at the Israeli-Egyptian border, as about 0.3 million Africans have been walking across,*

> yes indeed, can you believe it, they were walking! So these are infiltrators. Most of them are from Sudan or Eritrea. Few have a permit. The remaining are illegal – mostly unemployed, have no special rights – it is sad in so many ways."[50]

While the Separation Wall now effectively separates Palestinians and Israelis, the Israeli authorities also recently finished a Separation Fence on Israel's southern border with Egypt to stop African refugees from entering through the Sinai. This has been very effective and has caused a major problem for the Sinai hostages, as they are no longer able to find safety after being released and face a treacherous and long route. If they are caught by Egyptian police they will be detained and deported, and have to pay for their own deportation. If they stay out of the hands of the police, they face a dangerous situation in Cairo where they remain vulnerable to criminal gangs.

The use of the word 'infiltrator' has transformed what is perceived as 'the problem' for Israel in its survival and security as a nation state. The anxiety about the safety of the State of Israel is translated to keeping society clean from illegal aliens and their influence. Those who try to 'help' the African infiltrators – an offence under Israeli law – are publicly scorned. On the website <http://mistanen.com/> citizens expose Israelis who employ 'infiltrators', publicizing addresses and phone numbers. By referring, especially, to the term that was introduced to 'accompany' Israel's very foundation and has continued to label its relationship to the Palestinians, the situation of African refugees has become associated with the underpinning of the state of Israel. As an informant writes, reflecting the use of the word 'infiltrators':

> "The Israeli approach to the African migrant's issue has been defined as an existential threat among some decision makers. The usage of the word, which was associated with early Israeli-

Arab border clashes and state formation and consolidation, is not a surprise."[51]

Spewed out

The Nation State's struggle for survival, aided by the narrative that it provides safety for its citizens, can turn against its own citizens by enclosing them: the Separation Wall, the Separation Fence, the Eritrean border with its shoot to kill policy, but still producing 5000 refugees each month (Summer 2013) escaping from a country that is sometimes called an 'open air prison'.

Eritrea is a tiny country of four million people on the Red Sea in an immensely strategic position. Journalist Shoshana Kordova points out how the English expression 'asylum seekers' focuses on what refugees are looking for, a safe haven in another country, while the Hebrew word *plitim* emphasizes what makes them refugees in the first place:

> *"They were 'spewed out' (nifletu) of their homelands. The root of plitim is used in a wide variety of disgorgement-related contexts, including baby spit-up, environmental emissions, and plitot peh, or slips of the tongue."*[52]

Eritrea is a former Italian colony, long a part of the old empire of Ethiopia, populated by the Habeshia people from Abyssinia, thought to be the descendants of Ham, the son of Noah, and built on the old civilization of the Aksum Empire. These are the ancient peoples of the Middle East, among whom are the Philistines (Palestinians), and the descendants of Ham governed the longest-ever dynasty of Emperor Menelik, son of King Solomon and the Queen of Sheba. Next of kin to the Israelis, indeed:

> *"At the time of the first European intervention in Ethiopia, ... the Beta Israel did not perceive themselves as Jews (ayhud*

> in Ge'ez). They thought of themselves as Israelites. In earlier periods ayhud had been used as one of several derogatory designations of the Beta Israel by the Christians, but the term was equally used to describe pagans or Christian heretics."[53]

The Temple that King Solomon built in Jerusalem has been imagined as a haven of justice and peace (cf. Psalm 122). At that time, in the eighth century BCE, Palestine was divided between the Kingdom of Israel in the north and the Kingdom of Judah in the south of what is now the West Bank. Around that time the stories of Adam and Eve, and Cain and Abel were written in two different versions by two different authors, one from the Kingdom of Judah ("J"), the other from the Kingdom of Israel ("E"), which were combined in what was probably the earliest version of what we now call the Bible. From the very beginning, therefore, there was no single message in the Bible: J and E interpreted the history of Israel differently and the differences in accent, focus and interpretation were preserved by the editors. Thus from the very beginning diversity is inherent in the biblical tradition.

Judaism still has a strong influence in Ethiopian and Eritrean – Orthodox – Christianity. Ethiopia has its own national religious book, the *Kebra Nagast*, which provides a strong national identity and legitimizes the Solomonic Dynasty. The 1955 Constitution of Ethiopia – which at the time included Eritrea – rests on the belief of its Israeli identity. African and Jewish history expert, Tudor Parfitt notes:

> "The national epic of Ethiopia celebrates the Israelite origins of the royal house, and this became 'the basic metaphor for legitimacy and authority within Ethiopian culture'".[54]

Even the Constitution of Ethiopia (1955) refers to this origin as a definition of the country:

> *"The imperial dignity shall remain perpetually attached to the line... [which] descends without interruption from the dynasty of Menelik, son of the Queen of Ethiopia, the Queen of Sheba, and King Solomon of Jerusalem."*[55]

The Habeshia - Beta Israel and Christians – consider themselves Israelites. Parfitt cites the observations of Jewish-French Orientalist and traveler, Joseph Halévy (1827-1917), on his contact with Jews in Ethiopa:

> *"... I managed to ask them in a whisper 'are you Jews?' They did not seem to understand my question, which I repeated under another form, 'Are you Israelites?' A movement of assent mingled with astonishment, proved to me that I had stuck the right chord."*[56]

There is therefore, a plurality of narratives on who is Jewish, or Israelite, and what that means to the identity of a person, a people or a nation.[57]

Karen Armstrong describes how authors 'J' and 'E' brought the local stories together to weave them into a "sustained epic" which has become a "founding story" of Western – and, we should add, African – culture:

> *"Abraham, his son Isaac and grandson Jacob (also known as 'Israel') lived in the Promised Land as resident aliens but during a famine, Jacob's twelve sons, founders of the twelve tribes of Israel, were forced to migrate to Egypt. At first they prospered there, but eventually, threatened by their great numbers, the Egyptians oppressed and enslaved the Israelites until Yahweh commanded Moses to lead his people back to Canaan. With Yahweh's miraculous help, they managed to*

> *escape Egypt and lived a nomadic life for forty years in the wilderness of the Sinai Peninsula. On Mount Sinai, Yahweh delivered his teaching (Torah) to Moses, and adopted the Israelites as his own people."*[58]

If we listen to the journey of Moses, who led his people out of slavery after being called by a God who saw the misery of his people heard their cry, and knew their suffering (Ex. 3:7), and if we start realizing that it is our story, we may begin to recognize those who are 'spit out' as truly and deeply 'bone of our bones and flesh of our flesh.' We will weep with them over their fate, we will want to see and understand their oppression, hear their cries, and know their suffering. We will stand side by side to ask them to be recognized, to fight for them, to seek justice for them. We will become aware of their naming of us and we can start to build a world in which both we and they have the companionship we crave, for the community that gives us life and the help and the care we all need.

This is probably what the Letter to the Hebrews calls "the city which has foundations, whose architect and builder is God" (Heb. 11:10), but we will not elaborate on that here. For now it suffices, we think, to give our attention to the stones, which the builders of the world as it is today, have rejected, be they Palestinians or Ethiopians. Indeed we are convinced that they are meant to be the cornerstones of our common future (cf. Ps. 118:22).

14

Home, Land, and Homeland As Social Values

George Rivera

In August 2013, the ARTNAUTS (an art collective from the United States) had an art exhibition entitled *Home/Land: Art Exhibition of Home, Land, and Homeland* at the International Center of Bethlehem in Palestine as part of Diyar's 7th International Conference at Dar-Annadwa, Bethlehem. Since the Conference focused on "Palestinian Identity in Relation to Time and Space," the collective decided to address the concepts of home, land and homeland as a theme for the exhibition. The central idea was to address these concepts from our point-of-view as residents of the United States and other countries outside Palestine. We hope that by sharing our views and presenting visual images, a better understanding of similarities and differences in the human condition might prevail.

The ARTNAUTS were founded in the mid-1990s and have been exhibiting art at the International Center of Bethlehem since 2004. The group consists of artists/professors who teach in university art departments throughout the United States and includes other art faculty who are from Mexico and South America. The ARTNAUTS are dedicated to exhibitions that stimulate a visual dialogue about common issues of social change with international others. In pursuit of this goal, the ARTNAUTS have had exhibitions in Brazil, Chile, China, Colombia, Guatemala, Mexico, Palestine, Peru, Russia, and Spain. In this exhibition thirty-four artists (and thirty-three pieces of art) are represented.[1]

All societies have a concept of home, land, and homeland. Artists treat these concepts under the rubric of "place." Robertson and McDaniel (2010) consider "place to be a major theme addressed by contemporary artists and maintain that:

> *"Where you hail from and where you now reside are two of the most significant facts about anyone. Place can be a central facet of someone's identity. The place or places where one has lived, with their attendant physical, historical, and cultural attributes, condition what one knows and how one sees."*[2]

The ways in which a society views home, land and homeland depends on how these concepts are valued. C. Wright Mills in his sociological classic, *The Sociological Imagination,* classified societies according to whether their values were cherished or not, and if there were perceived threats to these values. Thus, Mills theorized that societies experienced the following states: Well-being -- values are cherished and no threat to them exists; Crisis -- values are cherished and a threat to these values is present; Indifference --Values are not recognized, known, or cherished and no threat to them is perceived; and Anxiety -- values are not recognized, known, or cherished but a sense of threat is felt.[3]

Not all societies (i.e., social groups or individuals within a society) place the same value on these concepts. Everyday life involves multiple realities. One country's "crisis" can be perceived by another country with "indifference," "anxiety," or as not relating to them because they perceive themselves to be in a state of "well being." Usually there is consensus among countries on values that have world significance. In some situations, politics and power play a role in a particular country's deviation from world consensus.

Although most of the people living in the United States are of European ethnicity, there is a growing minority population of Hispanics, African Americans, Asian Americans and Native Americans. In addition, artists from other countries are included here because they are members of the ARTNAUTS. These differences are reflected in this exhibition because artists from all of these groups are represented. As a consequence, the values represented by each group reflect differences based on what each group member perceives to be threatened.

1. Land

Many people in the United States view the environment as an important value that is being threatened. Thus, some of the artists address environmental issues.

One artist who does this is Dj Lu who lives in Bogota, Colombia (**see Image 1**). Dj Lu is a street artist who uses a stencil technique to create artwork on the walls of buildings and other public places. The photograph he contributed to this exhibition is a wall mural addressing the current global addiction to fossil fuels. He references where coal, oil and gas came from, i.e., dead animals (including the wooly mammoth and the remains of dead plants) from millions of years ago. This work also contains images of oil wells, including the image of a man hanging from an oil well pump suggesting the consequences of our dependence on this fuel.

Other artists who focus on environmental issues are Warren (**see Image 2**), Brunvand (**see Image 3**), DiDomenico (**see Image 4**), and Roth (**see Image 5**). Warren includes a piece with two images: the top includes a darkened sky with torn pieces of sky and the bottom depicts a geological map of a terrain. Brunvand's art similarly consists of a window into two views of bare trees with four horizontal bands that appear to be fragile (made of paper or cloth) suggesting geological layers of time. DiDomenico presents a dry landscape with a broken umbrella suggesting the depletion of water supplies. In contrast, Roth presents a pristine scene of the Rocky Mountains in the state of Colorado interrupted by a hand-held photograph of a brochure advertising land development for home sales in the area.

Miranda (**see Image 6**) depicts two morphed disfigured beings surrounded by menacing objects in the air that they have inhaled, evidenced by the menacing objects seen within the bodies. Since Mexico City, where Miranda lives, is known for its air pollution, this piece suggests that the air we breathe is damaging our cellular structures and distorting our evolution.

2. Home

The importance of home as a place of residence is a value that frequently represents "well being" – a value that is highly cherished and is usually not perceived as being threatened. Artists who created work with an image of a house include Russo (**see Image 7**), Leisek (**see Image 8**) and C. Jackel (**see Image 9**).

Russo presents her home which includes photographs of her mother and other family members. Additional references to family and home include a diagram of their family tree, the dinner table and perhaps a favorite dish. All are memories that value home and family.

Another positive view of home is found in the work of Leisek who includes photographs of childhood memories, children in Halloween costumes, a favorite wooden toy, and other children playing. C. Jackel offers a photograph of a group of houses that are reflected on a shiny surface that appears to be water (a piece that she usually exhibits as a small paper-made sculptural work). The fragility of a home is evident here.

Other works with geographic and global references to home include Woo (**see Image 10**) and Mitchell (**see Image 11**). Woo entitles her work, "Traveler's Cup," which includes a luxury apartment building immersed in a glass of water, with a cup in a wooden box below it. A building crane is also evident in the background of the glass of water. Perhaps this work is suggesting nomadism and social and geographic mobility where the "new" replaces the historic in contemporary culture. Mitchell includes a living room chair with gold leaf wallpaper and a group of African children looking on as if waiting to be recognized and included in the room.

Tornatzky (**see Image 12**), Faris (**see Image 13**) and Dalton (**see Image 14**) present pieces that suggest that the values embedded in "home" are being threatened, and can be classified as "anxiety" in Mills' model. Tornatzky entitles her piece, "Home is where the heart is," and draws a heart surrounded on two sides by barbed wire with arrows pointing toward it as in war games. Faris drew an insect with the head of an elderly man slowly crawling toward a house. Both of these images are disturbing and do not depict "home" as a safe haven. In addition, Dalton's woodcut shows a woman at an amusement park, but there seems to be an undercurrent of uneasy apprehension in the face of the distracted subject. In the home series, del Carmen Vilchis (**see Image 15**) creates an altogether different image of "home." She views this concept as cosmological, or as a non-place as her title "Nothingness is home" suggests.

3. Homeland

Though the other concepts addressed in this exhibition refer to "home" and "land," the concept of "homeland" has the most resonance with Palestinian identity. Whether an artist views this value as being threatened depends on his/her point of view. Some see it as a wall or fence that dehumanizes cultural others and empathize with those who suffer such indignities.

In the United States there is an obsession with building a wall/fence along the United States-Mexico border to keep Mexican immigrants out of the United States. Though parts of this border fence have already been built in some areas of the southwestern United States, the U.S. plans to build a wall from the Gulf of Mexico on the Atlantic Ocean side in Texas to the Pacific Ocean in San Diego, California. These works reference the paranoia of some Americans who feel that their country (value of nationhood) is being threatened. For these individuals, a crisis results as they try to protect the U.S. from "foreign invaders." Works that allude to this issue are pieces by Carrejo (**see Image 16**), McMahan (**see Image 17**), Boord and Valdovino (**see Image 18**), and to a lesser degree by Thompson (**see Image 19**).

Carrejo's piece, entitled "Beyond Every Visa Lies Nothing," reveals a fence with a hole in it and a donkey hanging from a crane on the other side of the fence. Whatever barriers exist one can find a way to get to the other side though the other side may not be what it appears to be from a distance. McMahan's work also utilizes a barbed wire fence including it in the background with a robe and hood of the Klu Klux Klan (a vigilante White supremacy group who, along with the Minuteman, patrol the border) in the forefront, including stamps issued by the U.S. Government depicting values upheld by almost all Americans. These values include freedom, conservation, religion, and peace.

Boord and Valdovino exhibit a still image from a video that shows Mexican immigrants crossing the border between the United States and Mexico with one side of the border labeled "US" and the other side labeled "THEM." Thompson has a similar piece that declares "NO TRESPASSING KEEP OUT" as a sign warning others of private land.

Krensky (**see Image 20**) and Babcox (**see Image 21**) allude to the displacement and nomadic life of those who inhabit the land and are searching for a place to anchor their lives. Krensky's work includes an image of herself carrying a chair on her back through a sparse, dry territory to mountains in the distance. Babcox's work resembles quilts placed in a manner to cover or protect something; it also could be read as a "tent" for temporary housing. However, Babcox's title, "Cover the green heart," suggests that it could be an ecological land piece, which tries to cover the forest from further destruction such as deforestation or development.

Other artists in this exhibition addressed the issue of contested homeland and liberation from oppression. These are artists who directly or indirectly empathize with international others whose identity is being threatened by more powerful nations. Among these artists are B. Jackel (**see Image 22**), Caes (**see Image 23**), Rivera (**see Image 24**), Ortega (**see Image 25**), Rosete (**see Image 26**), and Dureese (**see Image 27**).

B. Jackel has a drawing that he made from researching maps of Palestine entitled "Plan of Partition" that was proposed by the Ad Hoc Committee On The Palestinian Question as noted in Map

No.103.1 (6) in February 1956, United Nations. This map is what was proposed for Palestine which includes the West Bank and Gaza with all Palestinian land being contiguous. Moreover, the city of Jerusalem is not noted as belonging to the Jewish state or the Arab state.

Ceas has a piece that references the biblical beginning of differences between Jews and Arabs. She sews passages from the Bible on her work. The threads that bind these biblical passages to the canvas are the colors of the Palestinian flag and the Israeli flag. These biblical references seem to refer to when God spoke to Abram on having a son, one born to Hagar (Sarai's slave) named Ishmael and another born to Sarai named Isaac. God promised both children and their descendants great nations. The Ishmaelites were to become Arab peoples residing in Arab territories with the descendants of Issac (and Jacob) becoming the physical and spiritual ancestors of Judaism.

In a piece by Rivera, the artist has two images, one placed on top of the other. The top contains the Palestinian flag with the black part of the flag made from the U.S.-Mexico border wall/fence as it fades in the distance. The bottom portion of the piece contains a photograph of the U.S. Border Wall in San Diego, California, with the separation wall extending into the Pacific Ocean. On the left side of the barrier is Mexico and on the right side is the United States. In an effort to show the common situation of Palestinians and Mexicans/Mexican Americans, Rivera entitled the piece, "Common Ground II."

Ortega presents a map of the United States with names of southwestern states replaced with other terms in English and Spanish. In particular, he renames Colorado and Montana, which respectively in Spanish are the words "red" and "mountain." On the other side of the border, Rosete (an artist residing in Mexico) repeats the Spanish word, "Patria," which translated into English means "country." However, her hands hold a bleeding Mexican flag. Mexico lost most of the land that Ortega labeled with words in his piece, and both artists refer to blood shed when land is lost.

In contrast, Dureese presents stereotypical images of Black people in a work entitled "Liberation." A Black girl holds a Haitian flag that references slaves in Haiti revolting against their French colonizers to obtain independence.

Fodness (**see Image 28**), Connelly (**see Image 29**), and Norambuena (**see Image 30**) created pieces that reference war and peace. Fodness has a camaflogued background with cartoonish figures grabbing and preparing to consume each other, which happens when "neighbors" make war and seize territory. Connelly has a piece entitled "Reconciling Fragments." Childhood toys are strewn on a beach, among other objects, with what appears as a target on the upper left hand corner. At the bottom of his work is a green line that might refer to the "Green Line" partitioning Palestine and the beaches of Gaza.

On a more positive note, Norambuena (an artist from Chile) includes text in Arabic and Hebrew along with Spanish words emphasizing "peace," sharing ancestral lands and stopping wars --an apt message in these troubled times in the world.

Gonzalez (**see Image 31**) has created a portrait drawing of a man that, by Western standards, appears to be dressed in foreign clothing. Martinez (**see Image 32**) presents a work entitled "HOME/LAND: 7 Steps Forward 7 Steps Back." This is a disturbing image of a skeleton with a furry animal on its head surrounded by psychedelic rays and pieces of paper with the word "mayonnaise" on them. In addition, Hongchang (**see Image 33**) offers an abstract piece on her Chinese background entitled "Empty Home in Heavy," and Wiggins (**see Image 34**) presents iconic American pop stars and other known political figures on a flag of the United States.

4. Conclusion

The ARTNAUTS brought an exhibition to Palestine to demonstrate that we wish to share our visualization of home, land and homeland as artists living in the Americas. As human beings, we have much in common. We hold many of the same values though we might define which values are being threatened differently.

Each time that members of ARTNAUTS visit Palestine, we witness injustice. After every visit, we return to our country and recount what we have seen and experienced in Palestine. We see injustice and we tell others in our country about it. Injustice is injustice. That much is clear.

We hope that sharing our visualization attests to the humanity in all of us. We create artwork that allows us to have a dialogue about what we have in common with Palestinians and the inhumanity that we witness in the human condition.

Biographies

Bader, Liana
Mrs. Liana Badr is a Palestinian author and film producer, born in Jerusalem and currently lives in Ramallah. Studied Philosophy and Psychology and got her MA degree in Contemporary Arabic Studies. Her writings were translated into many languages and she produced award- winning documentary films in international festivals. Among her novels: "a Compass for the Sunflower", "The Eye of the Mirror", "Jericho Stars" and "A Balcony over the Fakihani". She also has four collections of short stories, a book about the poet Fadwa Tuqan, and another book about the impact of place on the identity in the works of Mahmoud Darwish, in addition to two collections of poetic texts and ten children books.

Bechmann, Ulrike
(Germany/Austria) is since 2007 Professor for Religious Studies and Head of Religious Sciences Department at Graz University, Austria. Born in 1958 in Bamberg, Germany (Bavaria) she graduated in Catholic Theology at Otto-Friedrich-University, Bamberg. Prof. Bechmann holds an M.A in Arabic and Islamic Studies. Her post doctoral thesis was in Biblical Theology and Religious Studies on the figure of Abraham in interreligious dialogue at the University of Bayreuth, Germany. 2006 Prof. Bechmann received the Science Award for Inter-cultural Studies of Augsburg, for her thesis. From 1989 to 1999 she was the executive director and theological consultant of the "German Committee of Women's World Day of Prayer".

Borgman, Erik
Prof. Erik Borgman is a professor for Public Theology at the Tilburg School of Humanities, Tilburg University. He is endowed with the

Cobbenhagen Chair which aims to publicly present and promote the Christian and Catholic traditions as contributions to public discourse. He is a director of the valorization-project: Understanding Society-Religion and values. Previously he worked at the Heyendaal Institute for theology, science and culture at Radboud University, Nijmegen. Prof. Borgman is a specialist in Liberation Theology and the theology of Edward Schillebeeckx. He is a member of the Board of Editors of the international theological journal *Concilium*.

Callendar, Dexter
Dexter E. Callender, Jr. is Associate Professor of Religious Studies at the University of Miami, Miami, FL. He is also Associate Professor Extraordinary, Faculty of Theology, North-West University, Potchefstroom, South Africa. He earned his PhD from Harvard University and is the author of *Adam in Myth and History* (Harvard Semitic Studies, Eisenbrauns, 2001) and *Did the Israelites Believe in their Myths?* (forthcoming, Bloomsbury). With research interests in myth theory, political theology, and race and religion, he is a specialist in Hebrew Bible and the history and literature of the ancient Near East. He regularly teaches on the prophets, myth, religion and culture and was a recipient of the 2000 Provost's Excellence in Teaching Award and also was named "Professor of the Year" by the University of Miami Pan-Hellenic Association in 2001.

Fernandez, Eleazar
Prof. Eleazar S. Fernandez is Professor of Constructive Theology at United Theological Seminary of the Twin Cities, New Brighton, Minnesota. He also has experienced teaching in other parts of the world, such as Philippines, Myanmar, and Cameroon. Among his writings are Burning Center, Porous Borders: The Church in a Globalized World (2011), New Overtures: Asian North American Theology in the 21st Century (editor, 2012), Reimagining the Human: Theological Anthropology in Response to Systemic Evil (2004), Realizing the

America of our Hearts: Theological Voices of Asian Americans (co-edited with Fumitaka Matsuoka, 2003), A Dream Unfinished: Theological Reflections on America from the Margins (co-edited with Fernando Segovia, 2001), and Toward a Theology of Struggle (1994).

Fuchs, Ottmar
Prof. Dr. Ottmar Fuchs was Born in 1945, studied Philosophy and Theology in Bamberg and Würzburg. Ordination 1972 (Priest of the Archdiocese of Bamberg, He earned his Ph.D in Theology in 1977. From 1981-1998: Prof. (Chair: Pastoral Theology and Kerygmatics) at the Cath.-Theol. Faculty in the University of Bamberg. Since 1998 Prof. (Chair: Practical Theology) at the Cath.-Theol. His main researches tackle the Fundamental questions between Practical Theology and Human science; Religion and solidarity; Theology of diaconical institutions; Theology and church in front of the challenges of Modernism, Postmodernism and Pluralisation of life; Theology of the Second Vatican Council; Pastoral responsibility in the horizon of eschatology; Constitutive interdisciplinary relations between practical theology and biblical responsibility.

Jubeh, Nazmi
Dr. Nazmi Jubeh, was born in Jerusalem, 1955. He was the Co-Director of Riwaq, Centre for Architectural Conservation. Currently, the Chairperson of the Department of History, Birzeit University and lecturer at al-Quds University. Jubeh's research melds archeology, history, politics and architecture. He completed initial studies in Middle Eastern Studies and archaeologies at Birzeit University and received both a Masters degree in oriental studies and archeology and a PhD in archeology and history from the University of Tubingen in Germany. From 1991 to 1993 he was a member of the Palestinian delegation to the Bilateral Peace Negotiations in Washington DC. Jubeh is well known for his expertise on Jerusalem in general and the holy sites in particular. Jubeh currently serves on the board

of trustees of several cultural institutions in Jerusalem. He published several books and a large number of articles on history, archaeology, politics and architecture."

Musallam, Adnan
Dr. Adnan Ayyoub Musallam got his BA and Masters degrees from Indiana University Bloomington. He got his PhD from the University of Michigan- Anne Arbor. He has been working at Bethlehem University since 1981.He is an associate professor and lecturer in history and cultural studies in the humanities department at the university. He was the chairman of the humanitarian department in (1984-1990, 1996-1999, 2005-2009). He was the dean of the Arts College (1996-1999), and the chairman of the university employees union (1993-1996). He wrote several books and articles in Arabic and English that were published in Jerusalem, Bethlehem, the USA and Germany. He is an active member in several centers including Al-Liqa' Centre for Religious and Heritage Studies in the Holy Land, in Bethlehem/Jerusalem, as well as The Applied Research Centre in Jerusalem-Areej.

Raheb, Mitri
Dr. Mitri Raheb is the President of Diyar Consortium and of Dar al-Kalima University College in Bethlehem, as well as the president of the Synod of the Evangelical Lutheran Church in Jordan and the Holy Land in addition to being the Senior Pastor of the Evangelical Lutheran Christmas Church in Bethlehem, Palestine. The most widely published Palestinian theologian to date, Dr. Raheb is the author of 16 books including: I am a Palestinian Christian; Bethlehem Besieged. He is the Chief Editor of the Contextual Theology Series at Diyar. His books and numerous articles have been translated so far into 11 languages. The 50 year-old multilingual contextual theologian, received the prestigious Wittenberg Award from the Luther Center in DC (2003), an honorary doctorate from Concordia University in Chicago (2003), For and for his 'interfaith work toward

peacemaking in Israel and Palestine he received' the "International Mohammad Nafi Tschelebi Peace Award" of the Central Islam Archive in Germany (2006) and in 2007 the well-known German Peace Award of Aachen. In 2012 the German Media Prize, a Prize granted mainly to head of states, was awarded to Dr. Raheb for his "tireless work in creating room for hope for his people, who are living under Israeli Occupation, through founding and building institutions of excellence in education, culture and health."

Rivera, George

Dr. George Rivera attained his doctorate degree from the State University of New York at Buffalo. Dr. Rivera is presently a professor in the Department of Art & Art History at the University of Colorado at Boulder. He received the Governor's Award for Excellence in the Arts from the State of Colorado and is a Fulbright Scholar. Dr. Rivera has published articles in national and international journals and has had exhibitions in Brazil, Bulgaria, Canada, Chile, China, Colombia, Germany, Guatemala, Mexico, Palestine, Peru, Russia, Spain, and throughout the United States. In addition to being an artist, Professor Rivera is an art critic and a curator. In 1964 Dr. Rivera organized an art collective known as the ARTNAUTS, and the collective has had exhibitions at the International Center of Bethlehem since 2004.

Shomali, Qustandi

Prof. Dr. Qustandi Shomali is Full Professor at Bethlehem University, he teaches Palestinian literature, Journalism and Translation. With degrees from universities in Algeria, Canada and the Sorbonne in France, he possesses a wide range of personal and academic interests that include history, literature and arts. He published many books including a series of academic studies about the Palestinian Press (1990-96), Literary and Critical Trends in Modern Palestinian Literature (Jerusalem 1990) and The Nativity in Bethlehem and Umbria (Perugia, 2000). He published also many research papers in

Comparative Literature, Communication & Information in Arabic, French and English.

Smith, Robert
Rev. Robert O. Smith, PhD, is a pastor in the Evangelical Lutheran Church in America. He recieved his PhD in Religion, Politics and Society from Baylor University in 2010. He received both the Masters of Divinity and MA in Islamic Studies in 2003 from Luther Seminary in St Paul, Minn. Currently, he serves as Special Adviser to the President of the Lutheran World Federation (Bishop Munib A. Younan). He is a Co-Moderator of the Palestine-Israel Ecumenical Forum of the World Council of Churches.He has published *More Desired than Our Owne Salvation: The Roots of Christian Zionism* (Oxford, 2013), and *Christians and a Land Called Holy: How We Can Foster Peace, Justice and Hope* (Fortress, 2006, with Charles P. Lutz).

Staubli, Thomas
Thomas Staubli (*1962) studied Theology, Religious Science, Egyptology and Assyriology in Fribourg, Jerusalem, Berlin and Bern and received a Ph.D. from the University of Fribourg, where he established the BIBLE+ORIENT Museum whose first director he was until 2012. The services of the museum include among others an online-database (www.bible-orient-museum.ch/bodo) with actually more than 25'000 Objects open to public. He teaches Old Testament studies at the University of Fribourg (Switzerland). His areas of expertise include: Iconography and Religious History of the Levant, Biblical Realia and Anthropology, Palestinian Ethnography, Didactics of the Bible. He wrote many popular scientific books. Available in English: Body Symbolism in the Bible (written together with Silvia Schroer.

Stegeman, Janneke

Janneke Stegeman is a theologian and researcher on the Old Testament, conflict and identity and VU University, Amsterdam. Her interest is in the interaction between conflict and religious identity. She will finish her dissertation on Jeremiah 32 early 2014. She spent two years living in Jerusalem doing research for her PhD and felt very much drawn towards and inspired by initiatives of non-violent resistance against the occupation. She is involved with the Dutch Kairos committee and board member of the Dutch Friends of Sabeel.

Van-Reisen, Mirjam

In October 2010, Prof. Mirjam van Reisen was appointed the Endowed Chair in honor of Marga Klomp on International Social Responsibility at Tilburg University, School of Humanities. Prof. Mirjam van Reisen is the founding director of Europe External Policy Advisors (EEPA), a research center of expertise on European Union external policy based in Brussels. In addition, she is also a Member the Supervisory Board of SNV, serves on the board of the Transnational Institute (TNI), has been an elected member of the International Coordinating Committee of Social Watch and has accumulated 20 years experience working both in and alongside European Commission institutions. She received the Golden Image Award by HE President Ellen Johnson Sirleaf from Liberia for support to women in peace-building in 2012.

Endnotes:

1. The Palestinian Identity:

1. In this intervention, identity does not dilute identities.
2. Brug, John Frederick. *A Literary and Archaeological Study of Philistines.* In British Archeological Reports International Series 265, Oxford, 1985; Derger-Jalkotzy, Sigrid. *Griechenland, die Aegaeis, und Levante waehrend der "Dark Ages".* Vienna: Austrian Academy of sciences press, 1983, 99-120.
3. Berlin, Andrea M.. *Between Large Forces: Palestine in the Hellenistic Period..* In Biblical Archeologist 60.1, Boston: American Schools of Oriental Research, 1997, 2-51.
4. Wilkinson, John. *The Streets of Jerusalem.* In Levant 7, London: Maney Publishing, 1975, 118-136.
5. Hirschfeld, Yizhar. *The Palestinian Dwelling in the Roman-Byzantine Period.* Jerusalem: Israel Exploration Society/Fransiscan Press, 1995.
6. Shahid, Irfan. *Rome and the Arabs: A Prolegomenon to the Study of Byzantium and the Arabs.* Washington, D.C.: Dumbarton Oaks Research Library and Collections, 1984, 22 ff.
7. Beebe, H. Keith. *Ancient Palestinian Dwellings.* In Biblical Archeologist 31, Boston: American Schools of Oriental Research, 1968, 38-58; Beebe, H. Keith. *Domestic Architecture and the New Testament.* In Biblical Archeologist 38, Boston: American Schools of Oriental Research, 1975, 89-104.
8. Al-Muqaddasi, Muhammad Ibn-Ahmad. *Ahsan al-Taqsim fi Ma'rifat al-Aqlim.* Leiden: Leiden University Press, 1904.
9. For further details on this subject and discussion, see: Athamina, Khalil. *Filistin fi khamsat qurun.* Beirut: Beirut Institute for Palestine Studies, 2000, 212 ff.
10. Peters, Francis Edwards. *The Arabs on the Frontier of Syria before Islam.* In Proceedings of the First International Conference on Bilad al-Sham, 20-25 April 1974, Amman: University of Jordan, 1984, 141-173.
11. Manna', Adel. *Tarikh Filistin fi awakhir al-'ahd al-'uthmani.* Beirut: Institute of Palestine Studies, 2003, 47ff.
12. Manna', Adel. *Tarikh Filistin fi awakhir al-'ahd al-'uthmani.* Beirut: Institute of Palestine Studies, 2003, 26-37.

Endnotes

13. Khalidi, Rashid. *Palestinian Identity: The Construction of Modern National Consciousness.* New York: Columbia University Press, 1977, 89ff.
14. It is worth noting the government of Common Palestine in Gaza after 1948, which was a total failure.
15. In the 1960s some Palestinian national movements declared the idea of establishing a democratic state in Palestine for both Palestinians and Jews; this actually was the same idea of the representative of Palestine in the negotiations that took place before the Partition Plan of 1947.
16. Khalidi, Walid. *All That Remains: The Palestinian Villages Occupied and Depopulated by Israel in 1948.* Beirut: Institute for Palestine Studies, 1992. A monograph to document the destroyed villages. Other initiatives were taken by the refugees documenting their own villages. This wave began in the early 1990s reaching its peak in 1998 celebrating fifty years of Nakba and has continued up to the present.
17. The Arabic word 'ardi' (my land) has two meaning: my private land (property) or my homeland.
18. It is not intended here to undermine the importance of this long research, which is not the center of this discussion, rather the relationship between Western researchers and the development of the local Palestinian population and how much this effort helped them in developing their attachment to their cultural heritage.
19. Burgoyne, Michael. Mamluk Jerusalem: An architectural Study. London: World of Islam Festival Trust, 1987; Auld, Sylvia/Hillenbrand, Robert. Ottoman Jerusalem: an introduction. London: Altajir World of Islam Trust, 2000; Pringle, Denys. *Some Approaches to Study of Crusaders Masonry Makers in Palestine.* Levant 13, London: Maney Publishing, 1981, 173-199.
20. Ongoing renovation programs were conducted in/around major holy sites from the beginning of the twentieth century and a tremendous number of publications appeared.
21. Wilson, Charles Thomas. *Peasant Life in the Holy Land.* New York: Dutton and Company, 1906.
22. Dalman, Gutav. *Arbeit in Sitte in Palestina.* Gütersloh: Bertelsmann, 1928.
23. Canaan, Tawfiq. Palestinian *Arab House: Its Architecture and Folklore.* Jerusalem: The Syrian Orphanage Press, 1933.
24. Fuchs, Aharon Ron. *Palestinian Vernacular Architecture – the Ottoman Connection.* In: British Institute of Archaeology at Ankara Monograph 26, Warwick: University of Warwick, 1998; Kanáan, R. Patronage and Style in Mercantile Residential Architecture of Ottoman Bilad al-Sham: The Nablus

Region in the Nineteenth Century. Thesis Submitted in Partial Fulfillment of the Master Philosophy Degree of Oriental Studies. Oxford: Oxford University, 199; Khasawneh, Diala. *Palestinian Urban Mansions: Memoirs engraved in Stone.* Ramallah: Riwaq Center for Architectural Conversation, 2001; Amiry, Suad. *The Architecture of the Throne Villages.* Ramallah, Riwaq Center for Architectural Conversation, 2003.

25. Smith, George Adam. *The Historical Geography of the Holy Land. Especially in Relations to the History of Israel and of the Early Church.* New York: Armstrong and Son, 1902; Robinson, Edward. *Biblical Researches in Palestine.* Boston: Crocker & Brewster, 1841; Robinson, Edward. *Later Biblical Researches in Palestine and in the adjacent regions.* Boston: Crocker & Brewster, 1856.

2. Identity, Belonging, and Home (Land)

1. Gohar, Saddik M. *Narratives of Diaspora and Exile in Arabic and Palestinian Poetry*. In Rupkatha Journal on Interdisciplinary Studies in Humanities, 3.2, India: Kolkata, 240.
2. Sedmak, Clemens. *Doing Local Theology: A Guide for Artisans of a New Humanity*. New York: Orbis Books, 2002, 47.
3. Foucault, Michel. *The Foucault Reader*. New York: Pantheon Books, 1984, 51-57.
4. Lorde, Audre. *Sister Outsider: Essays and Speeches*. California: The Crossing Press, 1984, 115.
5. Khalidi, Rashid. *Palestinian Identity: The Construction of Modern National Consciousness*. New York: Columbia University Press, 1997, 146-147.
6. Abdel-Malek, Kamal/Jacobson, David C. *Israeli and Palestinian Identities in History and Literature*. New York: Saint Martin Press, 1999, 163.
7. Gohar, Saddik M. *Narratives of Diaspora and Exile in Arabic and Palestinian Poetry*. In Rupkatha Journal on Interdisciplinary Studies in Humanities, 3.2, India: Kolkata, 233.
8. Saracino, Michele. *Being about Borders: Christian Anthropology of Difference*. Minnesota: Liturgical Press, 2011, 106.
9. Al-Udhari, Abdullah. *Modern Poetry of the Arab World*. New York: Penguin Books, 1986, 136.
10. Abdel-Malek, Kamal/Jacobson, David C. *Israeli and Palestinian Identities in History and Literature*. New York: Saint Martin Press, 1999, 189; Gohar, Saddik M. *Narratives of Diaspora and Exile in Arabic and Palestinian Poetry*. In Rupkatha Journal on Interdisciplinary Studies in Humanities, 3.2, India: Kolkata, 230.
11. Gohar, Saddik M. *Narratives of Diaspora and Exile in Arabic and Palestinian Poetry*. In Rupkatha Journal on Interdisciplinary Studies in Humanities, 3.2, India: Kolkata, 230.
12. Said, Edward. *The Question of Palestine*. New York: Vintage Books, 1979.
13. Saloul, Ihab. *'Performative Narrativity': Palestinian Identity and the Performance of Catastrophe*. In Cultural Analysis 7, Middletown: The Pennsylvania State University, 2008, 5.

14. Ibid.
15. Edward Said. *Reflections on Exile and Other Literary and Cultural Essays*. London: Harward University Press, 2000, 173.
16. Mahmud Darwish. *Who Am I, without Exile?* In *The Butterfly's Burden*. Port Townsend: Copper Canyon Press, 2007.
17. Palestine-Israel Journal, Vol. 12, No. 2/3, Jerusalem: Palestine-Israel-Journal, 2005, 4.
18. Gohar, Saddik M. *Narratives of Diaspora and Exile in Arabic and Palestinian Poetry*. In Rupkatha Journal on Interdisciplinary Studies in Humanities, 3.2, India: Kolkata, 239.
19. Ibid., 240.
20. Abdel-Malek, Kamal/Jacobson, David C. *Israeli and Palestinian Identities in History and Literature*. New York: Saint Martin Press, 1999, 183.
21. Lindholm Schulz, Helena/Hammer, Juliane. *The Palestinian Diaspora: Formation of Identities and Politics of Homeland*. London: Routledge, 2013.
22. Emphasis supplied.
23. Abdel-Malek, Kamal/Jacobson, David C. *Israeli and Palestinian Identities in History and Literature*. New York: Saint Martin Press, 1999, 184.
24. Mahmud Darwish. *Who Am I, without Exile?* In *The Butterfly's Burden*. Port Townsend: Copper Canyon Press, 2007.
25. Yoder, Carolyn. *The Little Book of Trauma Healing: When Violence Strikes and Community Security is Threatened*. Pennsylvania: Good Books, 2005, 30.
26. Gopin, Mark. *The Heart of the Stranger*. In *Explorations in Reconciliation: New Directions in Theology*, England: Ashgate, 2006, 17.
27. Radford Ruether, Rosemary/Ruether, Herman J. *The Wrath of Jonah: The Crisis of Religious Nationalism in the Israeli-Palestinian Conflict*. Minneapolis: Fortress Press, 2002, 215.
28. Rose, Gilian. *The Broken Middle: Out of Our Ancient Society*. Oxford: Blackwell, 1992.
29. Saracino, Michele. *Being about Borders: Christian Anthropology of Difference*. Minnesota: Liturgical Press, 2011, 109.

3. Palestinian Identity in Relation to Time and Space:

1. Khalidi, Walid. *From Haven to Conquest: Readings in Zionism and the Palestine Problem.* Washington, D.C.: Institute for Palestine Studies, 1987.
2. Musallam, Adnan. *Nationalism and Religion. An Historical Overview.* In *Nationalism today: Problems and Challenges, Acts of Muslim – Christian Colloquium.* Organized by the Pontifical Council for Interreligious Dialogue and the Royal Academy for Islamic Civilization Research, Amman: Al-Bait Foundation, 1994, 27 – 44.
3. Banko, Lauren E. *The Legislative Creation of Palestinian Citizenship: Discourse in the Early Mandate Period.* In *International Journal for Arab Studies*, Vol. 2, No. 2, Exter: Institute of Arab and Islamic Studies, 2011, 2; 5; 6; 21; Banko, Lauren E. *The Creation of Palestinian Citizenship under an international mandate: Legislation, discourses and practices, 1918 – 1925.* In *Citizenship Studies*, Vol. 16, No. 5/6, London: Routledge, 2012, 641 – 655.
4. Hussein, Hammad. *Collection of Documents, 1909 – 1939.* Jenin: Palestinian Centre for Culture and Mass Media, 2003.
5. Preparatory Committee for the Defence of the Rights of Arab Emigrants to Palestinian Citizenship. *An Appeal to the Noble British People.* Jerusalem, 1928; Musallam, Adnan. *Folded Pages from Local Palestinian History: Developments in Political, Society, Press and Thought in Bethlehem in the British Era 1917 – 1948.* Bethlehem: Wi'am Palestinian Conflict Resolution Center, 2002, 57 – 66.
6. Palestine Royal Commission Report 5479, London: Her Majesty's Stationery Office, 1937.
7. Preparatory Committee for the Defence of the Rights of Arab Emigrants to Palestinian Citizenship. *An Appeal to the Noble British People.* Jerusalem, 1928; Musallam, Adnan. *Folded Pages from Local Palestinian History: Developments in Political, Society, Press and Thought in Bethlehem in the British Era 1917 – 1948.* Bethlehem: Wi'am Palestinian Conflict Resolution Center, 2002, 57 – 66.
8. Letter from 'Isa Khuri Bandak, dated September 15, 1971
9. For an investigation of the disturbances: Palestine Royal Commission Report 3530. *Report of Commission on the Palestine Disturbances of August 1929.* Presented by the Secretary of State for the Colonies to Parliament by Command of His majesty, London: Her Majesty's Stationery Office, 1930, 90; 192.
10. See for example the issue of Sawt ash-Sha'b, September 3, 1930 for details on Bandak's visit to Mexico

11. Sawt ash-Sha'b, Sana 14, No. 897, 1935. 3; Sawt ash-Sha'b, issues of June, September and October, 1935
12. Ibid., No 893, May 11, 1935, 3; ibid., No. 918, November 2, 1935.
13. Sawt ash-Sha'b, Sana 15, No. 947, July 25, 1936.
14. Sawt ash-Sha'b, Sana 16, No. 982, April 18, 1937.
15. Musallam, 'Adnan. *'Isa Baseel Bandak: His Life... His Works... His Memoires, 1898 – 1984*. Bethlehem: Diyar Publishers, August 2013, 46.
16. Baladiyyat, Sijjil Oararat. Bayta Lahm, Record of Bethlehem's municipal decisions for the years 1938 through 1946. All Bethlehem's municipal records preceding September 14, 1938 were destroyed by the September 13, 1938 fire, according to the Sijjil... for 1938; and Letter from 'Isa Bandak dated August 15, 1972 and conversation with Yusuf's sister, Mrs. Suad George Aburdenah, in Bethlehem on August 9, 1972 to the present
17. Musallam, 'Adnan. *'Isa Baseel Bandak: His Life... His Works... His Memoires, 1898 – 1984*. Bethlehem: Diyar Publishers, August 2013, 91-94.
18. *Under our Spotlight: American Civilization.* In Sawt ash-Sha'b, No. 4, December 21, 1947, 1.
19. Letter from 'Isa Bandak, dated September 15, 1971.
20. Mayor of Bethlehem concerning the situation of the refugees and the poor of Bethlehem. Report No. 30, 1948; Musallam, 'Adnan. *'Isa Baseel Bandak: His Life... His Works... His Memoires, 1898 – 1984*. Bethlehem: Diyar Publishers, August 2013, 154.

Endnotes 247

4. Palestinian Identity in the Diaspora:

1. The origin of the word 'Diaspora' comes from the Greek verb Speiro, meaning 'to sow', and dia, meaning 'over', suggesting networks of real or imagined relationships between scattered peoples, whose sense of community is maintained by transnational communication.
2. Bandaly Saliba Jawzi was born in Bethlehem on July 2, 1871. Orphaned in childhood, he was schooled in Greek Orthodox monasteries in Jerusalem and Lebanon. In 1891, he moved to Moscow, where he pursued his theological studies at the Theological Academy. He later transferred to Qazan, where he taught Arabic while continuing his education. After a short visit to Palestine in 1900, he returned to Qazan, married a Russian woman, and lectured at the University until 1920, when he joined the faculty of the University of Azerbaijan. It was during a sojourn in the Middle East that he wrote his major work. He died in Baku in 1942.
3. Sonn, Tamara. *Interpreting Islam: Bandaly Jawzi's Islamic Intellectual History.* Oxford/New York: Oxford University Press, 1996.
4. Jawzi, Bandali. *The History of Intellectual Movements in Islam.* Oxford: Oxford University Press, 1966, 44.
5. Khalil Sakakini was born into an Arab Christina family in Jerusalem on January 23, 1878. He received his schooling in Jerusalem at the Greek Orthodox School, at the Anglican Christian Mission Society (CMS) College, and at the Zion English College where he read Literature. Later, Sakakini travelled to the United Kingdom and from there to the United States to join his brother, Yusif, a travelling salesman in Philadelphia. During his nine-month stay in America, he translated and wrote for Arabic literary magazines on the East Coast, and did translations for Professor Richard Gottheil at Columbia University. He supported himself by teaching Arabic. He also worked as a street vendor. Upon his return to Palestine in 1908, he worked as a journalist for the Jerusalem newspaper al-Asmai', taught Arabic at the Salahiyya School and tutored expatriates at the American Colony.
6. Sakakini, Khalil. *The Diaries of Khalil Sakakini: Diaries, Letters, Reflections.* Ramallah: Institute of Jerusalem Studies & Khalil Sakakini Cultural Centre, 2006.
7. Segev, Tom. *One Palestine, Complete: Jews and Arabs under the British Mandate.* New York: Metropolitan Books, 2000.
8. Shomali, Qustandi. *As-Sihafa al-'arabiyya fi Filastin.* Jérusalem: Jam'yatad-Dirasat al-Arabyyah, 1990.

9. Shomali, Qustandi. *Al-Ittijahat al-Adabyyat wan-Naqdiyyah fi al-Adab al-Filastini.* Jérusalem: Dar al-Awdah, 1990.
10. Hanafi, Sari. *Here and There:* The Palestinian Diaspora from Social and Political Perspective. Ramallah: Muwatin and Beirut: Institute of Palestinian Study, 2003, 320.
11. Kodmani, Bassma. *La diaspora palestinienne.* Paris: Presses Universitaires de France, 1997, 264.
12. Greimas, Algirdas Julien. *Sémantique Structurale.* Paris, Librairie Larousse, 1966.

5. The Impact of Place on Identity in the Works of Mahmoud Darwish:

1. Shalhat, Antoine. Paper delivered at a Seminar held at Al Aswar, Acre, on Palestinian national culture, on the 60th anniversary of the Nakba.
2. Ibid.
3. Shalhat, Antoine. *On Top of a Volcano.* Palestine: Ministry of Arts, 1996, 50.
4. Ibid.
5. Ibid.
6. Darwish, Ahmad. *Cold June in AlBarweh, AlJdaideh.* Palestine: Abdul-Rahman Hijjawi and Sons Printing Company , 2006, 66.
7. Wazen, Abdo/Darwish, Mahmoud. *The Stranger Falls upon Himself.* Beirut/London: Riad El Rayes, 2009, 137.
8. Darwish, Mahmoud, *We Shall Be As We Want: Dialogue with Abbas Baidoon.* In Al Safir Daily, Beirut: Dar Al Safir, 2009.
9. Radwan, Abdallah/Darwish, Mahmoud. *The Stage of Maturity and Excelllence.* Amman: Arab institute for Studies and Publishing, 1998, 8.
10. Darwish, Mahmoud/El Qassem, Semeeh. *Letters.* Haifa: Arabesque Publishing House, 1990, 36.
11. Al Imam, Ghada/Blaschar, Gaston. *Aesthetics of a Picture.* Beirut: Dar El Tanweer, 2010, 296.
12. Darwish, Mahmoud. *TheNew Works.* London: Dar El Rayes, 2004, 285.
13. Wazen, Abdo/Darwish, Mahmoud. *The Stranger Falls upon Himself.* Beirut/London: Riad El Rayes, 2009, 123.

6. Biblical Narrative and Palestinian Identity in Mahmoud Darwish's Writings

1. The Complete Poems: The Mahmoud Darwish Anthology vol. 1-2, From "Bed of a Stranger" (1996-1997): "I Waited for No One"
2. Recorded poem: "In Praise of the High Shadow" (1983)
3. From "Bed of a Stranger (1996-1997): "I Waited for No One"
4. From "Fewer Roses" (1986): "Oh my father, I am Yusuf"
5. From "Why did you Leave the Horse Alone": "The Eternity of Cactus"
6. From "Why did you Leave the Horse Alone": "Strangers' Walk"
7. From "Why did you Leave the Horse Alone": "How Many Times Will it be Over"
8. Jidariyya "Mural" (1999)
9. From "Eleven Planets" (1992): "The Speech of the Red Indian"
10. Jidariyya "Mural" (1999); "In Praise of the High Shadow"
11. Jidariyya "Mural" (1999); "Why did you Leave the Horse Alone"; "The Raven's Ink"
12. "Almond Blossoms and Beyond"
13. From "End of the Night" (1967): "A Woman from Sodom"
14. Jidariyya "Mural" (1999)
15. From "Lover from Palestine" (1966): "Waiting for the returning refugees"
16. Recorded poem: "In Praise of the High Shadow" (1983)
17. From "Lover from Palestine" (1966): "Anthem"
18. "Almond Blossoms and Beyond"; "Mural"
19. From "Why did you Leave the Horse Alone": "The Eternity of Cactus"
20. From "Fewer Roses": "God, Why Have you Forsaken Me?"
21. Jidariyya "Mural" (1999)
22. From "End of the Night" (1967): "Naïve Song on the Red Cross"; and from "Leaves of Olives" (1964) including: "To the Reader", "Allegiance", "On Man", "On Steadfastness", "*Rubaiyyat*"
23. mahmouddarwish.com/Arabic.live.htm
24. From "Leaves of Olives" (1964): "On Man"; and from "Mahmoud Darwish. Translation source: "Mahmoud Darwish: Poet, author and politician who helped to forge a Palestinian consciousness after the six-day war in 1967" by

Endnotes 251

Peter Clark. Published at the Guardian; 11 August 2008. Anthology vol. 1-2". Translation Source: Lyrics to Sabreen's "On Man" [online]

25. From "The Singer Said". Translation source from Khaled Mattawa's, "When the Poet is a Stranger", 2009
26. Recorded poem: "In Praise of the High Shadow" (1983)
27. Recorded poem: "In Praise of the High Shadow" (1983)
28. Recorded poem: "In Praise of the High Shadow" (1983)
29. Recorded poem: "In Praise of the High Shadow" (1983)
30. Recorded poem: "In Praise of the High Shadow" (1983)
31. Recorded poem: "In Praise of the High Shadow" (1983)
32. From "Fewer Roses" (1986): "Oh my father, I am Yusuf". Translated from the Arabic by Fady Joudah
33. From "Fewer Roses" (1986): "God, Why Have you Forsaken Me?"
34. From "Fewer Roses" (1986): "The Last Supper Lingers"
35. From "Fewer Roses" (1986): "They'd Love to See Me Dead"
36. From "Fewer Roses" (1986): "We have on this earth what makes life worth living"
37. From "Why did you Leave the Horse Alone": "The Raven's Ink"
38. From "Why did you Leave the Horse Alone": "Abel's Space"/"Isamel's *Oud*"
39. Jidariyya "Mural" (1999)
40. Jidariyya "Mural" (1999)
41. Jidariyya "Mural" (1999). Translated from the Arabic by Rema Hammami and John Berger (Mural: pp46-48)
42. Jidariyya "Mural" (1999). Translated from the Arabic by Rema Hammami and John Berger (Mural: p54)
43. From "Almond Blossoms and Beyond": "A Wedding Over There". Translated from the Arabic by Mohammad Shaheen
44. From "Almond Blossoms and Beyond": "Exile (2)"
45. From "Almond Blossoms and Beyond": "Exile (3)"
46. From "Almond Blossoms and Beyond": "Exile (4)". Translated from the Arabic by Mohammad Shaheen

7. Holy Places and the Formation of Identity

1. Bechmann, Ulrike. *Gestörte Grabesruhe. Idealität und Realität des interreligiösen Dialogs am Beispiel von Hebron / al-Khalil.* In Kleine Texte 24, Berlin: AphorismA, 2007.
2. Assmann, Jan. *Das kulturelles Gedächtnis: Schrift, Erinnerung und politische Identität in frühen Hochkulturen.* München: C.H. Beck, 1999; Assmann, Aleida. *Das Gedächtnis der Orte.* In: Borsdorf, Ulrich, Orte der Erinnerung.Denkmal, Gedenkstätte, Museum. Frankfurt am Main: Campus Verlag, 1999,59–77.
3. Cf. the concept of a „Holy Land": Bieberstein, Klaus. *Zum Raum wird hier die Zeit. Drei Erinnerungslandschaften Jerusalems.* In: Jahrbuch für biblischeTheologie 22, Neukirchen-Vlyn: Neukirchener Verlag, 2007, 3–39.
4. The concept of "Vertical Ecumenism" was developed by Othmar Keel and Thomas Staubli. Staubli, Thomas. *Vertikale Ökumene. Erinnerungsarbeit im Dienst des interreligiösen Dialogs*, Fribourg: Academic Press Fribourg, 2005.
5. Busse, Heribert. *Der Islam und die biblischen Kultstätten.* In: Islam 42, Berlin: De Gruyter, 1966, 113-147.
6. The Arab name *al-khalīl* ("the friend") is related to Qur'an, in Sura 4,125 *Ibrāhīm* is the only person who is called "friend of God." The mosque first was called "Mosque of Ibrahim", later *masdjid al-khalīl*, „mosque of the friend (of God)" and finally the town was called after the mosque. cf. Nagel, Tilman. *Abraham, der Gottesfreund. Deutungen muslimischer Korankommentatoren.* In: Kratz, Reinhard/Nagel, Tilman, *Abraham, unser Vater. Die gemeinsamen Wurzeln von Judentum, Christentum und Islam*, Göttingen: Wallstein, 2003, 150–164; Al-Jubeh, Nazmi. Hebron (al-Halīl): Kontinuität und Integrationskraft einer islamisch-arabischen Stadt. Tübingen: Eberhard-Karls Universität Tübingen, 1991, 4-6.
7. Foucault, Michel. *Dispositive der Macht: Über Sexualität, Wissen und Wahrheit.* Berlin: Merve-Verlag, 1978.
8. Gutting, Gary. *Michel Foucault.* In: Stanford Encyclopaedia of Philosophy. August 2013. http://plato.stanford.edu/entries/foucault/.
9. Jericke, Detlef. *Abraham in Mamre. Historische und exegetische Studien zur Region von Hebron und zu Genesis* 11,27-19,38. In: Culture and History of the Ancient Near East 17, Leiden: Brill Academic Pub, 2003, denies that combination. But even if there is no clear archaeological evidence does not seem possible to have such a place without a veneration of a goddess or god.
10. Keel, Othmar/Küchler, Max. *Orte und Landschaften der Bibel. Ein Handbuch und Studienreiseführer zum Heiligen Land,* Vol. 2, Zürich: Vandenhoeck &

Ruprecht, 1982–1984, 696-713. The cult of stones, wells or trees are rooted in the tradition of Arabia and were also present in Mecca before Islam, Busse, Heribert. *Der Islam und die biblischen Kultstätten.* In: *Islam* 42, Berlin: De Gruyter, 1966, 115.

11. Busse, Heribert. *Die Patriarchengräber in Hebron und der Islam.* In: Zeitschrift des Deutschen Palästina-Vereins 114, Wiesbaden: Harrassowitz Verlag, 1998, 71–94.

12. Sozomenos, Historia Ecclesiastica: Kirchengeschichte II. Turnout: Brepolis-Verlag, 2004; Mader, Evaristus. Mambre. Die Ergebnisse der Ausgrabungen im heiligen Bezirk Râmet al-Ëalîl in Südpalästina 1926–1928, Vol. 2, Freiburg: Gregorian Biblical Press, 1957.

13. For the Islamic tradition of Hebron: Al-Jubeh, Nazmi. *Hebron (al-Halīl): Kontinuität und Integrationskraft einer islamisch-arabischen Stadt.* Tübingen: Eberhard-Karls Universität Tübingen, 1991, 99-253.

14. Zertal, Idith/Eldar, Akiva. *Die Herren des Landes. Israel und die Siedlerbewegung seit 1967.* München: DVA, 2007; Hagemann, Steffen. *Die Siedlerbewegung. Fundamentalismus in Israel.* Schwalbach am Taunus: Wochenschau Verlag, 2010.

15. http://www.theparentscircle.com/

8. Land of Sprouting Twigs Vertical ecumenism in Palestinian art and culture

1. fig. 1: Wall painting, Gaza. http://pulitzercenter.typepad.com/.a/6a00d834520 a2e69e20111684e9ec5970c-pi.
2. fig. 2: Qabeh from a refugee with twigs, flags, Dome of the Rock and the letters, "PLO." In Kawar. Widad Kamel. *Threads of Identity. Preserving Palestinian Costume and Heritage*, Nicosia: Rimal Publications, 2011, 431.
3. fig. 3: Al-Adawi, Zuhdi. PrisonArt. Crayon on pillowcase linen. http://www.stationmuseum.com/Made_in_Palestine-Zuhdi_Al_Adawi_Mohammed_Rakouie_files/Made_in_Palestine-Zuhdi_Al_Adawi_Mohammed_Rakouie.htm.
4. fig. 4: Mansour, Suleiman. Ismael. Mud on wood, 1997. http://www.stationmuseum.com/Made_in_Palestine-Suleiman_Mansour/Made_in_Palestine-Suleiman_Mansour.htm.
5. fig. 5: Tamari, Vera. *Tale of a tree*. Ceramics and phototransfer on plexiglass, ceramic trees, 1999. http://www.stationmuseum.com/Made_in_palestine-Vera_Tamari/tamari.html.
6. fig. 6: Al Mozayen, Abdel Rahmen. From the series Jenin, 2002. Ink on paper. http://www.stationmuseum.com/Made_in_Palestine-Abdel_Rahmen_Mozayen/Made_in_Palestine-Abdel_Rahmen_Mozayen.htm.
7. fig. 7: *HaGosherim*. In Getzov, Nimrod. *Art. Ha-Gosherim.* In *New Encyclopaedia of Archaeological Excavations in the Holy Land,* Vol. 5, 2008, 1760.
8. fig. 8: *Nahal Mischmar.* In Schroer, Silvia/Keel, Othmar. D*ie Ikonographie Palästinas/Israels und der Alte Orient. Eine*

Religionsgeschichte in Bildern. Bd. 1, Freiburg: Academic Press Fribourg, No. 60, 2005

9. fig. 9: *Bab edh-Dhra.* In Schroer, Silvia/Keel, Othmar. *Die Ikonographie Palästinas/Israels und der Alte Orient. Eine*

Religionsgeschichte in Bildern, Bd. 1, Freiburg: Academic Press Fribourg, No. 100, 2005.

10. fig. 10: *Stamp seal amulets*, Geser. From Schroer, Silvia. *Die Zweiggöttin in Palästina/Israel. Von der Mittelbronze II B-Zeit bis zu Jesus Sirach.* In: Küchler, Max/Uehlinger, Christoph, *Jerusalem. Texte - Bilder – Steine, Novum Testamentum et Orbis Antiquus 6*, Freiburg: Fribourg Academic Press, No. 6, 1989, 201-225.

Endnotes 255

11. fig. 11: *Southern Levant*. In Schroer, Silvia, Die Zweiggöttin in Palästina/ Israel. Von der Mittelbronze II B-Zeit bis zu Jesus Sirach. In Küchler, Max/ Uehlinger, Christoph, *Jerusalem. Texte - Bilder – Steine, Novum Testamentum et Orbis Antiquus 6*, Freiburg: Fribourg Academic Press, No. 0101, 1989.

12. fig. 12: *Tell el-Ajjūl*. In Keel, Othmar. *Corpus der Stempelsiegel-Amulette aus Palästina/Israel (CSAPI I). Von den Anfängen bis zur Perserzeit,* Katalog Band I: Von Tell Abu Farʿa bis ʿAtlit. With Three Contributions by Baruch Brandl, Orbis Biblicus et Orientalis. Series archaeologica 13, Freiburg: Fribourg Academic Press, 1997, No. 955.

13. fig. 13: *Southern Levant*. In Schroer, Silvia. Die Zweiggöttin in Palästina/ Israel. Von der Mittelbronze II B-Zeit bis zu Jesus *Sirach.,* In Küchler, Max/ Uehlinger, Christoph, *Jerusalem. Texte - Bilder – Steine, Novum Testamentum et Orbis Antiquus 6,* Freiburg: Fribourg Academic Press, No. 53

14. fig. 14: *Bet Mirsim*. In Keel , Othmar. *Corpus der Stempelsiegel-Amulette aus Palästina/Israel (CSAPI II). Von den Anfängen bis zur Perserzeit.* Katalog Band II: Von Bahan bis Tel Eton. Mit Beiträgen von Daphna Ben-Tor, Baruch Brandl und Robert Wenning, Orbis Biblicus et Orientalis. Series archaeologica 29, Freiburg: Fribourg Academic Press, 2005, No. 54.

15. fig. 15: *Farʿa South*. In Keel Othmar, *Corpus der Stempelsiegel-Amulette aus Palästina/Israel (CSAPI III). Von den Anfängen bis zur Perserzeit.* Katalog Band III: Von Tell el-Farʿa bis Tel el-Fir, Orbis Biblicus et Orientalis. Series archaeologica 31, Freiburg: Frbourg Academic Press, 2010, No. 6.

16. fig. 16: *Farʿa South*. In CSAPI III, 2010, No. 26.

17. fig. 17: *En Samije*. In CSAPI II, 2005, No. 7.

18. fig. 18: *Amman*. In Eggler, Jürg/Keel Othmar. *Corpus der Siegel-Amulette aus Jordanien (CSAJ). Vom Neolithikum bis zur Perserzeit*. In Orbis Biblicus et Orientalis. Series archaeologica 25, Freiburg: Fribourg Academic Press, 2006, No. 27.

19. fig. 19: *Emmaus*. In CSAPI II, 2005, No. 1.

20. fig. 20: *Tell el-Ajjūl*. In CSAPI, 1997, No. 1122.

21. fig. 21: *Farʿa South*. In Keel, Othmar. *Corpus der Stempelsiegel-Amulette aus Palästina/Israel. Von den Anfängen bis zur Perserzeit.* Einleitung, Orbis Biblicus et Orientalis. Series archaeologica 10, Freiburg: Fribourg Academic Press, 1995, 273.

22. fig. 22: *Dor*. In CSAPI II, 2005, No. 21.

23. fig. 23: *Lakhish*. In Schroer, Silvia. *Die Zweiggöttin in Palästina/Israel. Von der Mittelbronze II B-Zeit bis zu Jesus Sirach,* In Küchler, Max/ Uehlinger, Christoph, *Jerusalem. Texte - Bilder – Steine, Novum Testamentum*

et Orbis Antiquus 6, Freiburg/Göttingen: Fribourg Academic Press/ Vandenhoeck&Rupprecht, 201-225, 1987, fig. 14.
24. fig. 24: *Tell Der Alla*. In CSAJ, 2006, No. 42.
25. fig. 25: *Akko*. In: CSAPI I, No. 17.
26. fig. 26: *Lakhish*. In Keel, Othmar/Uehlinger, Christoph. *Gods, Goddesses, And Images of God*. New York: Bloomsbury Academic, 1998, fig. 323.
27. fig. 27: *Jerusalem*. In Keel, Othmar/Uehlinger, Christoph. *Gods, Goddesses, And Images of God*. New York: Bloomsbury Academic, 1998, fig. 355.
28. fig. 28: *Juda*. In Keel, Othmar/Uehlinger, Christoph. *Gods, Goddesses, And Images of God*. New York: Bloomsbury Academic, 1998, fig. 317c.
29. fig. 29: *Samaria*. In Meshorer, Yakov/Qedar, Shraga. *Samarian Coinage*. In *Numismatic Studies and Researches 9*, Jerusalem: Israel Numismatic Society, 1999, fig. 206.
30. fig. 30: *Wadi ed-Dalije*. In CSAPI II, 2005, No. 4.
31. fig. 31: *Alexander Jannäus*. In Madden, F.W. *History of Jewish Coinage and of Money in the Old and New Testament*. London: Ktav Pub Inc, 1864, No. 66, 3 Obv.
32. fig. 32: *Herodes Antipas*. In Madden, F.W. *History of Jewish Coinage and of Money in the Old and New Testament*. London: Ktav Pub Inc, No. 97, 1864, 2 Obv.
33. fig. 33: *Simon bar Gamaliel*. In Madden, F.W. *History of Jewish Coinage and of Money in the Old and New Testament*. London: Ktav Pub Inc, 1864, 178, 1 Obv.
34. fig. 34: *Herodes*. In Madden, F.W. *History of Jewish Coinage and of Money in the Old and New Testament*. London: Ktav Pub Inc , No. 83, 1864, 2 Obv.
35. fig. 35: *Herodes*. In Madden, F.W. *History of Jewish Coinage and of Money in the Old and New Testament*. London:Ktav Pub Inc, No. 88, 1864, 6 Obv.
36. fig. 36: *Claudius*. In Madden, F.W. *History of Jewish Coinage and of Money in the Old and New Testament*. London: Ktav Pub Inc , No. 152, 1864, 2 Obv.
37. fig. 37: *Simon bar Giora*. In Madden, F.W. *History of Jewish Coinage and of Money in the Old and New Testament*. London: Ktav Pub Inc, No. 167, 1864, 2 Rev.
38. fig. 38: *Eleasar*. In Madden, F.W. *History of Jewish Coinage and of Money in the Old and New Testament*. London: Ktav Pub Inc , No. 164, 1864, 4 Rev.
39. fig. 39: *Hadrian*. In Madden, F.W. *History of Jewish Coinage and of Money in the Old and New Testament*. London: Ktav Pub Inc, No. 212, 1864, 5 Rev.
40. fig. 40: Abd el-Malik, In Madden, F.W. *History of Jewish Coinage and of*

Endnotes 257

Money in the Old and New Testament. London: Ktav Pub Inc, No. 231, 1864.

41. fig. 41: Münze aus Aschkelon, Julia Domna. Umzeichnung des Autors, In Meshorer, Yacov. *City-Coins of Eretz-Israel and the Decapolis in the Roman Period,* Jerusalem: The Israel Museum, 1985, fig. 49.

42. fig. 42: Terracotta figure. From Parlasca, Ingemarie. *Terrakotten aus Petra. Ein neues Kapitel nabatäischer Archäologie.* In Zayadine, F., *Petra and the Caravan Cities,* Amman: Department of Antiquities of Jordan, No. 12, Taf. IV, 1990, 87-105.

43. fig. 43: Detail of Samarian stone coffin. École Biblique, Jerusalem; photo by the author.

44. fig. 44: Māskah, silver amulet. Southern Palestine, early twentieth cent. CE, coll. I. Hroub, Dēr Samit-

45. fig. 45: Gold amulet, workshop Hroub. Dēr Samit. early twenty-first century CE

46. fig. 46: Hābie/soma'a, crop shrine made of adobe, decorated with a twig, southern Palestine, early twentieth century CE , coll. I. Hroub, Dēr Samit.

47. fig. 47: Twig decor on big water jar, southern Palestine, early twentieth century, coll. I. Hroub, Dēr Samit.

48. fig. 48: Twigs as elements of a piece of embroidery on a tobacco bag, southern Palestine, early twentieth century, coll. I. Hroub, Dēr Samit.

49. fig. 49: Twigs as decoration on a shawl, Bet Mirsim, early twenty-first century CE.

50. fig. 50: Fresh grave with palm brances in the Muslim cemetary in Jerusalem, 2012. Photo of the author.

51. fig. 51: Sarma, wedding dress, early twentieth CE. In Kawar, Widad Kamel. *Threads of Identity. Preserving Palestinian Costume and Heritage,* Nicosia: Rimal Publications, 2011, 177.

52. fig. 52: State seal of Israel. Israeli, 1999.

53. fig. 53: State seal of Palestine. http://4.bp.blogspot.com/-YMHA4cGsP2A/ T0fD1VB40RI/AAAAAAAAEN8/nw3XWRk_l1U/s1600/Stamp+State+of+ Palestine%231_2011KJarrar.jpg.

258   *Palestinian Identity*

8. Land of Sprouting Twigs Vertical ecumenism in Palestinian art and culture / Figures

1. Wall painting, Gaza

2. Qabeh from a refugee with twigs, flags, Dome of the Rock and the letters PLO

3. PrisonArt, Crayon on pillowcase linen

   Dome of the Rock and the letters PLO

4. Ismael, mud on wood

5. Tale of a tree, ceramics and phototransfer on plexiglass

6. From the series Jenin, ink on paper plexiglass

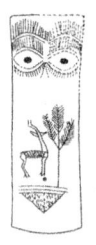

7. HaGosherim

8. Nahal Mischmar

9. Bab edh-Dhra

Foreword

10. Stamp seal amulets, Geser
11. Southern Levant
12. Tell el-Ajjūl
13. Southern Levant
14. Bet Mirsim
15. Far'a South
16. Far'a South
17. En Samije
18. Amman
19. Emmaus
20. Tell el-Ajjūl
21. Far'a South
22. Dor
23. Lakhish

260

24. Tell Der Alla

25. Akko

26. Lakhish

27. Jerusalem

28. Juda

29. Samaria

30. Wadi ed-Dalije

31. Alexander Jannäus

32. Herodes Antipas

33. Simon bar Gamaliel

34. Herodes

35. Herodes

36. Claudius

37. Simon bar Giora

Foreword

38. Eleasar

39. Hadrian

40. Abd el-Malik

41. Coin from Aschkelon

42. Terracotta figure

43. Detail of samarian stone coffin

44. Māskah

45. Gold amulet, workshop Hroub

46. Hābie/somàa, crop shrine made of adobe, decorated with a twig

47. Twig decor on big water jar, Southern Palestine

48. Twigs as elements of a piece of embroidery on a tobacco bag

49. Twigs as decoration on a shawl, Bet Mirsim

50. Sarma, wedding dress

51. Fresh grave with palm brances in the Muslim cemetery in Jerusalem

52. State seal of Israel

53. State seal of Palestine

9. Reading Palestine Rwalities with American Indian eyes:

1. Dylan, Bob. *With God On Our Side. The Times They Are A-Changin'*. Waner Bros. Inc., Apr 12, 1963; renewed by Special Rider Music, 1992.
2. U.S. Census Bureau, "American Indian and Alaska Native Poverty Rate About 50 Percent in Rapid City, S.D., and About 30 Percent in Five Other Cities, Census Bureau Reports," February 20, 2013. http://www.census.gov/newsroom/releases/archives/american_community_survey_acs/cb13-29.html.
3. Aspen Institute. *Fast Facts on Native American Youth and Indian Country.* http://www.aspeninstitute.org/sites/default/files/content/images/Fast%20 Facts.pdf.
4. Indian Country Today editorial board. *Middle East Conflict Calls Out for Insightful U.S. Leadership*. In Indian Country Today, New York: Media Network, April 5, 2002.
5. Robideau, Robert. God Given Right: Palestine and Native America. In Counterpunch, Petrolia: CounterPunch, February 1, 2006. For a history of the movement: Smith, Paul Chaat/Warrior, Robert Allen. Like a *Hurricane: The Indian Movement from Alcatraz to Wounded Knee.* New York: New Press, 1997.
6. Newcomb, Steven. *American Zionism*. In Indian Country Today, New York: Media Network, May 23, 2008.
7. Salberg, Michael.*Different Circumstances.* In Indian Country Today, New York: Media Network, June 20, 2008. Salberg's contribution drew a further response from Stanley Heller, chair of The Middle East Crisis Committee.
8. *National Pundits Sadly Ignore American Indian History*. In Indian Country Today, New York: Media Network, February 2, 2006.
9. Ibid.
10. Wallace, Anthony, F.C. *The Long, Bitter Trail: Andrew Jackson and the Indians*. New York: Hill and Wang, 1993, 11; 56; 62.
11. Robertson, Lindsay G. *Conquest by Law: How the Discovery of America Dispossessed Indigenous Peoples of Their Lands.* New York: Oxford University Press, 2005, 135. See also Banner, Stuart. *How the Indians Lost Their Land: Law and Power on the Frontier.* Cambridge, MA: Belknap/Harvard, 2005.
12. Weinberg, David M. *A win-win for Bedouin and the Negev.* In Israel Hayom Newsletter, Tel Aviv, June 30, 2013.
13. Browning, Noah. *Israel's Arab Bedouin citizens feel betrayed by eviction plan. Thomsen Reuters,* New York, August 28, 2013.

14. Rosenberg, Mica. *Native American Rallies for Israel, But Few Share His Enthusiasm.* In Jewish Telegraphic Agency, New York, December 3, 2002.
15. Warrior, Robert Allen. *A Native American Perspective: Canaanites, Cowboys, and Indians.* In Sugirtharajah, Sharada, *Voices from the Margin: Interpreting the Bible in the Third World*, New York: Orbis, 1991, 283–84.
16. Navajo Nation Press. *Navajo President Ben Shelly Meets with Deputy Minister at Knesset, and Honors Survivors of Holocaust at Yad Vashem,* December 13, 2012. http://www.navajo-nsn.gov/News%20Releases/OPVP/2012/Dec12/12712_PR_ShellyYadVashem.pdf.
17. Kane, Jenny. *Navajo, Israel conference seeks farmers.* In The Daily Times, Farmington: NM, March 27, 2013.
18. Yazzie, Janene. *Navajo Janene Yazzie: Solidarity with Palestine.* December 12, 2012. http://bsnorrell.blogspot.com/2012/12/navajo-janene-yazzie-solidarity-with.html.
19. Toensing, Gale Courey. *Indigenous Scholars Oppose Navajo President 'Becoming Partners' With Israel.* In Indian Country Today, New York: Media Network, April 06, 2013. http://indiancountrytodaymedianetwork.com/2013/04/06/indigenous-scholars-oppose-navajo-president-becoming-partners-israel-148645.
20. Salaita, Steven, *The Holy Land in Transit: Colonialism and the Quest for Canaan.* Syracuse, NY: Syracuse University Press, 2006, 44–5. In this case "American expansionism" is a more appropriate object of comparison than "Manifest Destiny," but the point still stands.
21. Salaita, Steven, *The Holy Land in Transit: Colonialism and the Quest for Canaan.* Syracuse, NY: Syracuse University Press, 2006, 55f, 77, quoting Churchill, Ward. A Little Matter of Genocide. San Francisco: City Lights, 1997, 2; Masalha, Nur. *Imperial Israel and the Palestinians,* London: Pluto Press, 58.

10. Exil as Identity:

1. Among the projects comparing the experience of Palestinians with African-Americans see: Kook, Rebecca. *The Logic of Democratic Exclusion: African Americans in the United States and Palestinian citizens in Israel.* Lanham, MD: Lexington Books, 2002.
2. A comparable situation obtains for Latinos. Alexander, Michelle. *The New Jim Crow: Mass Incarceration in the Age of Colorblindness.* New York: The New Press, 2010, 6-7. Alexander points out, for instance, while blacks, whites, and Latinos sell drugs at the same rate, blacks and Latinos are incarcerated at significantly higher rates.
3. Ibid. 6.
4. All translations are modified NRSV.
5. For an overview and representative discussion of the issue, see Blenkinsopp, Joseph. *Sage, Priest, Prophet: Religious and Intellectual Leadership in Ancient Israel.* Louisville, KY: Westminster John Knox Press, 1995. They are lower priests in Numbers, while Deuteronomy draws no such distinction. See Grabbe, Lester. *Priests, Prophets, Diviners, Sages: A Socio-Historical Study Of Religious Specialists in Ancient Israel.* Valley Forge: Trinity Press International, 1995, 41-53. See the recent collection of essays, in Leuchter, Mark/Hutton, Jeremy. *Levites and Priests in Biblical History and Tradition.* Leiden/Boston: Brill Publishers, 2012.
6. Cook, Steven. *Those Stubborn Levites: Overcoming Levitical Disenfranchisement.* In Leuchter, Mark/Hutton, Jeremy. *Levites and Priests in Biblical History and Tradition.* Leiden/Boston: Brill Publishers, 2012, 155-170.
7. Rousseau, for example, associated the inception of language with the corruption of nature's voice. From this perspective, the primitive cry is the voice of nature emanating from the individual, who becomes alienated from his former self when that cry is incorporated into a system of communication. The inception of language proper, then, "introduces a deferral, a loss, an otherness into the voice of nature, which no longer coincides perfectly with itself." The system socializes the individual into a subject "subsumed within social convention and influenced by the power of others." Calder, Martin. *Encounters with the Other: A Journey To The Limits of Language through Works By Rousseau, Defoe, Prévost And Graffigny.* Amsterdam /New York: Rodopi, 2003, 49.
8. As Lacan explains the primordial sense of essential unity, "the rupture of the circle in which *Innenwelt* and Umwelt are united generates that inexhaustible attempt to square it in which we reap the ego." As quoted by

Frederic Jameson, in: Jameson, Frederic. *Imaginary and Symbolic, in Lacan: Marxism, Psychoanalytic Criticism, and the Problem of the Subject.* In Yale French Studies 55/56, New Haven: Yale University Press, 1977, 338-95; 358.

9. In Lacanian terms, "the unconsciousness structured like a language," consisting solely of "a 'chain' of signifying elements, such as words, phonemes, and letters, which 'unfold' in accordance with very precise rules over which the ego or self has no control whatsoever." Fink, Bruce. *The Lacanian Subject: Between Language and Jouissance.* New Jersey: Princeton University Press, 1995. For discussion of Lacan's notion of split subjectivity, see.
10. Ibid., 11.
11. Ibid., 7.
12. Ibid., 11.
13. Ibid., 9.
14. Ezekiel presents traditional themes within the frame of the historical destruction of Jerusalem in ways that challenge the sensibilities of the reader in matters of responsibility. As Jacqueline Lapsley observes, "For Ezekiel, a significant tension is located in the area of human identity: the Babylonian Crisis, namely, the events of 605-586 B.C.E. in Judah, presented the occasion for a latent cultural tension concerning human moral selfhood to emerge as a central concern. This tension is discernible in the apparently contradictory ways in which human beings are depicted in the Book of Ezekiel: as capable of obedience (and thus subject to calls to repentance) on the one hand, and as fundamentally incapable of obedience (subject to a fairly strong determinism) on the other." Lapsley, Jaqueline. *Can These Bones Live? The Problem of the Moral Self in Ezekiel.* Berlin/New York: De Gruyter, 2000, 3-4.
15. For an accessible discussion of Lacan's approach to modeling the human psyche see Leader, Darian. Lacan's Myths. In Rabaté, Jean-Michel. *The Cambridge Companion to Lacan.* Cambridge: Cambridge University Press, 2003, 35-49.
16. Weinfeld, Moshe. *Deuteronomy and the Deuteronomic School.* Oxford: Clarendon Press, 1972. 307.
17. Weinfeld notes "Some scholars take the phrase to refer to the 'Israelite reconquest of the land that had become subject to foreign rule' and to express the Israelite desire of absolute dominance over all of the promised land. Others take it in an eschatological sense on the basis of its occurrences in Isaiah 57:13:13; 60:21." *Ibid.*,313.

Endnotes

18. Ibid., 315.
19. Ibid., 315f.
20. Ibid., 317f.
21. Studies from a variety of disciplines have demonstrated the importance of familiarity. When we speak of a psychotic break, the 'reality' is the recognition of the foundational temporal and spatial patterns that make up the social order.
22. There is an argument to be made against the idea of conservative scribal culture, the idea that scribes refused to destroy sacred texts but only added to them. First, the incident in Jeremiah of Jehoiakim burning the scroll suggests not that this was anathema, but that it was the most effective way to deal with rival ideas.
23. Leuchter, Martin. *From Levite to Maskil in the Persian and Hellenistic Eras.* In Leuchter, Mark/Hutton, Jeremy. *Levites and Priests in Biblical History and Tradition.* Leiden/Boston: Brill Publishers, 2012, 215-32.
24. Zimmerli writes of 44:10-16 regarding how the passage informs the history of priesthood. "Only when this context has been clarified can it be judged what the particular characteristic of the present regulation is and in what direction the tendency of what it is actually saying lies." Zimmerli, Walther. *Ezekiel II, Chapters 25-48.* Mineapolis: Augsburg Fortress Press, 1979, 459.
25. For a discussion of the phrase see: Block, Daniel. *The Book of Ezekiel, Chapters 1-24.* Grand Rapids: Eerdmans Publishing Company, 1997, 176-77.
26. On this point, Zimmerli notes "The reservation of the harsh judgment for an individual social class and the corresponding exoneration of another class do not…correspond in any way to Ezekiel's preaching about sin, which is directed in 22:23ff equally against all classes and found in chapter 8 its most trenchant expression with regard to the temple and those who served in it." Zimmerli, Walther. *Ezekiel I.* Mineapolis: Augsburg Fortress Press, 1979, 459.
27. Baden, Joel. *The Violent Origins of the Levites: Text and Tradition.* In Leuchter, Mark/Hutton, Jeremy, *Levites and Priests in Biblical History and Tradition,* Leiden/Boston: Brill Publishers, 2012, 103-116.

11. The text as a landscape and the landscape as a text:

1. Stegemann, Jannecke. *Remembering the land: Jeremiah 32 in Palestinian narratives of identity*. In Kirchliche Zeitgeschichte 26.1, Göttingen: Vandenhoeck & Ruprecht,2013, 41-54. Here I also discussed Palestinian-Christian appropriations of Jeremiah 32. The textual analysis can also be found in City of doom and *city of hope, landscape and identity in Jeremiah 32*, which will be published in Carstens, Pernilla, *Human Orientation*. My dissertation on Jeremiah 32, *Decolonizing Jeremiah*, will be published in January 2014.
2. See for a postcolonial approach for instance Segovia, Fernando F. *Decolonizing Biblical Studies: A View from the Margins*. New York: Orbis Books, 2000.
3. Note that both exile and return are ideological constructions with implications for how land and belonging are viewed.
4. As Nadim Khoury points out, the identity-costs of narrative negotiation are higher for those in power: Khoury, Nadim, 2005, 135.
5. Nussbaum, Marta. *Love's Knowledge*, Oxford: Oxford University Press, 1990, 38.

12. Religiouse Identity as Gift and Task:

1. Rosa, Hartmut. *Weltbeziehungen im Zeitalter der Beschleunigung.* Berlin: Suhrkamp, 2012, 382.
2. Fuchs, Ottmar, *Wer`s glaubt wird selig...Wer`s nicht glaubt, kommt auch in den Himmel.* Würzburg: Echter Verlag, 2012, 98-106.
3. Adorno, Theodor W. *Stichworte. Kritische Modelle 2.* Frankfurt am Main: Suhrkamp,1969, 98-99
4. Fuchs, Ottmar. *Wohin mit der „Angst im Abendland?* In Loretan, Adrian/ Luzatto, Franco, *Gesellschaftliche Ängste als theologische Herausforderung,* Münster: lit-Verlag, 2004, 119-135.
5. Richter, Horst-Eberhard. *Wer nicht leiden will, muss hassen.* Hamburg: Psychosozial-Verlag, 1993.
6. Döhling, Jan-Dirk. *Der bewegliche Gott.* Freiburg in Breisgau: Herder Verlag, 2009.
7. Arendt, Hannah.*Vita activa oder vom tätigen Leben* München/Zürich: Piper 2002, 167.
8. Wohlmuth, Josef: *Die Tora spricht die Sprache der Menschen.* Paderborn: Ferdinand Schöningh, 2002, 88.
9. Fehling, Ruth. *Jesus ist für unsere Sünden gestorben: Eine praktisch-theologische Hermeneutik.* Stuttgart: Kohlhammer, 2010.
10. Halik, Tomas. Geduld mit Gott. Freiburg in Breisgau: Herder Verlag, 2011, 5.
11. Fuchs, Ottmar, *Wer`s glaubt wird selig...Wer`s nicht glaubt, kommt auch in den Himmel.* Würzburg: Echter Verlag, 2012, 64-72.
12. Ochs, Robert. *Verschwendung: Die Theologie im Gespräch mit Georges Bataille.* Frankfurt am Main: P. Lang, 1995.
13. Bechmann, Ulrike. *Das Lied der Weisheit. In Bechmann,* Ulrike/Bieberstein, Klaus, *Weisheit im Leiden,* Stuttgart: Katholisches Bibelwerk e.V., 2007, 39-77; 60.
14. Sander, Hans-Joachim. *Einführung in die Gotteslehre.* Darmstadt: Wissenschaftliche Buchgesellschaft, 2006, 34.
15. Bonhoeffer, Dietrich. *Gesammelte Schriften I.* München: Chr. Kaiser Verlag, 1958, 303-304.

13. Infilators or Next of Kin:

1. The authors sincerely wish to thank colleagues and friends for their insightful contributions. We thank Tilburg University, Tilburg School of Humanities and Tilburg Law School for the support provided for the research. We especially thank Dr Conny Rijken (Tilburg Law School) and Meron Estefanos. All points expressed are the responsibility of the authors.
2. Battle, Michael. *Ubuntu: I in You and You in Me.* New York: Seabury, 2009.
3. Arendt, Hannah. *Between Past and Future: Eight Exercises in Political Thought.* London: Penguin Books, 1961.
4. voor Oorlogsdocumentatie, Rijksinstituut. *Het dagboek van Anne Frank.* Amsterdam: Bert Bakker, 1990, 515: "Voor ieder die bang, eenzaam of ongelukkig is, is stellig het beste middel, naar buiten te gaan, ergens waar hij helemaal alleen is, alleen met de hemel, de natuur en God. Want dan pas, dan alleen voelt men dat alles is zoals het zijn moet en dat God de mensen in de eenvoudige, maar mooie natuur gelukkig wil zien." (Feb. 23, 1944).
5. On the history of the codification and recognition of human rights in the period immediately after the Second World War, cf. Morsink, Johannes. *The Universal Declaration of Human Rights: Origins, Drafting and Intent.* Philadelphia: University of Pennsylvania Press 1999.
6. Patt, Avinoam. *Finding Home and Homeland: Jewish Youth and Zionism in the Aftermath of the Holocaust.* Detroit: Wayne State University Press, 2009.
7. Bunton, Martin. *The Israeli-Palestinian Conflict: A Very Short Introduction.* Oxford: Oxford University Press, 2013.
8. For background, see Avineri, Shlomo. *The Making of Modern Zionism: Intellectual Origins of the Jewish State.* New York: Basic Books, 1981.
9. Sand, Shlomo. *The Invention of the Jewish People.* London: Verso, 2009; Sand, Shlomo. *The Invention of the Land of Israel: From Holy Land to Homeland.* London: Verso, 2012. Of course, Palestinian nationalist identity is also a construction in this sense; see Khalidi, Rashid. *Palestinian Identity: The Construction of Modern National Consciousness.* New York: Columbia University Press, 1997.
10. Sand, Shlomo. *The Invention of the Jewish People.* London: Verso, 2009, 259-282. For documentation on the history of four hundred Palestinian villages and their fate during the establishment of the Israeli state, see Khalidi, Walid. *All That Remains: The Palestinian Villages Occupied and Depopulated by Israel in 1948.* Washington: Institute for Palestine Studies, 1992; Morris, Benny. *The Birth of the Palestinian Refugee Problem Revisited.* Cambridge: Cambridge University Press 2004.

Endnotes

11. Morris, Benny. *The Birth of the Palestinian Refugee Problem Revisited.* l.c., 505-548. For background, cf. Roberts, Jo. *Contested Land, Contested Memory: Israel's Jews and Arabs and the Ghosts of Catastrophe.* Toronto: Dundurn, 2013.
12. Handelzalts, Michael. *Word for word: By renaming migrants 'infiltrators', Israel is forging a new reality.* Haaretz, June 29, 2012.
13. Shavit, Ari. *Survival of the fittest. Haaretz*, Januar 8, 2004: "That has to be clear. It is impossible to evade it. Without the uprooting of the Palestinians, a Jewish state would not have arisen here."
14. "It was always my dream to reach Jaffa." Syrian infiltrator says, *Haaretz,* May 16, 2011.
15. http://www.executedtoday.com/2009/05/25/1948-witold-pilecki-auschwitz/. August 18, 2013.
16. http://www.jewishvirtuallibrary.org/jsource/biography/Witold_Pilecki.html. August 18, 2013.
17. http://www.thefreedictionary.com/infiltrator. August 18, 2013.
18. http://milog.co.il/%D7%9E%D7%A1%D7%AA%D7%A0%D7%A0%D7%99%D7%9D
19. http://www.executedtoday.com/category/where/israel/
20. http://www.timesofisrael.com/our-man-in-beirut-the-remarkable-story-of-isaac-shushan/. August 18, 2013.
21. Private e-mail communication.
22. Private e-mail communication.
23. Prevention of infiltration (offences and jurisdiction) Law 5714-1954. Passed by the Knesset August 16, 1954.
24. Ibid.
25. Israel Defence Forces, Order No. 329, Order regarding Prevention of Infiltration, 1969.
26. Handelzalts, Michael. *Word for word: By renaming migrants 'infiltrators', Israel is forging a new reality. Haaretz*, June 29, 2012
27. Al Haq, Legal Analysis of Israeli Military Orders 1649 & 1650: Deportation and Forcible Transfer as International Crimes. In REF: 61/2010, http://www.alzaytouna.net/en/files/Docs/2010/Al-Haq-April2010-Legal-Analysis.pdf.
28. A translation of the orders is available on http://www.alzaytouna.net/en/resources/documents/israeli-documents/114859-israeli-military-orders-1649-quot-order-regarding-security-provisions-quot-and-1650-quot-order-regarding-prevention-of-infiltration-quot-2010.html#1649.

29. Amnesty International. New Israeli military order could increase expulsions of West Bank Palestinians. April 28, 2010.
30. Khalil, Asem. *Impact of Israeli Military Order No.1650 on Palestinians' rights to legally reside in their own country.* Analytic and Synthetic Notes; 2010/46.
31. Strik, Tineke. *Lives lost in the Mediterranean Sea: Who is responsible? Parliamentary Assembly, Council of Europe.* Doc. 12895, 05 April 2012. The group UNITED for Intercultural Action, European network against nationalism, racism, fascism and in support of migrants and refugees, based in Amsterdam, documented 17,306 people who died during their attempts to enter the European Union since 1993 in "a list of deaths." August 18, 2013. http://www.unitedagainstracism.org/pdfs/listofdeaths.pdf.
32. Ibid.
33. BBC, Pope Francis visits Italy's migrant island of Lampedusa, 8 July 2013.
34. http://www.vatican.va/holy_father/francesco/homilies/2013/documents/papa-francesco_20130708_omelia-lampedusa_en.html.
35. CNN, Pope prays for lost refugees on visit to Mediterranean island, July 8, 2013. (the quotation is edited for readability).
36. Van Reisen, Mirjam/ Estefanos, Meron/Rijke, Conny. *Human Trafficking in the Sinai: Refugees between Life and Death.* Oisterwijk: Wolf Legal Publishers 2012. https://pure.uvt.nl/portal/files/1487709/Report_Human_Traf_Sinai.pdf.
37. Ibid.
38. AFP, Eritrean refugees kidnapped, killed: UNHCR chief, 12 January 2012. In this article AFP reports a UNHCR official stating: "They're being taken through the country by criminal groups and subject to kidnapping. This is happening here in the east of Sudan regularly", said Felix Ross, the UNHCR's senior protection officer.
39. United Nations, Report of the Monitoring Group on Somalia and Eritrea pursuant to Security Council resolution 2060. Eritrea, S/2013/440, 25 July 2013. http://www.securitycouncilreport.org/atf/cf/%7B65BFCF9B-6D27-4E9C-8CD3-CF6E4FF96FF9%7D/s_2013_440.pdf.
40. Hotline for Migrant Workers: 'Briefing note: African asylum seekers and refugees arriving in Israel via the Egyptian Sinai desert.' 2012.
41. Human Rights Watch: http://www.hrw.org/news/2012/06/10/israel-amend-anti-infiltration-law. September 16 2013 the Israeli Supreme Court decided unanimously that this amendment was unconstitutional; see http://elyon1.court.gov.il/files/12/460/071/b24/12071460.b24.htm. October 28, 2013. In response Prime Minister Netanyahu vowed to respect the decision,

but to continue to "put the brakes on infiltration". We did not research systematically the factual consequences of this decision, but clearly the labeling of Africans as 'infiltrators' goes on.

42. "Globally, 84% of applications filed by Eritrean nationals are determined to be genuine, and the respective figure for Sudanese applications is 64%. Indeed, should individual RSD procedures be conducted in Israel for Eritrean and Sudanese asylum seekers, the statistics are likely to be similar. It is noteworthy that a signatory state to the 1951 Convention that refrains from examining asylum applications may not deny such applicants rights under the Convention." Ziegler, Reuven.The New Amendment to the 'Prevention of Infiltration' Act: Defining Asylum-Seekers as Criminals. The Israel Democracy Institute. January 16, 2012. http://en.idi.org.il/analysis/articles/the-new-amendment-to-the-prevention-of-infiltration-act-defining-asylum-seekers-as-criminals.

43. Handelzalts, Michael. *Word for word: By renaming migrants 'infiltrators', Israel is forging a new reality. Haaretz,* June 29, 2012.

44. Ibid.

45. Note received from Bruck Teshome by email on August 9, 2013.

46. E-mails to author by different sources.

47. Handelzalts, Michael. *Word for word: By renaming migrants 'infiltrators', Israel is forging a new reality. Haaretz*, June 29, 2012

48. Kordowa, Shoshana. *Refugees: Are foreigners welcome in Israel?* Israeli Speak, November 19, 2010. http://www.tabletmag.com/scroll/50635/refugees.

49. Ibid.

50. Paraphrased from correspondence.

51. Comment received by authors.

52. Kordowa, Shoshana. *Refugees: Are foreigners welcome in Israel?* Israeli Speak, November 19, 2010. http://www.tabletmag.com/scroll/50635/refugees.

53. Parfitt, Tudor. *Black Jews in Africa and the Americas.* Cambridge: Harvard University Press, 2013, 145.

54. Ibid., 142. Quotation: Kaplan, Steven. *The Beta Israel (Falasha) in Ethiopia: From Earliest Times to the Twentieth.* New York: New York University Press, 1992, 23.

55. Parfitt, Tudor. *Black Jews in Africa and the Americas.* Cambridge: Harvard University Press, 2013, 142.

56. Ibid. 145-146.

57. Bruder, Edith. *The Black Jews of Africa: History, Religion, Identity*. Oxford: Oxford University Press, 2008.
58. Armstrong, Karen. *The Case for God: What Religion Really Means*. New York: Vintage, 2010, 39.

14. Home, Land, and Homeland As Social Values

1. Members in the 2013 ARTNAUTS Collective who had artwork in this exhibition include: Wendy Babcox, Dan Boord, Sandy Brunvand, Jaime Carrejo, Sandra Jean Ceas, Andrew Connelly, Dennis Dalton, Luz del Carmen Vilchis Esquivel, Rebecca DiDomenico, Francoise Duresse, Suzanne Faris, Donald Fodness, Quintin Gonzalez, Nicole Hongchang, Ben Jackel, Claire Jackel, Beth Krensky, Catherine Leisek, Jane McMahan, V. Kim Martinez, Arturo Miranda Videgaray, Susanne Mitchell, Marcela Norambuena, Enriqueta Rosete Ortega, Tony Ortega, Dr. George Rivera, Yumi Roth, Martha Russo, Jody Woods Thompson, Cyane Tornatzky, Luis Valdovino, Lori Ann Warren, Sherry Wiggins, and Joo Yeon Woo.
2. Robertsen, Jean/McDaniel, Craig. *Themes of Contemporary Art*. New York: Oxford University Press, 2010, 151.
3. Mills, Charles Wright. *The Sociological Imagination*. New York: Grove Press, 1959, 11-13.

276   *Palestinian Identity*

14. Home, Land, and Homeland As Social Values / Figures

1. Dj Lu

2. Warren

3. Brunvand

4. DiDomenico

5. Roth

6. Miranda

7. Russo

8. Leisek

9. C. Jackel

10. Woo

11. Mitchell

12. Tornatzky

Foreword 277

13. Farris

14. Dalton

15. del Carmen Vilchis

16. Carrejo

17. McMahan

18. Boord and Valdovino

19. Thompson

20. Krensky

21. Babcox

22. Ceas

23. B. Jackel

24. Rivera

278   *Palestinian Identity*

25. Ortega 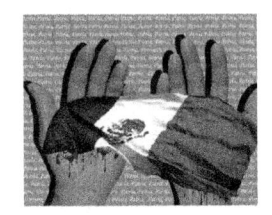   26. Rosete    27. Dureese

28. Fodness 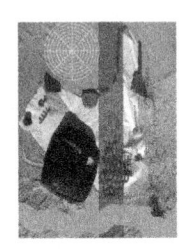   29. Connelly    30. Norambuena

31. Gonzalez    32. Martinez 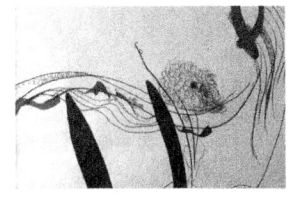   33. Hongchang

34. Wiggins

Index:

Aaron, 154, 159
Abd El-Malik, 130
Abel, 90, 99, 198
Abiram, 159
Abraham, 99, 109, 111, 112, 113, 114, 115, 122, 169, 220, 233
Adam, 96, 121, 197, 198, 219, 234
Adorno, Theodor W., 181
African-Americans, 151, 152, 153, 160, 225
al Bustani, Butrus, 47
al Carmel, 47
Al Muzayen, Abdel Rahmen, 123
Al Safir, 86
al-Adawi, Zuhdi, 122
al-Anshad, Nashid/al-Anashid, Nashid, 90, 91, 93
Al-'Arraj, Yusuf Abu, 56
Alexander, Michelle, 152
Alexander Yannai, 129
al-Filastini, 13
al-Ghareeba, Sareer, 90
Al-Haq, 209
al-Hilal, 68
al-Huayini, Saleem, 47
Al-Husayni, Musa Kazim, 57, 59, 60
Alienation, 45, 70, 151, 153, 155, 158
al-Jamiah, 71
al-Jamiah al-Arabiyyah, 50
al-Jamma'ily, 12
al-Jamma'iny, 12
al-Khali, 107, 109, 110, 111, 112, 115, 116, 117, 118, 119,
al-Kian, Abu, 145
al-Maqdisi, 13, 74

al-Maqdisi, 13, 74
al-Muktataf, 68
al-Muqqadasi, 115
al-Murr, D'ebis, 55
al-Nafa'is, 68
al-Najjar, Atallah Hannah, 51
al-Nakba, 35, 37, 38, 42, 142
al-Qudsi, 12
Al-Sihyounia, 48
al-'Umar az-Zaidani, Dahir, 16
al-Yaziji, Nasif, 47
Anton, Farah, 71, 72
Aqel, Musa, 47
Arabian Qedrenes, 112
Arafat, Yasser, 17
Aramairs, 15
Arendt, Hannah, 183
Armstrong, Karen, 220
ARTNAUTS, 223, 224, 225, 232, 237
Ashkelon, 122, 131
Asl al-Shaqa, 52, 55
Babcox, Wendy, 229
Baituna al-Talhami, 22
Balfour Declaration, 14, 48, 50, 66
Bandak, Isa Basil, 50, 52, 53, 54, 55, 56, 57, 58, 59, 60, 61, 62, 63, 64
Bandak, Mariam, 53
Banko, Lauren E., 50
Bataille, George, 189
Baydas, Khalil, 76
Bayta Lahm Newspaper, 52, 53, 54, 55, 56
Beirut, 47, 94, 95, 96
Benjamin, 165, 166, 167
Bethlehem, 223, 236, 237

Bethlehemite Young Men's Club, 57
Biblical Scholars, 151, 154, 158, 168, 172
Bismillah, 131
Blashard, Gaston, 87
Bonhoeffer, Dietrich, 190, 191
Book of Deuteronomy, 156, 157, 201
Boord, Dan, 228
British Mandate, 14, 21, 22, 63, 66, 83
Bruce Fink, 155
Brunvand, Sandy, 226
Bush, George W., 139, 140
Caes, Sandra Jean, 229
Cain, 90, 99, 198, 219
Cana, 90, 121, 123, 124, 125, 127, 131, 132, 133, 134, 145, 146, 188, 220, 237
Canaan, Tawfiq, 25
Carrejo, Jaime, 228
Caucus, Christian Allies, 146
Chaldeans, 166
Chickasaw Nation, 136, 141
Connelly, Andrew, 231
Counterpunch, 138
Dabdub, Yusuf Ya'qub, 56
dabka, 22
Dakkarat, Yuhanna Khalil, 52, 53, 54, 55
Dalman, Gustaf, 24
Dalton, Dennis, 227
Dao, Salim, 84
Dar at-Tifl al-'Arabi, 22
Dar-Annadwa, 7, 225
Darwish, Ahmad, 84
Darwish, Mahmoud, 96, 97, 98, 99, 100, 102, 103, 104, 233
Dathan, 159
David, 89, 112

Derrida, Jaques, 69
DiDomenico, Rebecca, 226
Dionysus, 128
Dj Lu, 225
Doumet, Aziz, 66, 73, 75, 76, 78
Dylan, Bob, 135
Ecce Homo, 92
Ethiopia, 218, 219, 220, 221
Eve, 197
Exodus, 38, 66, 145, 146, 159, 200, 216
Ezekiel, 151, 153, 154, 155, 156, 157, 158, 159, 160
Filastin Newspaper, 50
Fillister, 15
Flavius Josephus, 113
Fodness, Donald, 231
Foucault, Michel, 69, 111, 189
Francoise, Dureese, 229, 231
Frank, Anne, 201
Fried, Erich, 178
Friedman, Matti, 206
Gaza Strip, 11, 19
Ger/Gerim, 154
Gohar, Saddik, 31
Golden calf, 159
Goldstein, Baruch, 117
Golgotha, 94
Gomorrah, 90
Gonzalez, Quintin, 231
Gopin, Marc, 43
Greimas, Algirdas Julien, 77
Ha'aretz, 140
Habakkuk, 90
Habeshia, 218, 220
Hagar, 122, 230
HaGosherim, 125
Halevy, Joseph, 220

Index 281

Handelzalts, Michael,208, 214, 215
Hebrew,90, 197, 200, 204, 206, 208, 218, 221, 231, 234
Herod Antipas,130
Herodotus,11
Holy tree of Mamre,112
Homeland,224, 228, 229, 232,
Hongchang, Nicole,232
Human Subjectivity,155
Hussein, Taha ,76
Ibrahim,114, 115, 117, 119,
Ibrahim, Jabra ,40
In'ash al-Usra ,22, 23
Indian Country Today,138, 139, 140, 141
Indian Wars,140
Isaiah,90, 96, 160
Ishmael,89, 230
Islah' Movement,65
Ismael,122
Isma'il,115
Israel Hayom,144
Jabotinsky, Zeev,228
Jackel, Ben ,229
Jackel, Claire,226, 227
Jackson, Andrew,143
jahiliyya,124
Jaques Lacan,155, 156
Jawzi, Bendaly ,66, 67, 68, 69, 77, 78
Jeremiah,38, 157, 163, 164, 165, 166, 168, 169,
Jesus,89, 90, 92, 93, 94, 95, 97, 98, 100, 169, 188, 201
Job,90, 96, 121, 193, 214
Joseph,89
Joshua,89
Judah,112, 165, 166, 167, 219,
Judith,129

Kaabia, Hassam,144
Kabha, Safiq ,39
Kalis, Yusuf,54
Katz, Yaakov,216
Kawar, Widad ,122, 132
Khalidi, Rashid ,35
Khalidi, Rawhi ,66, 72, 73, 78,
Khoory, Elias,84
Kiryat Arba,116
Korah,159
Kordova, Shoshana,216, 218
Krensky, Beth,229
Lacanian Term,154
Lakhish,128
Lapsley, Michael ,31
Leisek, Catherine,226, 227
Leonard Peltier Defense Committee,138
Levites,151, 153, 154, 158, 159, 160
Leviticus,43
Lindholm Schulz, Helena ,41
Literary Gazette,70
Machpela,112
Madaba,113
Majallat at-Turath wal-Mujtama',22
Makari, Peter ,32
Mamre,112, 113, 114, 115
Mansour, Suleiman,122
Maoli, Kanaka,148, 149
Marcel, Gabriel,178
Maronites,133
Marshall, John,143
Martinez, V. Kim,231
Mary Magdalene,89, 96,
Matthew,180
McDaniel, Craig,224
McMahan, Jane McMahan,228
Meier, Golda,20

mestanen, 215
Mills, C. Wright ,224, 227
Mishmar, Nahal, 125
Mistanenim, 204, 216
Mizpah, 167
Moghannam, Moghannam, 55
Morcos, Khalil 'Issa, 51
Morris, Benny, 140, 141, 204
Morse, Jedediah, 142
Moscow, 94
Moses,159, 200, 220, 221
Munayyer, 132
mutasallil, 215, 216
Nabonid Babylonian Kingdom, 112
Nagast, Kebra, 219
Nassar, Najeeb, 47
Neo-Babylonian Period, 154
Netanyahu, Benjamin, 147, 148
Newcomb, Steven, 139
Nietzsche, Friedrich, 72
Noah, 90, 218
Norambuena, Marcela, 231
Nussbaum, Martha, 173
Omar ibn Al-Khattab, 46
Oppenheim, James, 122
Ortega, Enriqueta Rosete, 229, 231
Ortega, Tony, 229, 230, 231,
Oslo Accords, 96, 99
Oslo Peace Accords, 20
Ottoman Parliament, 16
Ottoman Period, 16, 66
Palestinian Liberation Organization (PLO), 19, 23, 122, 123
Parfitt, Tudor, 219, 220
Paul, 103
Pharaon, Henry, 133
Pilecky, Witold,205
Pope Francis, 212

Prawer Plan, 144
Ptah, 126
Quran, 96
Raheb, Mitri, 8, 194, 236
Rahner, Karl, 185
Refugee Camps, 36, 82, 152
Renan, Ernest, 69
Richter, Horst-Eberhard, 182
Rivera, George, 229, 230, 237
Robertson, Jean, 224
Robertson, Lindsey, 142
Robideau, Robert, 138, 139
Rohr, Richard, 43
Rosa, Hartmut, 178
Rose, Gillian, 43
Rosenstock-Huessy, Eugen, 124
Roth, Yumi, 226
Ruether, Herman, 43
Ruether, Rosmary, 43
Russo, Martha, 226
Sabra, 95
Said, Edward, 69, 99
Sakakini, Khalil, 66, 70, 71, 72, 73, 74, 76, 77
Salaita, Steven, 149
Samaritan, 89, 212
Saracino, Michelle, 37
Sawt ash-Sha'b, 56
Separation Wall, 203, 217, 218, 230
Shalhat, Antoine, 83
Shatila, 95
Shavit, Ari, 204
Shelly, Ben, 146, 147
Shimon bar Giora, 130
Shushan, Isaac, 206
Sidky, Nejati, 76
Skinner, Margarita, 132
Smith, Jonathan T., 136

Index 283

Solomon, 90, 99, 100, 101, 218, 219, 220
Soviet Union, 94, 97
Sozomenos, 113, 114
Stern, Avraham, 148
Suarez, Santos, 145
Sykes-Picot Agreement, 14, 18
Tel Rumeideh, 112
Thompson, Jody Woods, 228, 229
Tombs of Abraham, 109
Torah, 88, 90, 91, 156, 221
Tornatzky, Cyane, 227
Touqan, Ibrahim, 47
Turki, Fawaz, 40
Umayyad dynasty, 14
United States, 152, 205, 223, 225, 228, 229, 230, 232
Valdovino, Luis, 228
Vattimo, Gianni, 187
Vilchis, Carmen, 227
Wadi Abu Olleqa, 131
Wallace, Anthony, 141, 142
Warren, Lori Ann, 226
Warrior, Robert Allen, 145, 146, 147
West Bank, 19, 116, 117, 147, 152, 209, 210, 216, 219, 230
Wiggins, Sherry, 232
Wilson, Charles Thomas, 24
Woo, Joo Yeon, 227
Yabne, 128
Yahweh, 145, 146, 154, 155, 156, 157, 220, 221,
Yazzie, Janene, 147
Zealot, 113
Zerai, Mussie, 211, 213
Zionism / Zionist, 15, 17, 21, 36, 38, 46, 48, 49, 63, 66, 72, 76, 139, 149, 164, 166, 167, 170, 202, 204, 238